RENDEZVOUS WITH DEATH

The American Poetry Recovery Series

SERIES EDITOR

Cary Nelson

BOARD OF ADVISORS

Daniel Aaron · Houston A. Baker Jr.
Carolyn Forché · Karen Ford
Reginald Gibbons · Walter Kalaidjian
Paul Lauter · Philip Levine · Alan Wald

A list of books in the series appears at the end of this book.

RENDEZVOUS WITH DEATH

American Poems of the Great War

Edited by

Mark W. Van Wienen

University of Illinois Press

Urbana and Chicago

© 2002 by the Board of Trustees of the University of Illinois
All rights reserved
Manufactured in the United States of America
1 2 3 4 5 C P 5 4 3 2 1

∞ This book is printed on acid-free paper.

Library of Congress Cataloging-in-Publication Data
Rendezvous with death: American poems of the Great War /
edited by Mark W. Van Wienen.
p.   cm. — (The American poetry recovery series)
Includes bibliographical references and index.
ISBN 0-252-02744-2 (cloth : alk. paper)
ISBN 0-252-07059-3 (paper : alk. paper)
1. American poetry—20th century.
2. World War, 1914–1918—Poetry.
3. War poetry, American.
I. Van Wienen, Mark W. II. Series.
PS595.W63R46   2002
811'.52080358—dc21   2001006006

In Memory of

Margaret Fortuin DeYoung (1910–77)

Henry DeYoung (1911–92)

Martha Fieldhouse Van Wienen (1902–98)

Peter Van Wienen (1903–99)

My Great War Generation

We were so *cocky* in those days! I guess we've gotten knocked down a peg or two since then.

—MARTHA VAN WIENEN

✹ CONTENTS

CONTENTS

CONTENTS

CONTENTS

INTRODUCTION

This collection of poetry, the first representing the wide range of American poems published in response to the Great War, has arisen from motives both weighty and whimsical. I have compiled and selected the poems realizing that their authors saw them as weapons: literally, as tools of war that might bring U.S. citizens to kill their German counterparts; that might prevent such killing; that might protect the lives of U.S. citizens, their well-being, their rights; or that might conspire to take these away. Given such purposes, I have sought to deal seriously with these authors and their work. The arguments against as well as for American participation need to be heard and heard, also, in dialogue with each other much as they were during the war. Whether written for a popular audience or the most avant-garde, high-art one, each poem needs to be reconsidered with as much historical and biographical context as possible, to give the poem and its author ample chance to speak again with vital force. Creating these kinds of contexts and dialogues has been among my central responsibilities and aims in producing this collection. Moreover, the issues these poems explored—institutionalized violence, political repression, militarism, international relations and the lack thereof—remain vital. The United States of today is a dramatically different nation than the country of 99 million who observed and then participated in World War I. But the course set between 1914 and 1918 propelled us decisively into what has been called "the American Century," and the experiences of that century seem to have made us all the more determined, to the point of believing ourselves destined, to continue shaping history in our own, American image.

At the same time, readers of this collection will soon discover that American poets of the Great War could be wickedly satirical, exuberantly comic, and even downright silly. Not only would omitting such work mean leaving out an essential ingredient in the mix of American war poetry but it would also deprive readers of one chief pleasure of that poetry, the humor that has been a constant source of its appeal to me. Some delights are produced, admittedly, by anachronism. The hundreds of "sock songs" generated by a *Boston Globe* contest—to stimulate the knitting of socks for soldiers as well as the writing of poems about it—were intended for amusement, on the whole; but they are all the more charming in the age of MTV, machine-made hosiery, and Web surfing, and they profit as well by the twentieth-century flowering of Freudian interpretation. Another poem, Wallace Irwin's "A Few Words from Wilhelm," reflects xenophobic attitudes that are not simply dated but offensive today; yet Irwin's target of satire, Kaiser Wilhelm, is so ripe—and the parallels to Theodore Roosevelt so right—that for this one poem American mimicry of "foreign" accents seems forgivable. For still others, the particular cause that animated an author may be long past, yet the edge of satiric humor can still cut sharply today. Although the Industrial Workers of the World now does little more as an organization than keep its famous "Little Red Song Book" in print, IWW poet John Kendrick's "What For?" parodying Poe's "The Raven," speaks still to a culture of greed and exploitation.

Ironically, this anthology, some 150 poems grounded firmly in the history of the Great War, has needed a much later and distinctively different historical conjuncture to come into being. In the 1980s, when I moved from college to graduate work, the debate over "the canon" remained sharp; that the definite article *the* was still placed before *canon* without much self-consciousness indicates how much needed to be argued over. In this context, Barbara Herrnstein Smith's "Contingencies of Value," which shifted the question of literary worth from "is the poem any good?" to "what is it good *for?*" came as a revelation. So did Jane Tompkins's resuscitation of *Uncle Tom's Cabin* and other nineteenth-century popular novels in *Sensational Designs,* as she argued that the "cultural work" of Harriet Beecher Stowe's antislavery narrative was far more important than twentieth-century aesthetic principles of what does, or does not, comprise a great novel. As a student of modern poetry having worked through Richard Ellmann and Robert O'Clair's *Norton Anthology of Modern Poetry,* then still the only anthology covering my field, I read Cary Nelson's *Repression and Recovery* with relief bordering on exhilaration. It was possible, Nelson argued and himself demonstrated, to rediscover modern authors long neglected, even suppressed, who would address a broader range of issues than the formalist and high cultural questions prevalent in studies of modernism. It was possible to speak of history, politics, and society without recourse to torturous apologetics for T. S. Eliot or Ezra Pound. Poetry became more than a relation to literary tradition, as Eliot had figured it in his seminal, ubiquitous "Tradition and the Individual Talent." Poetry could, and should be, about the relationship between the poem and historical contingency; the poem itself became a historically grounded object, and not an object only but an action and a performance in and on history. The politics of literature became not just a legitimate topic, but the most necessary and essential literary topic. All of this many literary scholars now accept as perfectly obvious. Judging from the *Heath*

Anthology of American Literature inaugurated in 1991 (Lauter), I was not at all alone in my conversion experience; many others, many before me, were paving the way for what suddenly seemed a natural and inevitable opening, and then exploding, of the canon. But we do not often reckon fully just how much the landscape of literary studies has been altered, and we still have not entirely come to terms with the demands that the new, rapidly expanding constellations of texts now being read have placed upon our interpretive schemes.

The American poems contained in this anthology stand as both proof and test of how far we have come. In his 1964 dissertation, James Hart covered some of the same sources that I have drawn from. His research, assisted by prior work done by Hugh Morrison of the Library of Congress, was exhaustive. Restricted to publications between 1914 and 1920, his bibliography lists 80 different anthologies containing war poetry by American authors and an additional 704 volumes by individual American authors containing at least a single war poem (317); it also cites 86 U.S. periodicals in which he finds roughly 3,200 war poems by Americans (293). Yet after all his bibliographic work, Hart finds he must conclude that "although thousands of minor American authors felt moved to write about the First World War, none was transformed by the conflict into a true poet. More important writers, of course, composed a few war pieces, but none produced a major poem" (v). The hierarchies underlying Hart's terms— "minor authors," "true poet," "important writers," "major poem"—have by now been radically undermined. Even Hart's implied definition of "war poem" seems overly constraining; is not *The Waste Land*, as Sandra M. Gilbert and Susan Gubar have argued, a war poem (312–14)? What about Claude McKay's "If We Must Die?" published in the *Liberator* in 1919? To the extent the terms are useful at all, I would say the following: There were indeed minor authors of war poems, and many were among the writers we now see as the major modernists. There were many true poets of this conflict; their works appeared every month in American journals and every day in American newspapers. There were important American writers and major American poems of the Great War, though their names and titles have largely been forgotten: I should venture Lincoln Colcord, Arturo Giovannitti, Bernice Evans, John Curtis Underwood, and Sarah Norcliffe Cleghorn, to begin with, as a few poets who wrote such poems. That these and others should get another hearing decades after their war poetry was last published is itself a remarkable milestone.

But I hasten to add that much of this poetry violates both the strictures of literary value being formulated in the 1910s by the modernists and the conventions that continue to inform literary judgments, however implicitly, in the present. Most poetry in this volume was, in one or more senses, popular, and this sets the tenor of the collection. As such, many poems lack the layers of ambiguity or indetermination that are the persistent hallmarks of literary value even, or perhaps especially, in the era of the exploded canon. Certain poems were individually popular during the Great War, reprinted in dozens, even hundreds, of magazines and newspapers when editors and readers responded with particular enthusiasm. This enthusiasm was often linked to specific, emotionally charged events whose history, let alone significance, has been largely lost to us. Other poems, by flaunting the political or stylistic conventions of elite culture, pose themselves as defiant alternatives to it, and thus are poems of the people, the masses, rather than cultural elites. Poetry written by or for working-class people, in particular, often adopted a subcultural style or argot that was intentionally obscure, and these remain challenging for general readers today. Moreover, American culture was saturated with poetry in the 1910s, so when the war came, U.S. publications simply overflowed with war poems. With literacy rates climbing and modern entertainments such as film only beginning to pull people away from parlor recitations and public lectures, there were perhaps higher percentages of active writers and readers of poetry in the population than at any other time in U.S. history. Through syndication, a few poets such as Berton Braley and Edgar A. Guest achieved star status, having their poems published simultaneously in newspapers throughout the country, but newspapers as well as magazines relied on a steady stream of poems written by amateurs and their own editors. In 1914–16, daily newspaper poems were regularly concerned with the war; in 1917–18 they were almost exclusively devoted to it. In just the *New York Times* (for which I have compiled a complete log of poetry published during the war), in excess of 1,000 war poems appeared: over 400 prior to the April 1917 declaration of war, roughly 300 through the rest of 1917, and 300 again in 1918. Trying to understand the tumultuous events of the conflict, poets dashed off poems in a few hours and, not infrequently, newspaper editors published them the next day. Authors of all backgrounds, education, and abilities were writing poems about the war and having them published.

To sort out just what kinds of work this vast body of popular poetry includes and how we might make sense of its conventions, we can reasonably begin with the most popular of all the American poems published during World War I, and the inspiration for the title of this collection, Alan Seeger's "I Have a Rendezvous with Death." After first appearing in the October 1916 issue of the *North American Review,* Seeger's poem was rapidly reprinted in magazines and newspapers throughout the country, its fame helped along not a little by the poet's keeping his "rendezvous" while fighting in the Somme offensive. Seeger's posthumous *Poems* was a national best-seller: over 21,000 copies sold in its first year and more than 38,000 copies were purchased before it finally went out of print after World War II (Seeger, *Poems* manufacturing). Beginning in 1917 and 1918, it was a standard recitation piece in American schools and continued to be over the next three decades. A good many of my readers, then, will recall the poem's opening lines:

I have a rendezvous with Death
At some disputed barricade,
When Spring comes round with rustling shade
And apple-blossoms fill the air—
I have a rendezvous with Death
When Spring brings back blue days and fair.

But other than remembering, or recognizing for the first time, how good these lines sound, what are we to make of this poem, which uses the music of poetry to beguile poet and reader alike to embrace death in battle as gorgeous? Aside from Seeger's political and philosophical perspective—certainly central to the poem, but also hotly disputed in the United States at the time it was written—to renew the vitality of this poetry demands reorienting our conceptions of what poetry is and what it does. Seeger's objective throughout his brief career was the total identification of his poetic self with his personal and political selves, a fusion of art with action. Seeger took himself—and his poetic persona—utterly seriously, and his political commitment to French republicanism and French culture was such that when France was invaded in August 1914 he volunteered immediately for the Foreign Legion. Furthermore, he felt certain enough about his convictions to proselytize about the virtues of the Allied cause, as he did when he arranged to have his "Ode in Memory of the American Volunteers Fallen for France" publicly performed in Paris and Washington, D.C., on Decoration Day 1916 (Seeger, *Poems* 170–74). Seeger's gesture and his poetry were very much a part of important American poetic traditions, traditions amply documented in Aaron Kramer's *The Prophetic Tradition in American Poetry, 1835–1900*, Robert H. Walker's *The Poet and the Gilded Age: Social Themes in Late Nineteenth-Century American Verse,* and Cary Nelson's *Repression and Recovery: Modern American Poetry and the Politics of Cultural Memory, 1910–1945.* Yet the legacies of modernism and postmodernism mitigate against a serious reading of Seeger and company, for what is the modernist reader to do with a poet whose chief traits are engagement and emotion rather than detachment and irony? What is the postmodernist reader to do with a poet with such an unshakable sense of self-identity and such little inclination toward playful self-fashioning?

As it happens, Seeger's poetry is not wholly typical. His lack of irony certainly does not carry through with all, or even most, verse of the period, for parody and satire were common practice in many periodicals and were rampant in those affiliated with the political Left. The fervor of his commitment to France was certainly atypical of Americans, few of whom were ready to die for France, Belgium, or Great Britain in 1914. As this anthology shows abundantly, American poets tended at first to denounce the European conflict as a colossal waste of humanity and culture. Although in the minority in 1917, antiwar poets continued to make their voices heard in spite of government and civilian attempts to silence them. But the passion with which this debate was carried on, and the commitment that poets maintained toward their political and ideological positions—sometimes in spite of recognizing their ironies—nevertheless do recall Seeger.

Seeger and these other politically committed poets reversed conventional expectations about what poetry is supposed to accomplish: not the achievement of *timelessness*, of carving out a place in the canon of great literature, but the impact of *timeliness*, influencing historical and political conditions here and now. This is not to say that literary greatness was not on their minds or that transcendence was not an important poetic trope. But with models that included Romantic revolutionaries such as Lord Byron and Percy Bysshe Shelley and American public poets like John Greenleaf Whittier, Henry Wadsworth Longfellow, and James Russell Lowell, the achievement of greatness had as much to do with social and political involvement as with poetic craft. Seeger's "I Have a Rendezvous with Death" invokes the possibility of poetic and spiritual transcendence by its imagery of returning spring, which appears to promise the poet's incorporation into a cyclic, ongoing natural order even as he faces personal annihilation. Transcendence, however, is not portrayed as an end in itself; rather, it is mobilized to underscore the acceptability and nobility of patriotic sacrifice. While Seeger makes use of a literary tradition that longs for historical transcendence, he brings that tradition to bear on a particular sociopolitical context and a specific moment in history.

For Seeger and other poets who sought to respond to the Great War, the norm for poetry writing—and, at least in certain respects, the ideal—was not high art but journalism. The book of collected poetry, reflecting the values of deliberation, self-conscious craft, and historical durability, was not just rarer but also less capable: not able to respond to events quickly enough or to reach a large number of readers speedily enough. The single newspaper poem, however awkwardly crafted and hastily worked out, had the key strengths of immediacy, swiftness of response, and wide distribution. The poetry that met the crisis was oriented toward the spoken, or even sung, word rather than the printed word, intended more as public oracle than as private rumination. It was highly dialogic, both in the sense that poets imitated, quoted, parodied, and otherwise responded to other poets and poems and in the sense that poets sought to offer their own interpretations of the same political and historical circumstances, interpretations that were as often competitive with each other as complementary. Not always—but much more regularly and insistently than we have become accustomed to—the war poets were directly engaged with the social and political conditions of the moment; many willingly committed their poetic craft, their political allegiance, their very lives to one or another of the collective responses to the war. They actively supported Woodrow Wilson's "war for democracy"; they fought for international socialism or American labor; they championed women's rights or black Americans' rights; they struggled for world peace or against militarism or colonialism; and often, whether consistently or not, they spoke and acted on behalf of more than one cause.

BEYOND THE CULT OF THE SOLDIER-POET

The portrait I am painting of the U.S. Great War poet is not entirely unlike the much more familiar portrait of the British soldier-poet. The British soldier-poet is also thought to be politically committed—committed to the abolition of modern warfare. The recovery of American war poetry thus does not simply fill an empty niche in literary history because British soldier-poets already appear to have taken it. And why not? While Seeger presents us with the maddening image of a young man willing himself to an early grave, the well-known British soldier-poets protest vociferously against precisely this kind of death as a deluded, foolish sacrifice. In the most famous of their poems, Wilfred Owen's "Dulce et Decorum Est," the frightful death of a poison-gas victim is transformed into a most devastating antiwar indictment:

> If you could hear, at every jolt, the blood
> Come gargling from the froth-corrupted lungs,
> Obscene as cancer, bitter as the cud
> Of vile, incurable sores on innocent tongues,—
> My friend, you would not tell with such high zest
> To children ardent for some desperate glory,
> The old Lie: Dulce et decorum est
> Pro patria mori.
>
> (Fussell, *Norton* 166)

Wilfred Owen's horror of modern industrialized warfare, his testimony from the perspective of a soldier, and his incipient pacifism have come to define the proper attitudes of the war poet in the twentieth century. He, along with a handful of other British soldier-poets such as Siegfried Sassoon, Isaac Rosenberg, and Robert Graves, define the essence of the war poet: the lyric, ironic, antiwar, masculine voice that speaks from personal experience about the ghastliness of modern warfare.

The series of generalizations arising from this image have been applied not only to British Great War poetry but also to war poetry generally—including what consequently becomes a poor cousin, American war poetry. The prevailing assumptions go as follows: The experience of carnage on the Western Front was a necessary precondition to recognizing the reality of war, so much so that only frontline soldiers were properly equipped to understand the war. This understanding was described as so singular that it necessarily set apart soldiers, and soldier-poets, from civilians, opening a chasm between the experience of the soldiers and the innocence, ignorance, or mendacity of civilians. Thus, not only were soldiers alone capable of writing authentic war poetry but also they alone were capable of producing a credible critique of war and hence, also, only they could plausibly lead opposition to war (cf. Lewis; Bergonzi; Silkin). Paul Fussell's 1975 study, *The Great War and Modern Memory*, still the most influential single work on World War I poetry, positions verse and memoirs by British frontline soldiers as the very origin of modern understanding, not only of war literature or of warfare, but also of history generally: "I am saying that there seems to be one dominating form of modern understanding; that it is essentially ironic; and that it originates largely in the application of mind and memory to the events of the Great War" (35). Fussell, joined notably by Bernard Bergonzi, seems to postulate that once pre-combat innocence is shattered, British soldiers, British poetry, and even British culture could not look at warfare again with a comparable patriotic spirit.

Compared to these grand generalizations securely linking British war poetry to genuine antiwar activism and to the modernist revolution in arts and literature, the possibilities of American war poetry seem cramped indeed. For it follows, as a corollary of the soldier-poet paradigm drawn from the British context, that Americans, lacking combat experience, must have been unable to produce a coherent antiwar critique prior, at least, to U.S. intervention. Further, because American soldiers were involved in frontline combat in relatively small numbers and for a relatively short period, such American soldier-poets as might come forth were seriously handicapped. Hart describes the dominant trend: "In spite of all the prose accounts and photographs that presented the true horror of the campaigns, [American poets] demonstrated an unwillingness or even inability to see the slaughter in its true light. . . . They ought to have realized what the fighting, particularly that in the trenches, entailed; but it seems that at times of high emotion it is difficult for a nation, even a single person, to profit from the experience of others" (312–13). In his 1982 study, *American War Literature, 1914 to Vietnam*, Jeffrey Walsh does little more than draw an explicit parallel between American poets and the "facile" British poets who were superseded by the later, greater Sassoon, Owen, and Rosenberg (15). Alfred E. Cornebise's *Doughboy Doggerel*, an anthology drawn from the American Expeditionary Force newspaper *Stars and Stripes*, claims the authority of American poetry on the basis of battle experience, but then is compelled to admit that "the relatively short time that Americans were actively engaged in combat on a large scale" hampered their poetry (xii). With the important exception of Catherine W. Reilly's 1981 *Scars upon My Heart: Women's Poetry and Verse of the First World War*, which includes eight American poets among the eighty recovered, the trend to fill collections of war poetry almost exclusively with the works of soldiers—and hence to dismiss American poetry either implicitly or explicitly—has persisted through various recent additions and revisions of the war literature canon. Tim Cross's *The Lost Voices of World War I* asserts the primacy of frontline experience and battlefield death emphatically, limiting the collection to writers actually killed in combat and including just one American, Seeger.

Significantly, the near monopoly of soldier-poets in collections and studies of war poetry is broken only by a small selection of modernists. This is just what we would expect from Fussell's thesis linking soldier-poetry to modernism. Walsh writes, for example, "Only in the linguistic experiments and sophisticated ironies of modernist poets epitomised in Ezra Pound and E. E. Cummings do we find American poetry that comes near to enacting the historical realities of 1914–18" (15). Fussell himself apparently concurs, as the only American poets who appear in his *Norton Book of Modern War,* published in 1991, are E. E. Cummings and Ezra Pound. Much the same line of reasoning appears to inform Jon Silkin's *The Penguin Book of First World War Poetry,* published first in 1979 and reprinted in 1991, which includes two civilian modernists, F. S. Flint and Carl Sandburg; a third modernist who was also a volunteer ambulance driver, E. E. Cummings; and three American soldier-poets, Seeger, John Peale Bishop, and Archibald MacLeish.

It is surely curious that poems written and published after the war such as Pound's "Hugh Selwyn Mauberly" and Cummings's "my sweet old etcetera" should capture the "historical realities of 1914–18." In fact, Walsh's paradigm of American historical reality, along with Fussell's conception of modern irony, is historically selective and culturally narrow. The modern(ist) irony that Fussell describes as characteristic of the twentieth century generally derives, in fact, from the comeuppance of specific, historically privileged classes like the British gentry in Georgian England or (as Fussell himself eloquently acknowledges in his memoir *Doing Battle*) the portion of the American upper class that survived the Great Depression largely unscathed. Even while being sardonic about the euphemisms of modern mass warfare, the poetic irony favored by Fussell habitually underestimates the cultural pervasiveness and power of advertising copy, consumer culture, and technological discourses that have made terms like "precision bombing" not just credible concepts but, after the Persian Gulf War and the aerial campaign against Serbia, widely accepted as military achievements. At bottom, the logic upholding an ironic, disillusioned, and antiwar version of the war's experience begs the historical question: the horror of war is certainly the central subject of the antiwar British poets and of certain poems by modernists such as Pound, Cummings, and Eliot, but how do we know that an antiwar perspective is indeed historically representative of, or persuasive within, British or American culture? The chief evidence for the proposition is, simply, the poetry of the same antiwar British and American poets. But surely, given that Britain went to war in 1914 and remained at war through the Somme offensive and on to the armistice, and given that the United States joined the war in 1917 and stayed in the war to its conclusion, it would appear that presumptions about the historical evidence should, in fact, be shifted the other way around. Anyone will grant that the war caused immense human suffering and horror; the problem is, any sane adult living during the war also knew this, whether scraping by in the trenches or reading about them in the newspapers. The real historical issue is not how soldiers became disillusioned by, and opposed to, the horrors of war, but how the horrors of war did not sufficiently disillusion soldiers and citizens alike for them to cease supporting it. The answer to this puzzler, I would suggest, is not just that British and American cultures were overwhelmingly patriotic—a notion allowed, all along, by the chasm between home front and battlefront— or even that most soldiers remained patriotic and committed—quite empirically provable, in spite of the critics' generalizations—but also that the meaning of the "antiwar" poetry of the British soldier-poets is far different than we have supposed, and far more futile. British soldier-poets did indeed protest against the war's blasphemies, but few were able to act on their protest *except* through poetry, and often poetry not published until after the war, at that.

In being dominated by British soldier-poets, the war poetry canon is necessarily limited by nationality, gender, and, to a large extent, class. The history of that canon's selection has also led to an almost wholly antiwar body of work. But further, if less obviously, the difficulty of antiwar soldier-poets in getting their work published during the war, coupled with subsequent critics' preference for those beleaguered antiwar poets and for civilian modernists writing after the war, has produced an archaic and esoteric canon. One aim of this anthology, instead, has been to ask the critical consequences of focusing on the work historically repressed because of our fascination with the soldier-poet: What are the consequences of representing a much fuller range of perspectives on the war, reexamining patriotic as well as dissenting poetry? What do we learn, also, by reading civilian poets as well as soldier-poets, women as well as men, working-class writers as well as cultural elites, ethnic minorities as well as WASPs? What happens when we focus on poetry contemporary to the war years rather than retrospective of them? And what do American poems show about the distinctiveness of American war experiences?

From these opening questions, it rapidly becomes clear that the assumptions drawn from analysis of the British antiwar soldier-poets are at best misleading and often simply wrong. To begin with, the American poems collected here demonstrate, quite unequivocally, that frontline battle experience was *not* necessary to protest war effectively. The American civilians featured here were often well-established poets in the fall of 1914, and many were already— or soon to be—affiliated with political organizations holding significant influence over the direction of American public opinion. Their knowledge of war may have been third-hand, through censored newspaper reports, but their power to influence American society was direct and substantial. Moreover, unlike the young, naive soldier-poets, many American civilian poets did not need first-hand contact to turn against the war; they needed little time at all to develop into passionate and effective antiwar advocates. Granted, civilian poets in a neutral country might be expected to act very differently from soldiers or civilians in a country newly at war. But the thesis advanced by Fussell and others simply does not account for the passionate interest and antiwar activism that the war aroused in many Americans. Because they lacked direct knowledge of combat, one would expect them to produce only a disinterested, casual, and largely passive variety of pacifism. This is not what we find in the American poetry of 1914–16. American citizens and poets alike, responding to reports of the German advance through Belgium and the hundreds of thousands and then millions killed, became passionately engaged.

American readers during the Great War had not the benefit of Wilfred Owen's poetry; "Dulce et Decorum Est" reached the public only in 1920 with Owen's posthumous *Poems.* But already in the *Literary Digest* issue of 29 August 1914, Americans did have Edith M. Thomas's "The Woman's Cry," which urged Europe's soldiers to become conscientious objectors:

> Be ye not "mobilized" but stand like stones;
> And if to prison ye be haled, and if
> They rain upon your hearts their leaden rain
> Because ye will not serve, stand till ye fall!
> Ye can but die—but so, die innocent,
> Having, yourselves, slain no man innocent!
> So, fall, the protomartyrs Who Fought War,
> Glorious and sacred on the lips of men
> Who shall be, and their heritage *Your* Peace!
> "Red!" cried the women. Let them cry no more.

Well-read Americans could also encounter Louise Driscoll's "The Metal Checks," which won *Poetry* magazine's "war poem" contest in the fall of 1914 and was published in the November issue. More general readers would have found the poem, which represents the impersonal, mass destruction of Europe's soldiers by the identity disks each wore, in J. W. Cunliffe's *Poems of the Great War,* published in November 1916:

> That was a man a month ago;
> He could see and feel and know.
> Then, into his throat there sped
> A bit of lead.
> Blood was salt in his mouth; he fell

And lay amid the battle wreck.
Nothing was left but this metal check—
And a wife and child, perhaps.

By the assumptions of the soldier-poet paradigm, this kind of critical perspective should not be possible so early in the war—at a time when England was urged into battle with Rudyard Kipling's warning that "the Hun is at the gate" and comforted by Rupert Brooke's injunction that "If I should die, think only this of me: / That there's some corner of a foreign field / That is for ever England" (Silkin 81). Such responses to the war, so we are to assume, are not possible coming from civilians thousands of miles removed from the battlefield.

If truth be told, many British civilians actively protested the war from the very beginning: George Bernard Shaw was a vocal opponent, as were many writers affiliated with the *Nation* (including, in this collection, W. N. Ewer, the author of "Five Souls"). Only recently has this dissent been explored to some extent, most notably in Elisabeth A. Marsland's *The Nation's Cause*. It is inexcusable, though explicable, that critics of soldier-poetry have ignored this literature; it challenges directly the mythology of the soldier-poet. Yet American Great War poetry is instructive in other ways, for it also squarely challenges the assumption of Fussell and Bergonzi that, once a national poetry-writing culture becomes acquainted with the horrors of modern war and committed to war opposition, that culture can never again return to patriotic, jingoistic cant. American poets had established a poetry-writing culture in which antiwar attitudes were the norm and U.S. intervention was virtually unthinkable— near lunacy. Yet, prodded by outspoken public figures like former president Theodore Roosevelt and the poet, preacher, and ambassador to Holland, Henry van Dyke, and pushed by the threat of submarine warfare and its apparent challenge to national prestige, the United States would begin war preparations. By 1917 the massive preponderance of American poetry would be every bit as hysterically nationalistic as the poetry written by European poets at their florid best. The reversal was evident not just in national trends but also, quite remarkably, in the careers of individual poets: Edith M. Thomas was among the antiwar poets of 1914 who lent their support in 1917–18 to the Vigilantes, an organization of writers and artists who produced work dedicated to 100 percent loyalty of all Americans to the war effort.

The fickleness of antiwar poetic discourse ought, in fact, to be apparent from the instability of its core term—the painful, unlooked-for death of soldier-boys that seems, in Owen's "Dulce et Decorum Est," to provide such an unassailable condemnation. A further examination even of Owen's poem suggests the problem, for while the conditional "If you could hear" offers as a certainty that the knowledge of the frontline soldier would alter the perception of the non-soldier, the patriotic civilian, the speaker of the poem cannot in fact guarantee the then-undeluded civilian's response. The rhetorical force of the poem's conclusion masks what is, after all, a hypothesis about circumstances contrary to fact. Even if the sounds and sights of the battlefields *could* be brought home to civilians, the speaker of the poem does not actually make very expansive claims about how the home front perspective would be changed. The Horatian adage "sweet and fitting it is to die for one's country" would not be offered up to schoolchildren "with such high zest," but this does not exclude the possibility of its being doled out in some other fashion. Even if calling the adage an "old Lie" amounts to a more thorough rejection of it, then there remains the possibility that dying for one's country might be justified by some less hyperbolic, more measured, or practical reason—say, brute necessity. Owen's poem leaves open the possibility that under *some* circumstances a soldier ought to be willing to die in battle and registers the uncomfortable awareness that British commitment to its war effort was so powerful that even absolutely full disclosure about battlefield conditions might not be enough to sway a majority to an antiwar position. Owen himself *did* in fact willingly return to his unit on the Western front—if nothing else, out of a sense of obligation to his men— and there he was killed one week before the armistice. Furthermore, while one would never guess it from paging through any anthology of war literature published since the 1960s, the overwhelming majority of Britain's some 2,200 Great War poets and most of its 400 published combatant poets were supportive of their country's war effort (Reilly, *English Poetry* xix). Many soldier-poets, not to mention rank-and-file soldiers, saw and heard what Owen, Sassoon, and Rosenberg did but were not converted to pacifism.

LEST WE FORGET

The death of young men—and here especially we must add the brutal killing of women and children—has provided an argument *for* war as often as it has against it. The most cursory survey of triggering incidents, or not-so-artful pretexts, leading to declarations of war reveals the problem. Wars are often launched on account of a handful of one nation's citizens being killed by another nation's, under conditions ranging from the clearly outrageous to the merely accidental to the conveniently invented. The resulting conflicts have led to the sacrifice of a hundred or a thousand times more of the "defender's" populace as well as a similarly disproportionate number of the "aggressor" nation's citizens. Exhorted to "Remember the Maine!" we know now that its sinking in Havana harbor led the United States to declare war in spite of no conclusive evidence whatsoever of Spanish wrong-doing. Remember, also, Pearl Harbor. Or the Gulf of Tonkin. Indeed, we in the United States have waged self-proclaimed defensive wars many times not because American lives have, in fact, been lost, but because American lives were merely threatened or, remarkably, because an American "way of life" was threatened.

World War I was triggered by the assassination of a single man, heir to the Austro-Hungarian throne Archduke Franz Ferdinand, by a Serbian nationalist teenager. Once the war was well under way and initial expectations of a short, decisive campaign had been utterly blasted, the most powerful arguments for continuing the killing centered on the vast numbers of people already murdered: their deaths either called out for vengeance (the case especially for women and children killed as the Germans marched through Belgium) or demanded a national victory, lest those deaths be "in vain" (this instance applying to virtually everyone else). The appeal, however illogical, could be powerfully wrenching, as in this, one of the best-known and often reprinted poems written in English during the war, the Canadian poet John McRae's "In Flanders Fields":

> In Flanders fields the poppies blow
> Between the crosses, row on row,
>   That mark our place, and in the sky,
>   The larks, still bravely singing, fly,
> Scarce heard amid the guns below.
>
> We are the dead; short days ago
>   We lived, felt dawn, saw sunset glow,
> Loved and were loved, and now we lie
>   In Flanders fields.
>
> Take up our quarrel with the foe!
> To you from failing hands we throw
>   The torch; be yours to hold it high!
>   If ye break faith with us who die
> We shall not sleep, though poppies grow
>   In Flanders fields.

Immediately reprinted in 1916 throughout the United States as well as in Britain and the Commonwealth, the poem might well be read as a challenge not only to Britons to continue the fight but also to Americans to "take up our quarrel."

With significant exceptions, most Americans were swayed to support the Allies by the mass killing of Belgian, English, and French soldiers, who were obviously on the defensive in the war's opening months, and were moved as well by the highly exaggerated accounts of murder, mutilation, and rape in Belgium publicized through the British government's Bryce Commission report. The immediate trigger for intervention, however, centered on a few hundred American civilians who shipped passage to Europe on Allied vessels and were killed when those ships were sunk by German U-boats. The most spectacular sinking was of the British passenger liner *Lusitania,* which went down on 7 May 1915 off the coast of Ireland at the loss of some 1,200 civilians including 128 U.S. citizens. Whereas a majority of Americans—including the president—was not immediately persuaded that this sinking amounted to a *causus belli,* the event changed perceptions of the war and of its chief antagonists considerably. The predominant U.S. attitude toward the tragedy and its American dead was summed up, and stirred up, by Joyce Kilmer's "The White Ships and the Red." Published in the 16 May Sunday magazine section of the *New York Times,* the poem personifies the sunken ship to give unequivocal voice to the moral issues involved:

> "I went not forth to battle,
>   I carried friendly men,
> The children played about my decks,
>   The woman sang—and then—
> And then—the sun blushed scarlet
>   And Heaven hid its face,
> That world that God created
>   Became a shameful place!
>
> "My wrong cries out for vengeance,
>   The blow that sent me here
> Was aimed in Hell. My dying scream
>   Has reached Jehovah's ear.
> Not all the seven oceans
>   Shall wash away the stain;
> Upon a brow that wears a crown
>   I am the brand of Cain."

Never mind that in Genesis Cain was supposedly branded by God not as a mark of his moral depravity but as a seal of protection, so that anyone seeking vengeance for Cain's murder of Abel would be subjected to God's wrath. What counted, rather, for Kilmer and readers of the *Times* was a poem recording, in rough and ready fashion, their initial shock and moral outrage. Unless Woodrow Wilson and his administration could substantially alter the terms under which Germany was carrying on its submarine warfare, additional American citizens would inevitably be killed and the resulting public outcry would push the United States into the conflict. Wilson in fact achieved this change in German policy. In September 1915, after another passenger liner, the *Arabic,* was sunk and two Americans were among those killed, Wilson's diplomacy extracted a pledge from the German government that its submarines would attack passenger liners only with fair warning and with time provided for civilians to escape to lifeboats. The promise, kept almost unblemished for the next year and a half, effectively ended the U-boat blockade of England. But the 128 Americans lost with the *Lusitania* virtually guaranteed that when Germany returned to unrestricted submarine warfare—as it did in February 1917—the United States would enter the war on the side of the Triple Entente.

Yet abhorrence of modern war's death, destruction, and horror was only part of the story of how the United States became a participant, even as it was only part of the reason that the European powers continued to fight. As Eric Leed has suggested in *No Man's Land: Combat and Identity in World War I*, the liminality of war—its apparently complete discordance with civilian, peacetime life, which permits civilians of neutral nations to be swallowed up, in a flash, by the sea—produces not only revulsion in observers and participants but also fascination. The extreme liminality of massive, random death in modern war can have a seductive attraction: it sorts out the significant from the insignificant, "masculine" hardness from "effeminate" weakness, the alloy from the dross. We cannot underestimate the importance of this attraction in the ongoing popularity of works by Wilfred Owen and the soldier-poets, not to mention the much wider popularity in American society of action-adventure and war stories both in print and on film. American society in 1917, like European society in 1914, welcomed the conflict as an opportunity to refine itself. So, too, many American young men of 1917, like their European counterparts of 1914, saw the war as an adventure and essential proving ground for their manhood. The attractiveness of war as a test for human (and often specifically masculine) power, even though—or, really, *because*—its testing may prove fatal is treated straightforwardly as sex appeal in Alan Seeger's "I Have a Rendezvous with Death." Death is a rendezvous more vital than conventional romantic love:

> God knows 'twere better to be deep
> Pillowed in silk and scented down,
> Where Love throbs out in blissful sleep
> Pulse nigh to pulse, and breath to breath,
> Where hushed awakenings are dear. . . .
> But I've a rendezvous with Death
> At midnight in some flaming town,
> When Spring trips north again this year,
> And I to my pledged word am true,
> I shall not fail that rendezvous.

Seeger was eager for war; he could hardly wait for his accelerated military training to be over, let alone wait for the United States to get involved. Indeed, his keenness for danger is said to have alarmed his comrades in the French Foreign Legion. But lest Seeger's enthusiasm be thought merely the ravings of a romantic twenty-five year old, recall that "I Have a Rendezvous with Death" was enormously popular. Consider, also, Edgar Lee Masters's commentary in the May 1917 issue of *Poetry* magazine:

> And you, O young boys of eighteen and twenty, athletic and fearless, eager for battle, leaving this strange mixture of tragedy and comedy for the immediacy of Eternal Presences, Death and the Great Inspirations, may your blood be the atonement for us, and for ours to come. You will pass in such numbers over the threshold between this life and what is beyond that the great echo of your steps may give us the proof that death is not death, and that this Reality here is a Dream, and yours the Reality. (91)

Consider, further, an editorial published the next month in the same journal, when it was senior editor Harriet Monroe's turn:

> If we have war, devastating war that shall relieve us of surplus billions and drain some of our most precious hearts' blood, its huge and irresistible flood may wash away much of the accumulated materialism which clogs our souls. It is not enough that we fight, as of old but in a larger, more generous sense, for liberty; not only our own but the liberty of all men—for the freedom of the seas and the democratizing of the world. We must fight first and most persistently for that freedom of the spirit—the clear vision and stript athletic strength of mind and soul which alone will enable us to achieve our purpose and advance the freedom of the world. ("What War" 143–44)

Masters and Monroe, two founders of modern poetry in the United States, are hardly less keen than the romantic Seeger in embracing the Inspiration, Reality, Purgative, Reformer, Lover that they call, alternately, War and Death.

Kilmer's and Seeger's rationalizations for intervention, though similar in their fervor, are utterly contrary in their logic. For Kilmer, the United States must wage war to protect that which is precious on the home front: domestic harmony, safety, civil tranquility, and order. For Seeger, war must be waged because civilian life is defective or false; war is a purifier or a reformer of the base, the uncivil, and the impure. Yet these opposed attitudes worked in tandem to bring the United States into the conflict. While Kilmer's argument helped sway the larger number of Americans to support intervention—first because American lives were endangered on the seas and later because American soldier-boys were risking death in France—Seeger's style of argument appealed to the country's intellectual elites. The notion of war as purifier and reformer, illustrated in the ruminations of Edgar Lee Masters and Harriet Monroe, encompassed both aggressive, military-minded nationalists such as Theodore Roosevelt, who regarded warfare as the antidote for a society grown weak, womanly, and vacillating, and politic, diplomacy-minded reformers such as Woodrow Wilson, who in 1917 hoped to gain by battle the kind of egalitarian, law-abiding concert of nations that he had failed to orchestrate through neutrality. Wilson and the many reformers in his administration were, further-more, animated by the notion that the war provided unique opportunities for old domestic systems to be broken apart and more equitable or rational ar-rangements to be established instead. It was this kind of thinking that persuad-ed George Creel, the muckraking journalist from Denver, to join the admin-istration in 1917 as the head of the newly formed wartime Committee on Public Information—the U.S. purveyor of propaganda.

All of this should not suggest, however, that debate ended once interven-tionist American poets and political rhetoricians discovered that random, mass killing (whether one was repulsed or attracted to it) could be mobilized to support their causes. The arguments could still be readily enough reversed to argue against war involvement, and this is precisely what many poets did. The counterthrust against the Kilmerian position is roughly the same one devel-oped in the pacifist poems that we have already sampled. The disparity between the war's causes and its consequences were, indeed, greatly magnified as the fighting continued. In 1917, that one man's assassination should lead to the killing of millions of European soldiers and civilians was thought absurd. It continued to appear ridiculous even when set forth by an American poet such as Katharine Lee Bates, who by mid-1917 was generally in support of U.S. in-tervention. Her poem "The Retinue," published in the October 1917 issue of the *Atlantic Monthly*, may cast the Germans as the villains, but it hardly suc-ceeds in showing why, because hundreds of Americans are among the "dim civilians" in Hades, thousands of additional Americans ought to be conscript-ed, sent overseas, and killed. Just to join them?

> Archduke Francis Ferdinand, Austrian Heir-Apparent,
> Rideth through the Shadow Land, not a lone knight errant,
> But captain of a mighty train, millions upon millions,
> Armies of the battle-slain, hordes of dim civilians;
>
> German ghosts who see their works with tortured eyes, the sorry
> Specters of scared tyrants, Turks hunted by their quarry,
> Liars, plotters red of hand—like waves of poisonous gases
> Sweeping through the Shadow Land the host of horror passes.

In spite of the antimonarchist bent of the poem, very much in keeping with Wilson's "war for democracy," it is hard to see how the poem provides an in-terventionist argument. It is at least not difficult to see why the editors of the pacifist journal *Four Lights* should have appropriated it, reprinting it at the first opportunity, in the journal's penultimate issue of 20 October 1917.

Against the Seegerian idea that war provided an opportunity to purge American society of its ills, dissenters argued that a society as undemocratic, oppressive, and inequitable as the United States had no business whatsoever fighting for democracy, freedom, and opportunity abroad, and further, that the war was likely to entrench more deeply antidemocratic and unjust social tendencies. Sarah Norcliffe Cleghorn's "Peace Hath Her Belgiums," published in August 1917, compares the invasion of Belgium with the living conditions of the working class in U.S. cities and the figure of German militarism, "tall Uhlans," with capitalist "Profits":

> There is a Belgium in the bedrooms dark,
> Tiny dark bedrooms, feeders to the grave.
> Hark how the besieged Belgians cough and gasp
> Where those tall Uhlans, Profits, have cut off
> Their sunlight and their air!

As a consequence of the attention given the German-invaded Belgium, Americans ignore and thereby enable the perpetuation of home-grown "Belgiums." Ralph H. Chaplin, a poet, illustrator, and organizer in the syndicalist IWW, similarly foregrounds the disparity between the emerging, idealistic rationales for intervention and domestic conditions in "Preparedness," written in the summer of 1916 when Congress was deliberating expansion of U.S. armed forces:

> For freedom die? but we were never free
>   Save but to drudge and starve or strike and feel
>   The bite of bullets and the thrust of steel.
> For freedom die, while all the land can see
>   How strikers writhe beneath thy crushing heel
> And mothers shudder at the thought of thee!
>   For freedom die . . . ?

In Chaplin's poem, the charge that patriotism is a fatal trap is made still more explicit than in Cleghorn's. Nationalist cries of "freedom," as well as "defend the flag" and "protect our land" (the themes of the following two stanzas), are blasphemous distractions from the business of actually making the country more free, more representative, and more just.

Here we glimpse some possibilities for war poetry, and wartime debate, that are almost missed in the dichotomy of antiwar soldier-poets and pro-war civilian doggerelists. We see, first, the possibility that some writers will simply refuse to buy into the opposition of war/peace, between the violent battlefront that serves as a shield for the peaceful home front. For the Wobblies and other critics of U.S. involvement in war, the home front is as much a source of violence and exploitation. We see, also, alternatives emerging that are more complex and politically astute than simply the elimination of war—which, although poets like Owen and Rosenberg offer more complex solutions than this, is about all their critics propose to gain from their "antiwar" attitudes. Dissenters such as Cleghorn and Chaplin did not ultimately define their identities in national terms so much as in class terms: the key question was not, what will best serve the interests of my country? but rather, what will advance the cause of the dispossessed? Other political groups and communities of common interest within American society were asking similar questions and finding answers that likewise challenged whether their first allegiance, even in wartime, ought to be to their country. The Socialist Party of America, convening after the U.S. declaration of war, voted overwhelmingly for a resolution of opposition. Pacifists at their most radical were internationalists, putting understanding among nations ahead of national partisanship. Radical woman's suffrage advocates, particularly those affiliated with the National Woman's party founded in June 1916, would not give their support to the war effort before Woodrow Wilson acknowledged their struggle for democratic participation at home as essential to his war for democracy abroad. Activists for black civil rights, led by the fast-growing National Association for the Advancement of Colored People, which was still less than a decade old, were inclined to support intervention if only because they dreaded the consequences of black resistance. Yet many remained critical of a government that demanded blacks pay the full price of citizenship while it lagged in ensuring them the full benefits thereof.

All these struggles for equal rights predated the quarrel with Kaiser Wilhelm. All, for the most committed activists, transcended national loyalty. All had drawn volunteers who sacrificed much and risked much; some gave all. Jane Addams, for example, was arguably the best known and most widely revered woman in the United States when she agreed to head the Woman's Peace party in January 1915; by 1917, she was jeered at during public appearances even when she consented to speak on behalf of the U.S. Food Administration. In the suffrage movement were historic saints such as Susan B. Anthony and Elizabeth Cady Stanton, who had dedicated their entire lives to the fight for women's rights, and also contemporary political prisoners such as members of the National Woman's party who picketed the White House throughout 1917 and were jailed for "disturbing the peace." The histories of the black civil rights movement and of the labor movement were similarly marked by martyrs. Among African Americans were lynching victims, numbering nearly 3,000 between 1885 and 1917 by the NAACP's count and still ranging between 44 and 80 per year during the war ("Colored Men Lynched"). There were also many violent deaths suffered in labor's cause. Thirty-five thousand people were killed in industrial accidents in 1914; the federal report producing this statistic suggested that at least half of these were considered "preventable" and put the number of job-related injuries for the year at seven hundred thousand (Metzer 165). Smaller but more visible numbers of workers were killed in strike violence, and a few labor martyrs gained international fame. Foremost among these was Joe Hill, charged with murder in January 1915 on significant though circumstantial evidence, but convicted largely on the basis of his membership in the radical IWW. By the time Hill was executed in November 1915 he had become an international cause célèbre: as radical periodicals around the world championed him, Woodrow Wilson issued an eleventh-hour appeal for clemency. For his part, Hill telegrammed the IWW leadership hours before his execution, "Don't waste any time mourning. *Organize*" (qtd. in Dubofsky 311).

The often contentious attitudes of woman's suffrage workers, civil rights activists, Socialists, and union organizers toward the nation are reflected in the complicated ways they sought to appropriate the rhetorical power of patriotic discourses and, at the same time, reject the government's oppressive exercise of that power. The life-and-death sacrifices advocates made were described, within their respective movements, in virtually the same terms as were the sacrifices of soldiers and war workers. They, too, called upon the living to carry on the struggle. "Lest We Forget," borrowed from Rudyard Kipling's famous "Recessional" exhorting Britons to recall God's divine providence (supposedly) authorizing the empire, was common enough that it could be used with minimal gloss as the title for a patriotic anthology published in London (Elliott). Only *A War Anthology* needed to be appended as a subtitle; what was being remembered and why were obvious. By this time, however, the very same phrase had entered the lexicon of the political Left to demand an active remembrance of radical martyrs. It was used, for example, in a July 1914 *International Socialist Review* article commemorating the five strikers framed for the Haymarket Riot and executed by the state of Illinois in 1887 (Sadler). "Lest We Forget" was the title and the theme also of a 1918 article in the socialist *New York Call*, Pauline M. Newman's commemoration of the seventh anniversary of the Triangle Shirtwaist factory fire in which 146 working women had died.

Radical writers were self-conscious about the possible implications of making their causes parallel too closely the national causes tearing Europe apart. Recognizing that the calls for remembering the "millions . . . killed during the past four years" might well drown out the voices of the Triangle Shirtwaist victims, Newman asserts that they, unlike the dead in Flanders fields, point the way to the elimination of both economic injustice and war: "Some day, when the workers of the world will come to a realization of their own powers, possibilities of a Triangle fire, even the possibilities of a war, will be a thing of the past—never, never to return." Even more assertive is Arturo Giovannitti in his "When the Cock Crows," published in September 1917 to commemorate the lynching, little more than a month before, of IWW organizer Frank Little by a patriotic, antiunion vigilante gang in Butte, Montana. Although the poem is structurally similar to patriotic calls to arms, demanding that the union faithful commemorate their heroic dead by undying allegiance to their cause, the speaker is emphatic about not only the distraction provided by patriotism but also the *difference* between patriotism and political radicalism. The poem imagines what Little, who in 1917 did in fact season his union stump speech with advocacy of draft resistance, would say to any who dared shrink from his example:

> "Brothers[ ]—he will shout to them—["]are you then, the Godborn,
>   reduced to a mute of dogs
> That you will rush to the hunt of your kin at the blowing of a horn?
> Brothers, have then the centuries that created new suns in the heavens,
>   gouged out the eyes of your soul,
> That you should wallow in your blood like swine,
> That you should squirm like rats in carrion.
> That you, who astonished the eagles, should beat blindly about the
>   night of murder like bats?
> Are you, Brothers, who were meant to scale the stars, to crouch forever
>   before a footstool,
> And listen forever to one word of shame and subjection,
> And leave the plough in the furrow, the trowel on the wall, the
>   hammer on the anvil, and the heart of the race on the knees of
>   screaming women, and the future of the race in the hands of
>   babbling children,
> And yoke on your shoulders the halter of hatred and fury,
> And dash head-down against the bastions of folly,
> Because a colored cloth waves in the air, because a drum beats in the
>   street,
> Because six men have promised you a piece of ribbon on your coat, a
>   carved tablet on a wall and your name in a list bordered with
>   black?
> Shall you, then, be forever the stewards of death, when life waits for
>   you like a bride?
> Ah no, Brothers, not for this did our mothers shriek with pain and
>   delight when we tore their flanks with our first cry;
> Not for this were we given command of the beasts,
> Not with blood but with sweat were we bidden to achieve our
>   salvation.["]

The poem is conspicuously glib in its appropriation of pacifist icons (the woman giving birth to life being utterly opposed to death) and of Christian religious rhetoric (in a later line, the Frank Little persona proclaims, "Behold! I announce now to you a great tiding of joy"). The chasm between patriotism and radicalism, in contrast, is utterly unbridgeable: the former means "shame and subjection," delusion, blindness, bloodshed, "death"; the latter signifies humanity, progress, productive labor, "delight," "salvation," "life." Yet the discourses are far more closely related than all this suggests, not simply because the pro-Entente rhetoric that helped bring the United States into the war offered a similar divide between humanity and hate (note the title of a 1918 poetry anthology of French and German poetry: *Humanity or Hate: Which?* [Grumbine]) but also because patriotic rhetoric, like Giovannitti's poem, seldom actually asked soldiers to *kill,* but only to be willing to *die.*

Both the Second International and the Triple Entente claimed, finally, that their pledge to the dead would be redeemed by the creation of a better world—it was a war not just to "end war" but to "make the world safe for democracy." American rhetoricians, whether poets, politicians, political activists, government publicists, or common readers, used roughly the same terms for describing war: "democracy," "our boys," "our dead." They were in constant dialogue with one another, though they were also locked in continual struggle about the reality those terms referred to—which vision of democracy, which methods for arriving at it, which war was being actually fought, which war should be.

The struggles between these groups were also, inevitably, struggles between factions and struggles within individuals. Even so implacable a critic of official and civic racism as W. E. B. Du Bois was inspired by the patriotism of his fellow African Americans—and thus led to publish his infamous "Close Ranks" editorial of July 1918, in which he declared black civil rights to be "special grievances" and urged blacks to suspend their activism "while this war lasts." Women's rights advocates were divided over their role in war mobilization: far and away the largest organization, the National American Woman Suffrage Association, gave its wholehearted support to war work, on account of its members' patriotic sentiments as much as out of political tactics; the National Woman's party gave limited support to the war effort only after Wilson had come out in favor of the suffrage amendment in January 1918. Even Socialists were divided over a proper response. Many intellectuals dissented from the party's platform of war opposition, partly because in March 1917 the first wave of revolution had swept Czar Nicholas from power in Russia. That the most politically regressive member of the Triple Entente had suddenly moved to the political vanguard was all that was needed to sway a considerable number of Socialists already eager to reconcile patriotism with their ideological and political creeds. The poet Carl Sandburg, a regular contributor to the *International Socialist Review* as well as to *Poetry* magazine, wrote a poem in the fall of 1917 in which he proclaimed,

> Look! It is four brothers in joined hands together.
> The people of bleeding France,
> The people of bleeding Russia,
> The people of Britain, the people of America—
> These are the four brothers, these are the four republics.

Blood sacrifice could not only bind together Socialists in a common, undying cause but also entwine some in the sacred national causes that fueled the European war to its very end. The problem with sorting out just which cause deserved one's utmost loyalty—my country or my class?—was that no one cause could lay unequivocal claim to Life and Freedom, no cause could be unambiguously aligned with Death and Slavery. The questions were immeasurably more complex, having to do with hypotheses about political ideals and their future consequences: Which path leads to life and liberty? Which path leads to death and destruction? And hardest of all: what kind of life and liberty, what political cause, are you willing to die for?

POETIC DIALOGUE AND ITS LIMITS

It may fairly be said that poems giving voice to these questions—and charting answers—were engaged in a dialogue with one another, though it was not by any means a genteel exchange. This fiercely waged contest could hardly have had higher stakes. The poems included in this anthology demonstrate that this dialogue did not operate simply, or even especially, on the level of "thematic" concern. For precisely this reason, I have chosen to order the poems not by literary theme but by chronology, which highlights the ebb and flow of politics, history, and authors' responses to contemporary events. The primary orientation of this dialogue was not toward a literary community but a broader reading community and not toward the achievement of great literature so much as the practice of immediate politics. The subject of the dialogue was not literature but history: poems sought to interpret what the events reported in the papers meant, what the lived experience of the war mobilization meant, and what role the United States played, and should play, in those events and in the lives of its citizens.

When poets entered into direct dialogue with one another, they often did so through imitation, mimicry, and parody. The poets and songwriters of the IWW have long been recognized for their art of parody (see Salerno), and certainly the selections I have made for this anthology confirm this reputation: note, for example, John Kendrick's parodies of Poe's "The Raven" in "What For?" and of the evangelical hymn "Onward, Christian Soldiers" in his lyric of that name—a verse scandalous enough to be entered as prime prosecution evidence at the IWW sedition trial. What has not been so widely recognized, however, is just how widespread imitation and parody were. Written in 1914, Katherine Devereux Blake's "O say can you see, you who glory in war" was a pacifist and socialist version of the "Star Spangled Banner." Woman's suffrage prisoners held in the fall of 1917 at Occoquan Work House composed and sang a lyric reprinted here, "We Worried Woody-Wood," which ridiculed Woodrow Wilson's handling of his war for democracy to the popular song tune "Captain Kidd."

Besides popular songs, sacred hymns, and the national anthem, prime fare for voracious parodic appetites were the works of other poets, particularly of those who had gained notoriety as spokespersons for a certain point of view. Rudyard Kipling, who in the fall of 1914 established himself as Britain's de facto national oracle, provided one such sizable target for satire. Kipling's hortatory poem of fatherly advice, "If," published first in 1910, proved especially irresistible as a model, as it offered, in a single convenient package, a formula for both poetic versification and logical deduction. One version reprinted herein, by Florence Guertin Tuttle, quotes the stanzaic and metrical patterns of "If" almost exactly, appearing to pay some measure of homage to Kipling. Yet "IF. A Mother to Her Daughter" sets the verse in an entirely new context—a woman's admonitions to her daughter at the Red Cross office as opposed, perhaps, to a man's advice to his son on the polo grounds—and the poem's satiric tone slyly undercuts the conspiratorial masculinity of Kipling's original. Kipling's "If" concludes with the promise that a good man's virtues will be rewarded by national, even imperial, political power, and—what is supposedly "more"— the assurance of one's pure masculinity:

> If you can talk with crowds and keep your virtue,
>> Or walk with Kings—nor lose the common touch,
> If neither foes nor loving friends can hurt you,
>> If all men count with you, but none too much;
> If you can fill the unforgiving minute
>> With sixty seconds' worth of distance run,
> Yours is the earth and everything that's in it,
>> And—which is more—you'll be a Man, my son!

In comparison, Tuttle's parody suggests that the reward of the good patriot daughter, willing to sacrifice her time, her treasure, and her conscience for her country, is the forfeiture of both her femininity and her humanity. So runs Tuttle's final stanza:

> If you can sing "My Country first" and never
>> Observe that lands melt freely into one;
> If you can prove mankind is not united,
>> Led by one hope as by one rising sun;
> If you can doubt that greed of State must perish,
>> And God, the King, One Sovereignty unfurl,
> You'll be a "loyal patriot" my darling,
>> And which is more—a thing of stone, my girl.

As a parody, Tuttle's poem gestures to the fact that Kipling and most Britons were anything but temperate, independent-minded, and honest when their country entered the war. As a commentary on American political culture, the poem criticizes both the nationalist and the jingoist direction of current policies and the ready accommodation of most women to the needs of the war effort.

Poems of this kind, in which a poet responds directly to the form as well as the content of another's work, abounded in American wartime writing and are well represented among the poems that follow. But this direct mimicry naturally constitutes a distinct minority among the thousands of American war poems. In most, authors responded to the pull of current events, which demanded constant watchfulness and ongoing exploration, and to the push of political commitments, which compelled constant redefinition of positions, renewal of arguments, and recruitment of political converts and new allies. A significant number of poems responded to journalistic or personal accounts of the war offered explicitly as epigraphs: poems as various as Columbia undergraduate Morrie Ryskind's "Ten Thousand Tommy Atkinses" Edith M. Thomas's "The Woman's Cry," and Wallace Stevens's "Lettres d'un Soldat." Still others responded to diplomatic pronouncements, as when, in the fall of 1914, Henry van Dyke's "A Scrap of Paper" (which he wrote as Civis Americanus) angrily countered German chancellor Bethmann-Hollweg's comment that Britain would be going to war "just for a scrap of paper" in defending Belgian neutrality (Tuchman 129), or as when, in the fall of 1917, McLandburgh Wilson's "Made Safe for Democracy" translated Woodrow Wilson's high-minded political justifications for war into a plain, folksy, visceral idiom. A still larger number responded to a specific political or military action or program. Many, many poems, for example, responded to the Russian Revolution—five appear in this collection. More mundane, but perhaps materially more important, were the many poems that bolstered, commented on, or critiqued the national mobilization on the American home front. Prominent in this collection are poems that support patriotic knitting, including selections from the *New York Sun*'s "Sock Songs" competition of May–November 1918, and a poem that ridicules the practice, soldier-poet Sidney G. Doolittle's "Enthusiasts." Several others preach food conservation—for one, Alice Corbin Henderson's "The Planting of the Green" (which she published as plain Alice Corbin)—while others, such as Lola Ridge's "Bread," suggest enough Americans are starving without inventing special government programs to encourage it.

The exchanges should not suggest that wartime dialogue took place on a level political terrain. The editorial policy of national publications tended to follow rather than lead the mainstream of popular opinion—even when such publications professed to be above the vicissitudes of such opinion. *Poetry* magazine was willing to publish a high percentage of distinctly antiwar poems in November 1914, but at that point, as the associate editor Alice Corbin Henderson explained, "The American feeling about the war [was] a genuine revolt against war," so the magazine was taking no particularly bold stance as an advocate. When in 1917 *Poetry* editor Harriet Monroe was chided "for printing no war poems at the very moment of the nation's dread decision," she asserted that war poems would be published, regardless of their viewpoint, only when those submitted met the magazine's high artistic standards: "[Any] interpretation of the present crisis . . . which, in the opinion of the editors, *is* poetry," she promised, "*Poetry* will print promptly" ("Will Art" 203, 205). Yet during the succeeding year *Poetry* apparently found almost no true poetry of a pacifist hue (so abundant in 1914) but ended up publishing a good deal of poetry highly partial to the Allied war cause, including Baker Brownell's "Freebourne's Rifle," Ajan Syrian's "The Prayer Rug of Islam," and John Curtis Underwood's "At Bethlehem."

Editorial balance in mainstream publications seems to have been possible only when the country was poised uncertainly between war and peace. Among the few places where dialogue about the war was carried out on anything like an equal footing were war poetry anthologies and literary journals published in 1916 and 1917. In anthologies such as J. W. Cunliffe's *Poems of the Great War,* W. Reginald Wheeler's *A Book of Verse of the Great War,* and George Herbert Clarke's *A Treasury of War Poetry* and in a few periodicals—not only in an avant-garde little magazine like *Poetry* but also in magazines as popular as *Scribner's* and as venerable as the *Century*—poems that propagandize for the Allied cause are invariably mixed with some that are unequivocally pacifist. At all times during the war, however, definite limits restricted content. Already during *Poetry*'s pacifist phase, while Karle Wilson Baker's "Unser Gott" could express sympathy with war victims in Germany as well as in Russia, Serbia, England, and France, the poem still singled out Germany as the model for misguided, hysterical nationalism. Similarly, even in 1917, magazines like *Scribner's, Outlook, Century,* and the *Atlantic Monthly* published poems underscoring the pathos of war, even to a degree suggesting pacifist attitudes. But poems that expressed revulsion at the institutions of war and their hypocrisies were acceptable only if they attacked militarism and autocracy as the root causes of war—permissible since autocratic rule and militarism were assumed to be altogether European phenomena. Unacceptable were poems that attacked the *American* institutions of war or that proposed solutions to the wartime crisis (pacifist internationalism, international socialism) that were at odds with U.S. government policy. The poems published in anthologies and more prestigious journals did indeed bring different perspectives together, but, virtually for the war's duration, antiwar attitudes in poetry remained almost entirely nonspecific about, and uncommitted toward, any substantive political alternative.

To obtain a more comprehensive view of the cultural and political work being done through American poetry during World War I, we must examine partisan poetry that appeared in less elite contexts, like daily newspapers and party organs, as well as in politically committed journals such as the *Masses* and *Seven Arts.* These journals' editors were far less eclectic in their tastes for war poetry. In a sense, they were utterly discriminating, but their primary criteria were oriented less to literary craft than to political acuity. The IWW's *Solidarity* and *Industrial Worker* wanted revolutionary fare, just as the *New York Times* sought, from the *Lusitania* disaster onward, pro-intervention and pro-war verses. The editors of periodicals such as these applied political and ideological litmus tests freely. The partisan stance taken by the author was, simply, an essential feature of a poem's goodness or badness; within the right ideological frame, the more partisan a poem was, the better. Insofar as their readers already shared a perspective on the war, the periodicals' rhetorical goal was not so much to convince them to think about the war differently as to enjoin them to act according to their established convictions. The IWW's organs, and the poems published therein, encouraged its readers to go out on strike, to recruit new members, to contribute to the strike fund or prisoners' fund, and to wait patiently for the expected revolution. The National Woman's party organ, the *Suffragist,* specifically encouraged participation in the picketing campaign and gave succor to the embattled and jailed picketers of the summer and fall of 1917. Meanwhile, mainstream newspapers across the country, which after the *Lusitania* only rarely gave space to poems questioning the Allied cause, let alone American preparedness measures, let loose a flood of poems with clear, instrumental intent: first hundreds, and by the end of the war thousands, of poems not only encouraging 100 percent American loyalty but also specifically promoting the Red Cross, socks for soldiers, liberty bonds, food conservation, and other government programs.

But again, even as the methods and aims of these partisan poets and editors were similar, the conditions under which they worked to proselytize and mobilize readers could hardly be more different, especially as 1917 wore on and the government's hard-line policy against dissent solidified. Any movement linked with internationalism (read: foreign interests) or any cause imagined to compete with the national crusade was under suspicion. Meanwhile, business interests and conservative politics were profiting; their causes, with no real reform agenda, were easier to harmonize with the nationalist status quo. When in the middle of June 1917 Congress passed the Espionage Act, which outlawed advocacy of draft resistance and allowed mailing privileges to be denied to "seditious" periodicals, the law was used primarily, and almost immediately, to attack leftist periodicals: by the end of the summer, Postmaster General Albert Burleson had halted circulation of the *International Socialist Review,* the *Masses, Solidarity,* and *Industrial Worker.* The government's war for democracy abroad became a war to silence dissent at home. The entire leadership of the IWW was arrested on federal conspiracy charges in September 1917, held in federal prisons in Chicago, Leavenworth, and San Francisco, convicted of treason in August 1918, and given sentences ranging from five to twenty years. The union never recovered. The Socialist Party of America was similarly crippled.

The party's membership declined from its high of 123,000 in the election year of 1912 to 81,000 by 1918 and rebounded to 100,000 in 1919 only on the strength of its foreign-language federations, which comprised 57 percent of union membership in 1919 as compared to just 13 percent in 1912 (Bell 291). In the year of the Red Scare and after a war that popularized "100 percent Americanism," this high percentage signaled the party's effective demise as a viable contender for national power. While other groups were not put down as ruthlessly as the Socialists and labor radicals, dissent was suppressed even when direct government action was not taken. Many newspapers practiced self-censorship; only a few ventured to criticize some features of war mobilization, and even then only those few scandals, like food hoarding and profiteering, which Woodrow Wilson himself spoke against in public, were targeted.

American political discussions were increasingly dominated by publications and poetry that opposed substantial criticism of war mobilization. Amid suspicion of all things foreign—German agents, for example, were thought responsible for introducing influenza to the United States—jingoist effusions were written more or less spontaneously by poets, both avocational and professional, whose productions filled editorial pages across the country. Meanwhile, the syndicate system of distributing newspaper editorials and poetry nationally was exploited effectively by the Vigilantes, a group of patriotic writers and artists who published the anthology of prose and poetry *For France* in April 1917 and an all-poetry collection, *Fifes and Drums,* in June, but thereafter resorted to daily press releases of patriotic poems and editorials provided gratis. Organizations that came to the Vigilantes with requests for propaganda included the Red Cross, the YMCA, the American Bankers' Association, the League to Enforce Peace, the U.S. Chamber of Commerce, and the Boy Scouts, as well as the group's original backers, the National Security League and the American Defense Society (Browne 67–68). After the war George Creel remarked that "their patriotism was a thing of screams, violence and extremes, and their savage intolerances had the burn of acid" (qtd. in Peterson and Fite 18). But Porter Emerson Browne, one of its four cofounders, reports that the Vigilantes worked with two different subcommittees of Creel's own Committee on Public Information, the American Alliance for Labor and Democracy, which provided material for labor newspapers, and another that produced anti-German propaganda for distribution in Russia (68). The free, unofficial publicity the Vigilantes provided the Food Administration, the Fuel Administration, and Liberty Loan campaigns was simply too helpful to be dismissed. The director of the Liberty Loan publicity division wrote to thank the Vigilantes for its publicity help in "papers all over the country from Texas to New York" (Meetings).

The prominence of the Vigilantes and allied groups such as the National Security League and the American Defense Society provides important context for understanding the gains made, and the limitations placed on, progressive political groups and their causes. For example, the most reactionary of "progressive" causes—Prohibition—received an unexpected boost from wartime conservation of grains and wartime prejudice against German breweries. Women's rights activists finally attained the main prize, suffrage, that had eluded them for over seventy years of activism; but after a combination of women's wartime service and direct action won the vote in 1920, further activism stalled and did not reemerge cohesively on the national level until the late 1960s. NAACP membership expanded rapidly, in part because life remained so perilous for African Americans: black communities were buffeted by race riots during and after the war, black soldiers faced bigotry in the segregated army (and were not even permitted into the Coast Guard, marines, or the navy except as coal-shovelers and stevedores). And the war years also saw the rebirth of the Ku Klux Klan. Catalyzed by D. W. Griffith's pro-KKK film *The Birth of a Nation* as well as by the wartime rise in xenophobia, the Klan sprang up this time throughout the nation and played a hand in the highly restrictive, prejudicial immigration quotas of the Immigration Reform Act of 1924. In contrast, the NAACP's ambitious programs for economic and political justice went largely unrealized until the midfifties and sixties, by which time W. E. B. Du Bois, utterly frustrated by American injustice, had joined the Communist International and renounced his U.S. citizenship. Progressive groups and causes ensured their survival only by acknowledging the primacy of the national interest, a move that sometimes resulted in political gains but almost always meant distorting principles and compromising interests. Thus, the American Federation of Labor moved into uncontested leadership of American labor after collaborating with the government in wartime, but its primacy meant that labor leaders would pursue collective bargaining by relinquishing any claim to parliamentary political power and any direct challenge to market capitalism. The Woman's Peace party, during the war the largest pacifist organization in the United States, survived the conflict, but it did so by lapsing into virtual silence by 1916; in 1918 party members changed the name of the organization to the Woman's International League.

ENVOI TO THE READER

The mixture of dialogue and conflict characteristic of wartime poetry in the United States has had important consequences for the organization of this anthology. First, as already noted, I have organized this collection chronologically to reveal the poems as a record of developing American analyses of the war. Second, because the partisanship of the author and the audience plays a crucial role in a poem's reception and because this orientation is established through each poem's site of publication, I have included information on the initial place of publication preceding the poem and even its author and title. Moreover, in deference to the poems' first editors, I have as far as possible located the original printings of the poems and faithfully reproduced them as they appear here. Only in rare instances have I supplied punctuation to avoid confusion or corrected spelling errors (indicated by brackets); the designer has regularized only the placement of poem's authors and titles, the treatment of epigraphs, and the ornament used in poems. Third, biographical information is relegated to endnotes, a point of organization that reflects the secondary importance of that information in the original sources. Even journals rarely provided author bios in the 1910s. While many authors would have been quite well known to their readers, political affiliation counted at least as much as name recognition. Fourth, I have chosen to represent most poets by one or two poems, just a few by three, one by five. In this decision, I am to some extent following the practice of virtually all wartime anthologists, whether their motive was an attempt at evenhandedness or a show of massive, univocal support for their viewpoint. My own impulse is, I hope, toward evenhandedness, even as I confess to believing the political-poetic voices of the Great War that most need a hearing today are dissenting ones. In any case, I have taken pains to avoid the impression that the bulk of wartime verse protested against it. By including all these poetic voices, the anthology reflects the multiplicity of American perspectives.

As my quotations of Harriet Monroe and Edgar Lee Masters should imply, proponents of what we now think of as modernism certainly have their place here, although they do not by any means enjoy a monopoly on the Great War's "historical realities," as Fussell and Walsh suggest they do. While such inclusions invariably invite aesthetic comparisons, they also help demonstrate the pervasiveness of political engagement and aesthetic immediacy, for these qualities were necessarily the province of the "new poetry" as well as of the genteel, popular, and other demotic poetries. Furthermore, instead of reinforcing the modernists' long-assumed aesthetic superiority, I would assert that quite different ends are served by the proximity of these well-known American poets and their less heralded peers. In some instances, the new context reestablishes the political and historical force of modernist poems. In others, it compels us to consider their limitations. Reading Carl Sandburg's "The Four Brothers" as well as his imagist, antiwar classic "Buttons" and his still more vehemently antiwar "Ready to Kill" forces us to recenter Sandburg's career at the very fulcrum of wartime political debate. Such a comparison also brings us to feel the power of historical, political, and human pressures that can bring a poet to protest, one year, against a general "holding a flag in the air" who is "Ready to kill anybody that gets in his way, / Ready to run the red blood and slush of the bowels of men all over the sweet new grass of the prairie" and just three years later to sing,

I stand on sidewalks and you go by with drums and guns and bugles,
You—and the flag!
And my heart tightens, a fist of something feels my throat
When you go by,
You on the kaiser hunt, you and your faces saying, "I am ready to be
    killed."

Reading Robert Frost's fairly familiar poem "Not to Keep" as one of many poems about the departure and return of soldiers, including Dana Burnet's "The Return," John Gould Fletcher's "The Last Rally," and Marion Patton Waldron's "Victory," means both restoring a lost conversation among poets treating the same set of historical circumstances and reassessing whether Frost's treatment of the subject is so transcendently superior to justify the entire neglect of the others.

Fussell may indeed be right about the influence of the war's brutality and irrationality on the direction of modernist aesthetics. For writers such as Pound, Eliot, Frost, and Stevens, already disenchanted with the world of technological progress and mass culture, the war confirmed the pessimistic, alienated sensibility they had already cultivated. And—what is perhaps more— for the generation of American writers and artists who would soon be flocking to postwar Paris, it proved the validity of that perspective. But viewed in a wider context, this modernist sensibility is revealed as only one of many poetic options; that it was triumphant in American high culture proves only that its practitioners later became the principal shapers of postwar American letters. *Rendezvous with Death: American Poems of the Great War* is designed to explore the other varieties of poetic response coexisting with modernism-in-the-making that were, indeed, much more pervasive culturally. The book is meant to consider the proposition, furthermore, that the terrible historical contingencies of the conflict may have been faced more honestly, bravely, and constructively by the likes of Arturo Giovannitti, Sarah Norcliffe Cleghorn, or Alan Seeger than by Sandburg or Eliot. As with the participants in the 1916 Easter Sunday uprising recounted by Yeats, a "terrible beauty" is born in the political-poetic commitment of Giovannitti pledging defiance toward the state and fidelity, in spite of all odds and circumstances, to the cause of international labor as figured in the martyr Frank Little:

And if you spring the trap under my feet and hurl me into the gloom,
    and in the revelation of that instant eternal a voice shriek madly
    to me
That the rope is forever unbreakable,
That the dawn is never to blaze,
That the night is forever invincible,
Even then, even then, I shall not deny him.

For a poem such as this, the high modernist selections serve as foils.

Precisely because a poet such as Giovannitti is so uncompromising, his aesthetic and political sensibilities so much at odds with our dominant literary paradigms, this anthology cannot offer up all of its contents for straightforward critical acclamation, as the great majority of anthologies still do. Here, even when aesthetics and craft are not strongly marked by the urgency and murkiness of a particular historical moment, the conflicting political positions laid out demand that the reader, no less than the poet, take sides. Some poems may invite aesthetic and political admiration, but not all of them can. And a poem one reader finds particularly agreeable, another will almost as likely find loathsome. However similar their purpose of political mobilization might be, Arturo Giovannitti, Claude McKay, and the Vigilantes do not allow much space for ideological temporizing or political negotiation.

In imagining the kinds of readers that might pick up this volume, I have found instructive the cases of two readers and amateur editors of Great War poetry, discovered by chance while digging through newspaper microfilms and archive boxes. The first of these, a correspondent to the *New York Times* of 30 August 1918, was flushed with enthusiasm for the unequivocally nationalistic and patriotic poetry that the paper had been publishing for more than two years. This reader from Jersey City, identified only by the initials R. Y. W., relates that her or his reading has naturally progressed to anthologizing: "As a long and constant reader of your paper, I should like to express my admiration of the splendid poems appearing daily in THE TIMES, and also to thank you for giving your readers such a rare treat. I am carefully clipping these and pasting them in a blank book which I call 'War Poems,' and I am sure the result will be a very interesting little volume." R. Y. W. might be taken to represent the reader looking for a univocal, partisan perspective: a reader much like the imagined audiences for anthologies such as *The Spirit of Democracy* (Powell and Powell) and *Verse for Patriots, to Encourage Good Citizenship* (Broadhurst and Rhodes), published during or soon after the war, but also not unlike the intended audiences for antiwar soldier-poetry published mostly since the 1960s. More to my taste, and closer to my anthology-making practice, was the avocational anthologist Grace W. Greene, a 1913 alumna of Swarthmore College whose "Poems of the War" is today preserved in the archives of that college's Peace Collection. Greene's compilation includes the English poet Harold Begbie's patriotic "Fall In!" as well as the American Benjamin F. Leggett's "A Word for Peace" and George Sylvester Viereck's "The German American to His Adopted Country," a pro-German plea first printed in his newspaper, *Fatherland: Fair Play for Germany and Austria-Hungary.*

In R. Y. W.'s anthology, the poems become a mirror, a medium for reader identification—with poets and their achievements and also with the national cause and national achievements. In Greene's collection, in contrast, the poems reflect not necessarily her own identity but rather a range of American (and also British) positions—by which the anthology becomes a medium for political debate, deliberation, and choice. There were, and are, liabilities as well as opportunities in either kind of reading. The "writerly" reader such as Greene risks indecision and inaction in striving for political discernment and critique. The "readerly" reader such as R. Y. W. risks purely ideological reproduction.

Yet while constructing an anthology more like Greene's, that attempts, by richness of contents and context, to preclude easy generalization about wartime experiences in the United States, I am compelled to recognize the importance of the kinds of emotional and personal investments in reading and writing poetry that are highlighted by R. Y. W.'s response. While the poems in the *Times* may well speak merely for and through R. Y. W., never allowing her or him to gain critical purchase, they may also speak *on behalf of* R. Y. W., with her or his full and examined assent. Moreover, in spite of their differences, Greene's experiences of reading and anthologizing almost certainly had much more in common with R. Y. W.'s than with ours of many decades later. We may reasonably suspect that Greene, by her affiliation with the Quaker-founded Swarthmore and the eclecticism of her poetry selections, was a pacifist sympathizer if not herself an activist. Even if she was not politically active, she was immersed in the conflicting pressures of the historical moment in ways that she shared with R. Y. W.—however differently they might have been situated in relation to those pressures and however differently they might have responded. From Greene as from R. Y. W., a passionate and political response was directly called for: to refuse to act on the injunctions of the poems would also have been a type of political response. Both were called to play their part in the national mobilization or to define their role in opposition to it, to take up the cause they felt most compelled to live and die by.

The clearest legacy of these readers and the poems they read is their passionate investment in social and political action. We see it summoning both R. Y. W.'s response and Grace Greene's, calling out clearly in the poetry of Edith M. Thomas as well as of Ralph H. Chaplin. While I am well aware of the political possibilities in modernist irony and detachment and postmodern indeterminacy and playfulness, I also dread the possibility that professional and avocational readers alike are being trained into adopting a hypersophisticated political passivity. Whatever their diversity of perspective, whatever their strengths and weaknesses, the poems in this collection provide a nearly united summons to throw off passivity. My hope is that this collection will contribute not only to an expanded estimate of those writers who were important to American culture at a particular time and place but also to an ongoing debate about how poetry should be read and to what uses it can and should be put. These poems are a call to their readers not just to be, but to do.

The historical circumstances encountered by the Great War poets are not, of course, precisely ours. But political and social issues important to the 1910s persist, and the experiences of the Great War continue to define key landmarks on our cultural horizon. After the turn of the millennium, in a global political arena in which national self-interest remains an unquestioned good, the United States can advance its economic and political agendas confident in its unequaled power. As I compose these final introductory comments on November 11, 2001, eighty-three years removed from the World War I armistice but two short months after the September 11 terror attacks, I realize that many Americans would demur. Americans feel themselves uniquely under threat; our media, our politicians, and our military experts are consumed with a new and vigorous "homeland defense." But clearly, little has changed in Americans' capacity to write history when U.S. warplanes can bomb Afghanistan day and night with minimal risk to their flyers, when the U.S. military can send its special forces into the country at will, and when the United States and its allies can confidently devise plans for postwar Afghan nation-building prior to any significant ground advance against the Taliban. The United States has tremendous opportunities for shaping the world, and retains considerable potential for arrogance, when Afghanistan can be invaded and terrorism combated on a hundred fronts while the president urges Americans to shop and entertain themselves as usual and rest assured that there are enough anthrax-killing antibiotics to go around. This powerful self-assurance has its roots in the heady experience of intervening in World War I and tipping the military balance decisively in favor of Britain and France. It was tested by the agony of Vietnam but revived by the end of the cold war and the brutal yet antiseptic Persian Gulf War. We might draw a nearly unbroken line of influence from Woodrow Wilson's dream of fighting a "war to end war" to the vision of a United States protected from nuclear attack by a high-tech missile shield. The link is still more uncanny between the Great War rhetoric of "Lest We Forget" and President Bush's promise that the dead civilians being exhumed from the World Trade Center and the solders killed in Afghanistan "will not have died in vain."

Given such parallels, the historical roots and precedents found in American poems and experiences of the Great War may prove instructive. Even an interventionist like Edith Wharton or an enthusiast such as the Carl Sandburg of 1917 remind us plainly of the blood spilled even in a just war. Florence Guertin Tuttle, Arturo Giovannitti, Sarah Norcliffe Cleghorn, and Claude McKay would have us ask just how much injustice will be overlooked at home, how long attention to the struggles of the disadvantaged will be suspended so that the United States can fight its war against terrorism. What will be the cost in suffering for the rest of the world so that Americans can insulate themselves from suffering? Lincoln Colcord's *Vision of War,* whose cantos reprinted here describe the indifference of Great Britain to the calamities of the opium trade it fostered, might have us ask: How many Afghan people, in the midst of a war featuring American "precision bombing" will become sick or die from malnutrition because food apparently cannot be distributed so precisely? Such questions are not inspired by idealism only but by the historical facts of the Great War and the realistic assessments of them by American poets. The unmatched power of the United States does not, after all, automatically translate into safety for its individual citizens—something demonstrated all too clearly when the twin towers fell. Certain questions must be asked when we consider the consequences of Germany's annexation of Alsace-Lorraine in 1870 or of the Versailles Treaty that was supposed to end the Great War once and for all in 1918. If we feel certain that the deaths in New York, Pennsylvania, and Washington, D.C., call for war halfway around the world, we can feel no less confident that the dead in Kabul, Baghdad, and even Hebron will call for a response. That the dead cry out to the living is manifested by the American poets of the Great War. Equally manifest is that the dead cry out *through* the living. The poems testify that we have some choice, considerable power, and a responsibility to cry out well and to act wisely on their behalf—and that how we respond defines not just our remembrance of the dead but our commitment to the living and our hopes for the future.

PART 1

PRESENTIMENTS

It has been the time-honored custom to attribute unjust wars to the selfish ambition of rulers who remorselessly sacrifice their subjects to satisfy their greed. But . . . it remains to be seen whether or not democratic rule will diminish war. Immoderate and uncontrolled desires are at the root of most national as well as of most individual crimes, and a large number of persons may be moved by unworthy ambitions quite as easily as a few. If the electorate of a democracy accustom themselves to take the commercial view of life, to consider the extension of trade as the test of a national prosperity, it becomes comparatively easy for mere extension of commercial opportunity to assume a moral aspect and to receive the moral sanction. Unrestricted commercialism is an excellent preparation for governmental aggression. The nation which is accustomed to condone the questionable business methods of a rich man because of his success, will find no difficulty in obscuring the moral issues involved in any undertaking that is successful. It becomes easy to deny the moral basis of self-government and to substitute militarism.

—Jane Addams, *Newer Ideals of Peace,* 1911

The following six poems suggest a fundamental tension in prewar U.S. society between an acquisitive, aggressive nationalism and a moralistic, populist reformism. These twin, usually contrary impulses were as often located within particular social movements and individuals as between them. They were embodied, for instance, in the dominant political figure of the period, Theodore Roosevelt, famous both for taking on the powerful business trusts and for asserting a robust, masculine, and newly assertive version of American nationalism. They emerge strikingly, as well, in the familiar patriotic hymn "America the Beautiful" by Katharine Lee Bates, which celebrates manifest destiny and patriotic self-sacrifice but also progressive ideals: every "flaw" is "mended," "liberty" is enshrined in "law," and cityscapes are "Undimmed by human tears!" These tensions would inform much in American culture and poetry during the Great War.

Emerging criticisms of both nationalism and reformism were likewise drawn quite distinctly prior to the war. These carried over into the wartime debate often in particular ways, in quotations or reprintings of earlier poems. Though no less patriotic than Bates's "America the Beautiful," Paul Laurence Dunbar's "Black Samson of Brandywine" concerns a subject—African American citizenship—that tested the nation's readiness truly to realize its ideal of "liberty in law." Dunbar's poem asserts that it is the exemplary conduct of the black Revolutionary War hero, not his legal status, that proves his fitness for citizenship. However dangerous this argument (it appears to make citizenship something earned—and possible only for men to earn—rather than claimed by right), Dunbar's poem was reprinted in June 1917 by the *Crisis*. It fit closely the NAACP's wartime agendas to gain recognition for the contributions of black soldiers and to further, by virtue of this war service, the civil rights claims of black Americans generally, though the editor, W. E. B. Du Bois, did need to omit the stanza that describes with gusto the "bloody swath" that Black Samson supposedly cut through the "human harvest" of *British* soldiers. Meanwhile, race issues abroad formed the basis for another criticism of the too-easy conjunction of nationalism and progressivism. A satirical version of "Onward, Christian Soldiers" written by William Lloyd Garrison Jr., son and namesake of the abolitionist activist, responded to the first U.S. colonial war outside the Western Hemisphere, the seizure of the Philippines during the Spanish-American War. Garrison's poem scouts the compatibility of American manifest destiny and human equality, indicating that missionary and military zeal to subdue the earth must inevitably mean subjection and destruction for colonized people. Not only did the poem's analysis of colonialism and national aggrandizement strike at two key causes of the Great War in Europe but the poem was also close enough to the wartime perspective of the Industrial Workers of the World (IWW) that in December 1915 it was reprinted in the union's organ *Solidarity* along with another "Onward, Christian Soldiers" parody by one of the IWW's own.

Many political groups and social movements that were to play an influential role in American politics and society during the Great War were founded during the two decades represented by these opening selections. The IWW was formed in 1905. American pacifists grew in strength, inspired by the international peace congresses held at The Hague in 1899 and again in 1907. The American Peace Society, a genteel organization founded in 1828 and dominated by aging Bostonians, began to gain in membership after decades of quiescence (Marchand 8–9, 16). In 1907, funded by the Carnegie Endowment for Peace, Columbia University president Nicholas Murray Butler began to publish a monthly pamphlet, *International Conciliation,* that was to run right through the war. About the same time, influential business owners and philanthropists led by the publisher Hamilton Holt founded the New York Peace Society, a group later to merge with the American Peace Society and dominate its policies (Marchand 37–38, 132–33). Also in 1907, Jane Addams turned her settlement house experience to the problem of world peace, publishing a book, *Newer Ideals of Peace,* in which she argued that the peaceful assimilation of foreign immigrants into U.S. society provided a model for international cooperation and industry, but also warned that democratic institutions in the United States did not necessarily guarantee a pacifist, or even a benign, foreign policy: "A large number of persons may be moved by unworthy ambitions quite as easily as a few" (222). In 1909 another settlement house worker, Mary White Ovington, cofounded the NAACP; Du Bois was recruited as the sole African American representative on the board of directors and began to edit and publish the *Crisis* in the fall of 1910. In 1911 the Boy Scouts opened its first chapters in the United States. In the United States as in Great Britain, where the organization was founded by retired lieutenant general Sir Robert S. S. Baden Powell, the Boy Scouts was to provide an important ideological stimulus and practical vehicle for military preparedness. When in 1916 public pressure mounted for universal military training of American youth and retired U.S. general Leonard Wood ran paramilitary camps at Plattsburg, New York, Scoutmaster James E. West could argue that "a great proportion of the program of the Plattsburg and other strictly military training camps is [already] included in the program of the Boy Scouts of America" (806).

So the struggles between militarism and pacifism, nationalism and internationalism, were longstanding debates. But much would change when the European war broke out in August 1914. Like the Boy Scouts, the U.S. military tried to prepare for war in the years leading up to 1914, increasing its personnel by almost 71 percent and its expenditures by 64 percent between 1900 and 1914. But the U.S. Army remained puny compared with the European armies measured in absolute numbers: its 164,000 personnel made it smaller than the Austro-Hungarian army by 300,000, the German army by over 700,000, and the Russian army by more than 1 million (Q. Wright 670–71). Before U.S. soldiers would be sent to fight, the army would have to grow significantly to be taken seriously by the European powers and the political landscape would need to shift. To be sure, in "A Few Words from Wilhelm" published in *Collier's* in 1905, the political satirist Wallace Irwin finds much to ridicule in the pompous, autocratic, and militaristic emperor of Germany. This would not change during the war; indeed, Irwin's poem may indicate a general predisposition against Germany that had much to do with the wartime alliance with the Triple Entente. What did change—or at least became irrelevant to Irwin—was his attitude toward Theodore Roosevelt, whom Irwin sees as a counterpart to the kaiser in his moralism and quest for personal and national aggrandizement. In 1917 and 1918 Irwin was to become one of the Vigilantes, who not only advocated a Rooseveltian brand of nationalism but had Roosevelt himself as its key financial and political supporter.

For proponents of intervention to succeed in bringing the United States into the war, they needed not only American xenophobia but also militarism. The kind of national pomp and pretension that the kaiser symbolized had to be embraced by a far greater proportion of the public. Katherine Devereux Blake's pacifist and socialist national anthem, written in 1914 and sung to the same tune as Francis Scott Key's anthem, closely resembles any number of the parodies the U.S. Justice Department used to convict the IWW on conspiracy charges in 1918. But Blake's anthem seems remarkably uncynical and nonsubversive with respect to its source, as if to demonstrate no great ideological contradiction between patriotic values and those of pacifism and socialism; indeed, Blake's anthem seems not to have been considered scandalous by its readers and singers, for it was actually approved by the New York City School Board for use in its schools and was sung throughout the period of U.S. neutrality (Blake). If Katharine Lee Bates's vision of "America the Beautiful" is revealing in its blindness to how American expansion flattens other cultures in its path, it is also revealing in its inability to imagine that American development could ever be anything but truly progressive, egalitarian, and peace-loving.

1895
KATHARINE LEE BATES

AMERICA THE BEAUTIFUL

O beautiful for spacious skies,
  For amber waves of grain,
For purple mountain majesties
  Above the fruited plain!
    America! America!
  God shed His grace on thee
And crown thy good with brotherhood
  From sea to shining sea!

O beautiful for pilgrim feet,
  Whose stern, impassioned stress
A thoroughfare for freedom beat
  Across the wilderness!
    America! America!
  God mend thine every flaw,
Confirm thy soul in self-control,
  Thy liberty in law!

O beautiful for heroes proved
  In liberating strife,
Who more than self their country loved,
  And mercy more than life!
    America! America!
  May God thy gold refine,
Till all success be nobleness,
  And every gain divine!

O beautiful for patriot dream
  That sees beyond the years
Thine alabaster cities gleam
  Undimmed by human tears!
    America! America!
  God shed his grace on thee
And crown thy good with brotherhood
  From sea to shining sea!

1899
WILLIAM LLOYD GARRISON JR.

[THE ANGLO-SAXON CHRISTIANS, WITH GATLING GUN AND SWORD]

The Anglo-Saxon Christians, with Gatling gun and sword,
In serried ranks are pushing on the gospel of the Lord.
On Afric's soil they press the foe in war's terrific scenes,
And merrily the hunt goes on throughout the Philippines.

What though the Boers are Christians; the Filipinos, too;
It is a Christian act to shoot a fellow-creature through:
The bombs with dynamite surcharged their deadly missiles fling,
And gayly on their fatal work the dum-dum bullets sing.

The dead and mangled bodies, the wounded and the sick,
Are multiplied on every hand, on every field are thick.
"O, gracious Lord," the prayer goes up, "to us give victory swift;"
The chaplains on opposing sides the same petitions lift.

The mahdis and the sirdars along the great Soudan
Are learning at the cannon's mouth the brotherhood of man;
The holy spirit guides aloft the shrieking shot and shell,
And Christian people shout with joy at thousands blown to hell.

The pulpits bless the victor arms and praise the bloody work,
As after an Armenian raid rejoiced the pious Turk.
The Christian press applauds the use of bayonet and knife;
For how can social order last without the strenuous life?

The outworn, threadbare precept, to lift the poor and weak,
The fallacy that this great earth is for the saintly meek,
Have both gone out of fashion: the world is for the strong;
That might shall be the Lord of right is now the Christian song.

The Jesus that we reverence is not the lowly man
Who trod in poverty and rags where Jordan's waters ran:
Our savior is an admiral upon the quarter-deck,
Or else a general uniformed, an army at his beck.

How natural that a change should come in nineteen hundred years,
And Bibles take a place behind the bullets and the beers!
We need a new Messiah to lead the latest way,
And gospel version well revised to show us how to prey.

Then onward, Christian soldier! through fields of crimson gore,
Behold the trade advantages beyond the open door!
The profits on our ledgers outweigh the heathen loss;
Set thou the glorious stars and stripes above the ancient cross.

Collier's, [1905]
WALLACE IRWIN

A FEW WORDS FROM WILHELM

Man vants put leedle hier pelow
   Und vants dot leedle Dutch—
Der vishes vich I vish, I know,
   Are nicht so fery much:
Choost Europe, Asia, Africa,
   Der Vestern Hemisphere
Und a coaling-station in Japan—
   Dot vill pe all dis year.

Hi-lee, hi-lo, der vinds dey plow
   Choost like Die Wacht am Rhein;
Und vat iss mein pelongs to Me
   Und vat iss yours iss mein!

Jah also, ven I vloat aroundt
   Mitin mein royal yacht

I see so much vat iss nicht Dutch
  Dot—ach, du lieber Gott!—
It gif me such a shtrange distress
  I gannot undershtand
How volks gan lif in happiness
  Mitout no Vaderland!

Hi-lee, hi-lo, der vinds dey plow
  As I sail round apout
To gif der Nations good adwice
  Und sausages und kraut.

Each hour I shange mein uniform,
  Put I never shange mein mindt,
Und efery day I make ein spooch
  To penefit mankindt:
Race Soosancide, der Nation's Pride,
  Divorce und Public Sins—
I talk so much like Roosenfeldt
  I dink ve must pe tvins!

Hi-lee, hi-lo, der vinds dey plow
  Der maxim Rule or Bust—
You gannot wreck our skyndicate
  Ven Gott iss in der Trust!

Being ein kviet Noodral Power,
  I know mein chob, you bet—
I pray for Beace, und hope for War
  Und keep mein powder wet;
Put ven I've nodings else to do
  Put shtandt around und chat
Den der Right Divine talks nonsense t'rough
  Mein military hat.

Hi-lee, hi-lo, der vinds dey plow
  Und softy visper dis:
"Der Kaiser he iss more as yet
  Und all iss right vat Iss!"

Life and Works of Paul Laurence Dunbar [1907]
PAUL LAURENCE DUNBAR

BLACK SAMSON OF BRANDYWINE

> "In the fight at Brandywine, Black Samson, a giant Negro, armed
> with a scythe, sweeps his way through the red ranks."
> —C. M. Skinner's "Myths and Legends of Our Own Land."

Gray are the pages of record
   Dim are the volumes of eld;
Else had old Delaware told us
   More that her history held.
Told us with pride in the story,
   Honest and noble and fine,
More of the tale of my hero,
   Black Samson of Brandywine.

Sing of your chiefs and your nobles,
   Saxon and Celt and Gaul,
Breath of mine ever shall join you,
   Highly I honor them all.
Give to them all of their glory,
   But for this noble of mine,
Lend him a tithe of your tribute,
   Black Samson of Brandywine.

There in the heat of the battle,
   There in the stir of the fight,
Loomed he, an ebony giant,
   Black as the pinions of night.
Swinging his scythe like a mower
   Over a field of grain,
Needless the care of the gleaners,
   Where he had passed amain.

Straight through the human harvest,
   Cutting a bloody swath,
Woe to you, soldier of Briton!
   Death is abroad in his path.
Flee from the scythe of the reaper,
   Flee while the moment is thine,

None may with safety withstand him,
   Black Samson of Brandywine.

Was he a freeman or bondman?
   Was he a man or a thing?
What does it matter? His brav'ry
   Renders him royal—a king.
If he was only a chattel,
   Honor the ransom may pay
Of the royal, the loyal black giant
   Who fought for his country that day.

Noble and bright is the story,
   Worthy the touch of the lyre,
Sculptor or poet should find it
   Full of the stuff to inspire.
Beat it in brass and in copper,
   Tell it in storied line,
So that the world may remember
   Black Samson of Brandywine.

*Songs of the Workers on the Road, in the Jungles,
   and in the Shops,* 5th ed. [1913]
JOE HILL

SHOULD I EVER BE A SOLDIER

(Tune: "Colleen Bawn.")
We're spending billions every year
   For guns and ammunition,
"Our Army" and "our Navy" dear,
   To keep in good condition;
While millions live in misery
   And millions died before us,
Don't sing "My Country 'tis of thee,"
   But sing this little chorus.

(Chorus)
Should I ever be a soldier,
   'Neath the Red Flag I would fight;
Should the gun I ever shoulder,
   It's to crush the tyrant's might.
Join the army of the toilers,
   Men and women fall in line,
Wage slaves of the world! Arouse!
   Do your duty for the cause,
For Land and Liberty.

And many a maiden, pure and fair,
   Her love and pride must offer
Our Mammon's altar in despair,
   To fill the master's coffer,
The gold that pays the mighty fleet,
   From tender youth he squeezes,
While brawny men must walk the street
   And face the wintry breezes.

Why do they mount their gatling gun
   A thousand miles from ocean,
Where hostile fleet could never run—
   Ain't that a funny notion?
If you don't know the reason why
   Just strike for better wages,
And then, my friends—if you don't die—
   You'll sing this song for ages.

1914
KATHERINE DEVEREUX BLAKE

[O SAY CAN YOU SEE, YOU WHO GLORY IN WAR]

[To the tune of the "Star Spangled Banner"]
O say can you see, you who glory in war,
   All the wounded and dead of the red battle's reaping?

Can you listen unmoved to their agonized groans,
   Hear the children who starve, and the pale widows weeping?
     Henceforth let us swear
     Bombs shall not burst in air,
Nor war's desolation wreck all that is fair,
   But the star spangled banner by workers unfurled
Shall give hope to the nations and peace to the world.

PART 2

AUGUST TO DECEMBER 1914

The first observation the reader will make is that the glamor of war has not touched these poems; here are no stirring battle songs and no hero- ic ballads. Perhaps the newspaper correspondent and the newspaper photograph have made war too frightfully real for any but a horrified treatment; perhaps warfare has ceased for the moment at least to be an idea of any sort, alluring or otherwise, and has become, or has tended to become, for the public consciousness simply an ugly and stupefying fact. But however we explain it, the absence of glamor from these verses on the war is a new and interesting phenomenon. . . .

Since this frame of mind prevails in these poems, it is not surprising that the "literary" manner is absent from them. Whatever else they are, these pieces are spontaneous and sincere; they impress the reader as vehicles of an urgent protest rather than as elaborations of a theme. . . . When we have become hardened to this war or have got further away from its horrors, we may begin to make literary use of them, but at present, it seems, the poets and their readers think it a kind of sacrilege to convert any of this stupendous misery to the purposes of art.

—John Erskine, Introduction to *Contemporary War Poems*, December

---

Throughout the summer and fall of 1914, most Americans saw the war unfold as if it were a serial novel available in daily installments. For inattentive readers, the story may have burst like a storm in August, but the first volume, mostly political farce, was plainly enough told in June and July. The *New York Times* reported the 28 June assassination of the Austro-Hungarian prince Franz Ferdinand on its front page. Though neither the *Times* reporters nor the paper's readers could see exactly where the plot was heading, all the key events were recounted and ed- itorialized upon: the Austro-Hungarian ultimatum, the pledge of Ger- man support for Austria-Hungary, the conciliatory Serbian reply, Rus- sia's declaration of solidarity with Serbia, the war declarations in the East, the German violation of Belgian neutrality, the French and En- glish declarations. With the onset of military operations, the plot took a new direction, joining sensational melodrama with high tragedy. Between August and December 1914, Americans devoured some four separate volumes of this epic: the Battle of the Frontiers, the Heroic Belgian Resistance, the Battle of the Marne, the Race to the Sea. The various episodes were distinguished starkly later by Barbara Tuchman in *The Guns of August*, but they were already delineated quite clearly in 1914. Americans doubtless read of the war with varying mixtures of fascination, horror, and bewilderment, but not really confusion over what was happening when and where, at least at this point. In most U.S. newspapers, the heroes and villains were even plainly drawn: the former wore outrageous, menacing spikes on their helmets and occupied ever larger areas of Belgium and northern France, as revealed by the campaign maps appearing daily; the latter chose to die rather than lose their honor, had their retreat at Mons covered by an angel host, and rode off to defend France on the River Marne in off-duty Parisian taxis. The defenders of civilization also had Rudyard Kipling, whose poem "For All We Have and Are," published on the front page of the *New York Times* on 2 September, on the eve of the first battle of the Marne, declared, "The Hun is at the gate," and therefore,

> There's but one task for all,
> For each one life to give.
> Who stands if Freedom fall?
> Who dies if England live?

Just as in Europe, where recruiting stations were swamped with eager young men and town squares were filled by patriotic crowds, currents of intellectual and emotional stimulation ran strong in the United States and touched American poetry immediately. Even as American poets tended to condemn the conflict and criticize the social causes underpinning it, they sensed that the war was encouraging literary production and creativity. On 11 August the *Times* commented on the volume of war poetry being written: "As always when deep emotions are stirred, a great number of people are now feeling an impulse, evidently irresistible, to express their opinions and their feelings in verse. Not since the loss of the Titanic have the mails brought to *The Times* office such numbers of metrical offerings as they have since Europe took up arms" ("Writing Poems"). Interviewed at length for a *New York Times Book Review* feature published on 13 September, Professor Brander Matthews of Columbia University went further, suggesting that the quantity of literary production catalyzed by the war would also result in increased quality: as the *Times* correspondent summed up, "the history of literature in many countries, both ancient and modern, attests

International News Service. "French soldier in the trenches continuing to
shoot though a stricken comrade had fallen into his arms." Photograph.
(From the *New York Times* 11 Oct. *1914.*)

the fact that great wars have exerted a quickening influence upon lit-
erary production. Society is stirred to its base by such conflicts, new
ideas gain currency, and creative work is welcomed by a larger audi-
ence than before" ("War Will Probably"). This notion of intellectual
quickening was to recur throughout the period of American neutrali-
ty, particularly among those inclined toward U.S. involvement. Later,
when the United States entered the war, the idea seemed to occur to
virtually all the literati at once.

But though the seeds of sympathy with the Triple Entente were al-
ready sown in these opening months of the war, and though the cru-
cial cultural rationalizations for war involvement were already being
formulated by Matthews and others, the overwhelming consensus re-
sponse was distinctly nonpartisan and pacifist. The first wartime dem-
onstration was a peace march in New York City, organized primarily
by suffrage activists and consisting entirely of women and children,
in which the sole banner unfurled bore the single word "Peace" and a
dove ("Protesting Women"). The march, for which most of the fifteen
hundred participants dressed in mourning and walked to the beat of
a muffled, funereal drum, impressed the *Times* editors as "evidence of

definite determination on the part of a considerable number of women to exert a practical influence on a field of public action from which in the past they have been almost wholly withdrawn" ("Women's Manifestation"). The *Times* also observed, however, that pacifist conviction was backed by an absolutely national consensus, and in this sense the parade was actually unnecessary: "As a demonstration of horror of war, of sorrow that it should be raging, of sympathy with the multitudes on whom it inflicts incalculable suffering, it may truly be said—and has been said by many since the plan was proposed— that it was needless. . . . There is no class that needs to be impressed by the strength of the essential antiwar cause; there are no converts to be made, as in political campaigns, no 'doubtful vote' to attract, no opponents to cow."

On this most commentators seem to have agreed. It was certainly the view of *Poetry*'s associate editor Alice Corbin Henderson in the war poetry issue of November 1914, in which she proclaimed, "Just as the neutrality of the United States is in no sense passive, so the spirit of her poets is one of active antagonism to the barbaric survival of war." She predicted, based on the 738 entrants in the magazine's "best war or peace poem" contest, that "no future historian of the United States will be able to use quotations from her twentieth-century poets in support for an imperial policy of conquest and slaughter" (Henderson 83, 84). This was also the finding of John Erskine, who edited what was almost certainly the first anthology of Great War poetry, part of the monthly *International Conciliation* series underwritten by the Carnegie Foundation for Peace. Soon the foundation, along with virtually all the peace societies formed prior to the war, would be supporting disinterested scholarly research and discussion about the war rather than offering concrete proposals or agitating for any particular policy. Erskine would eventually serve with the American Expeditionary Force in France as a director of educational programs. But in December 1914, Erskine's *Contemporary War Poems* was in fact thoroughly antiwar and seemingly representative of a nationwide pacifism: "It might have been expected that feeling so anti-military would have directed itself against one or another of the warring governments, as against the supposed nurse and citadel of militarism. Yet the poems in our newspapers have in this respect shown remarkable poise. . . . It has been militarism rather than any one country or government that has roused the indignation expressed in these poems" (5). And lest a reader imagine that Erskine refers only to a limited range of periodicals, the acknowledgments show that the collection reprints poems from the *Bookman, Outlook, Nation, Independent, Columbia Jester,* and *San Francisco Bulletin;* the *Boston*

Globe and *Evening Transcript;* and the *New York Times, Tribune, Globe, World, American, Evening Journal, Evening Post,* and *Evening Sun.*

By and large, then, variety in American war poems published in the fall of 1914 arises *within* the framework of pacifist, or at least antiwar, convictions. Variation depends on how particular poets chose to voice a nearly unanimous stance. So for political leftists such as Charles Ashleigh and Charles W. Wood the European war provided a textbook example of international capitalism in action—a stern warning to American labor to be, as Ashleigh puts it, "a wind of scorn" against patriotism so that U.S. workers would not end up cannon fodder like their socialist counterparts in Germany, France, and England. For Mary White Ovington, writing in a remarkably modernist, multivoiced idiom for an amateur poet usually absorbed in the day-to-day business of the NAACP, settlement house work, and sociological research, sympathy for the suffering nations of Europe demands a cease-fire, ordered in the poem by God—that is, until he hears the lament of peoples oppressed by European colonialism. Other poets, while filled with loathing toward the war, seem actually to bring into question Erskine's statement that the poems of this period lacked a "'literary' manner," which might develop only "when we have become hardened to this war or have got further away from its horrors" (4). Vachel Lindsay, in "Abraham Lincoln Walks at Midnight," and Louise Driscoll, in "The Metal Checks," appear genuinely appalled at the war, yet develop that response through lines crafted with particular care. Driscoll's poem, the prize-winner in *Poetry*'s November contest, is especially ambitious in its creation of a dramatic and symbolic structure for understanding the magnitude of the war: The "World" and "Death" are, respectively, a Bearer and a Counter of the "identity disks" worn by the warring nations' soldiers, used to keep track of fatalities and, in the poem, counted and stacked as a banker would count coins. Other poems are highly ambiguous, belying the notion that American poets, lacking first-hand contact with the fighting, were somehow incapable of a complex poetic or moral response to it. One such poem, Wallace Stevens's "Phases," offers such ambiguity where we might expect it, from one of the High Modernists. But so do the sonnets "Doubt" and "Destiny" by the now-obscure and nonmodernist Percy MacKaye. Though at first seeming quite straightforward, the sonnets juggle declarative, interrogative, and hypothetical statements and thus undercut whatever stable ground they may appear to build up for the reader. In "Destiny," for example, the octave uses the European preparations for war, the decades-old arms race, as proof that "Dreams of slaughter rise to slay, / And fate itself is stuff that fancy breeds." The sestet appears to play on the American experience as a counterpoint, but do these lines suggest that Americans' dreams *are* antimilitarist and democratic or that they *should* be?

> Mock, then, no more at dreaming, lest our own
> Create for us a like reality!
> Let not imagination's soil be sown
> With armed men but justice, so that we
> May for a world of tyranny atone
> And dream from that despair—democracy.

The final lines appear to grow in confidence and hopefulness, but the sentence that ends the poem begins with "Let not," implying that at present Americans' imagination is indeed inclined toward military power rather than justice. That fear about American culture was to prove well founded. Woodrow Wilson was to fashion intervention precisely as a "war for democracy," and MacKaye's poem "Doubt," while seeing militarism and democracy as antithetical, also associates the evil of war with the "lurking Hun" and, thus, suggests the rationale that would demand the United States go to war against Germany *because* of the nation's loathing for military power and war. It was, as Wilson declared in another memorable phrase, supposed to be a war to end war.

Fatherland: Fair Play for Germany and Austria-Hungary,
    17 August
George Sylvester Viereck

THE GERMAN AMERICAN TO HIS
ADOPTED COUNTRY

The great guns crashing angrily
    Sound, distant echoes, in our ear.
We pray for those beyond the sea
    Whose lives to us are very dear.

We catch a mother's smile. We seize
    In thought a father's hand again.
We see the house and, through the trees,
    A girl's face in the window pane.

May God above them st[r]etch His hand,
    For men are mowed as fields of rye.
Destruction rides on sea and land
    Or drops, like thunder, from the sky.

Columbia, though thou shed no tear,
    Must thou fan hate with evil breath
Through ghouls in easy-chairs who sneer
    While these our brothers go to death?

Upon their page with hellish glee
    They prance their joy in black and red,
While Teutons strike for liberty,
    And Teuton mothers count their dead.

While Death and warring Cherubim
   O'er blood-red fields of battle flit[,]
Upon the shining mail of him
   Who leads God's hosts, they puke their wit.

Shall these that are thy children fling
   Their gibes upon our brothers' scars?
We taught our hearts thy songs to sing,
   Aye, with our blood we waged thy wars.

We fought thy fight when Britain's paw
   Upon thy country's heart was laid,
When the French eagle's iron claw
   Perturbed great Montezuma's shade.

The dry bones of our kinsmen rot
   In Gettysburg. Was it for this?
Are Schurz and Steuben both forgot?
   Nay, thine is not a traitor's kiss.

Let not thy words belie the right,
   Turn not from them that are thy kin!
Thy starry crown will shine less bright
   If freeman lose, if Cossacks win.

The Red Czar's blight shall never fall
   Upon the earth, nor freedom pale,
While the white blade of Parzival
   Still guards the Teuton's Holy Grail.

New York Evening Post, [August]
EDITH M. THOMAS

THE WOMAN'S CRY

> "All the posters were printed in red. 'Red!' cried the women, and
> there was some weeping among them; but the men for the most
> part took it quietly, seriously, and with sad submissiveness."
> —St. Petersburg newspaper.

"Red!" cried the women by the Neva's tide. . . .
And what they're crying by the Neva's tide

56

They're crying, too, in France, the Beautiful,
And 'neath the lindens of the Fatherland.
And farther yet, on ancient Danube's banks!
What boots it that you cry, O woman-souls,
Your strong ones going hence—(I mark it well
In "sad submissiveness" they're going hence!)
Your strong ones are a herd; the lash is swung,
And dumb they go—they dream no other way!

"Red!" cried the women. I cry, too—in vain. . . .
I know what I would do, if but my wit
Equaled my swelling heart—and if my tongue
The Pentecostal gift of tongues might seize—
Not speech of courts, nor sinuous subtle phrase,
But peasant power of straight appeal to hearts.
Words like to glowing coals that neighbors pass,
From heart to heart—words like the ringing ax
When the arm swings it through the heart of oak,
Words like the fervid plowshare, driven deep—
Might I but speak their native speech to them,
In some four countries of this world, gone mad,
The children of the soil should hear me cry:—
Now, wherefore are ye driven forth to War?
Ye have not made it, and ye hate no man.

That ye would go to hunt him to his death
(He hunting you—yet bearing you no hate)!
Stand in your fields, your shops, and do not go!
Be ye not "mobilized," but stand like stones;
And if to prison ye be haled, and if
They rain upon your hearts their leaden rain
Because ye will not serve, stand till ye fall!
Ye can but die—but so, die innocent,
Having, yourselves, slain no man innocent!
So, fall, the protomartyrs Who Fought War,
Glorious and sacred on the lips of men
Who shall be, and their heritage *Your* Peace!
"Red!" cried the women. Let them cry no more.

Poetry, September
CARL SANDBURG

READY TO KILL

Ten minutes now I have been looking at this.
I have gone by here before and wondered about it.
This is a bronze memorial of a famous general
Riding horseback with a flag and a sword and a revolver on him.
I want to smash the whole thing into a pile of junk to be hauled away to the
    scrap yard.
I put it straight to you,
After the farmer, the miner, the shop man, the factory hand, the fireman and
    the teamster,
Have all been remembered with bronze memorials,
Shaping them on the job of getting all of us
Something to eat and something to wear,
When they stack a few silhouettes
  Against the sky
  Here in the park,
And show the real huskies that are doing the work of the world, and feeding
    people instead of butchering them,
Then maybe I will stand here
And look easy at this general of the army holding a flag in the air,
And riding like hell on horseback
Ready to kill anybody that gets in his way,
Ready to run the red blood and slush the bowels of men all over the sweet
    new grass of the prairie.

Memphis Commercial Appeal, 6 September
SARA BEAUMONT KENNEDY

THE CALL TO THE COLORS

Like the seeds of wind-flowers, lightly blown
  On vagrant, gypsying breeze,
They are scattered wide throughout our land—
  Aliens from over the seas.

They came from the crowded fatherlands
    To share in our broader sphere,
And they built their nests and reared their broods
    Through many a changing year.

But a vibrant cry comes unaware
    From over the crested wave—
The voice of the warring motherlands
    Calling their children to save:
"On our grain-grown fields War plants its guns
    And lights its torch on the crag;
We need you, sons in the Other Lands,
    Come back and fight for the flag!"

And deep in each listener's heart there stirs
    A memory that has slept
'Neath blush of blossom and pallor of snows
    While the years have onward crept;
And he sees in a flash his native hut,
    Where the foeman's banners float—
And he's German again, or French, or Slav
    At thrill of a bugle note!

For a man may wander across the world
    And dwell 'neath a stranger's sky,
But the call of the blood will cleave all space
    When it comes in a battle-cry;
And the nest he built and the brood he reared
    Are left to an alien flag
While he turns him home, with his soul aflame,
    To die for a silken rag.

Independent, 21 September
VACHEL LINDSAY

ABRAHAM LINCOLN WALKS
AT MIDNIGHT

It is portentous, and a thing of state
    That here at midnight, in our little town

A mourning figure walks, and will not rest
  Near the old court-house pacing up and down,

Or by his homestead, or in the shadowed yards
  He lingers where his children used to play,
Or thru the market, on the well-worn stones
  He stalks until the dawn-stars burn away.

A bronzed, lank man! His suit of ancient black,
  A famous high top-hat and plain worn shawl
Make him the quaint great figure that men love,
  The prairie-lawyer, master of us all.

He cannot sleep upon his hillside now.
  He is among us, as in times before!
And we who toss and lie awake for long
  Breathe deep, and start, to see him pass the door.

His head is bowed. He thinks on men and kings.
  Yea, when the sick world cries, how can he sleep?
Too many peasants fight, they know not why,
  Too many homesteads in black terror weep.

The sins of all the war-lords burn his heart.
  He sees the dreadnoughts scouring every main.
He carries on his shawl-wrapt shoulders now
  The bitterness, the folly and the pain.

He cannot rest until a spirit-dawn
  Shall come;—the shining hope of Europe free;
The league of sober folk, the Workers' Earth
  Bringing long peace to Cornland, Alp and Sea.

It breaks his heart that kings must murder still,
  That all his hours of travail here for men
Seem yet in vain. And who will bring white peace
  That he may sleep upon his hill again?

Springfield, Illinois

Boston Transcript, 26 September
PERCY MACKAYE
From Carnage: A Meditation on the European War

I. DOUBT

So thin, so frail the opalescent ice
Where yesterday, in lordly pageant, rose
The monumental nations—the repose
Of continents at peace! Realities
Solid as earth they seemed; yet in a trice
Their bastions crumbled in the surging floes
Of unconceivable, inhuman woes,
Gulfed in a mad, unmeaning sacrifice.

We, who survive that world-quake, cower and start,
Searching our hidden souls with dark surmise:
So thin, so frail—is reason? Patient art—
Is it all a mockery, and love all lies?
Who sees the lurking Hun in childhood's eyes?
Is hell so near to every human heart?

VI. DESTINY

We are what we imagine, and our deeds
Are born of dreaming. Europe acts today
Epics that little children in their play
Conjured, and statesmen murmured in their creeds;
In barrack, court and school were sown those seeds,
Like Dragon's teeth, which ripen to affray
Their sowers. Dreams of slaughter rise to slay,
And fate itself is stuff that fancy breeds.

Mock, then, no more at dreaming, lest our own
Create for us a like reality!
Let not imagination's soil be sown
With armed men but justice, so that we
May for a world of tyranny atone
And dream from that despair—democracy.

Cornish, New Hampshire, September 22

Crisis, October
MARY WHITE OVINGTON

WAR

Said the Lord of Hosts:

I am weary of this multitude of prayers.
They ascend to me through the sound of the cannon
And the sharp sound of the bullet.
The petitions of the warriors greet me,
They disturb me not at all;
But to-day came the prayer of a child,
A little child, a daughter.
She turned her face to the sky,
And held up her hands to heaven;
She cried: Give me back my father!
Descend thou, therefore, to the earth,
And tell me of the battle.

> Then the seraphim, his two wings outspread, dropped from the celestial heights. When he returned, the odor of smoke was upon his hair.
>
> I have seen the desolation of Russia, oh, Master, and have heard the cries of its women as alone they garner the grain.
>
> I have passed over the Emperor's dominion, he who calls upon Thy name; Thy name is continually in his mouth, and boys are left to stand guard at the city gates.
>
> In the land of the Flemmings are smoking houses and ravished daughters.
>
> The cannon thunders at the gateway of France, and Saxon and Gaul fall like nuts in an October storm.
>
> Desolation is in the East and the West is desolate. The pyres of the dead burn on the hillside where the violets bloomed, and the dead cover the meadows once azure with the forget-me-not.
>
> Then the Lord of Hosts entered into His temple and rested for a while in thought. And beneath His feet slowly the earth turned on its appointed round.
>
> And again He called to Him the seraphim, and said:

The prayers of the mothers and the children
Shall be answered.
The cannon shall cease and the rifles.

Again shall man rise in the morning
To till the soil.
He shall listen to the song of the lark,
And shall watch the low flight of the swallow.

But the seraphim raised his eyes to his Master, and answered:

I have visited the earth again, oh, Lord, and the face she now turns is full of gladness. The people cry, Rejoice, for the Lord of Battle hath revenged us on our enemies!

Ethiopia holds up her hacked limbs. They gathered our hands in their baskets, and now their dead hands rest on their cold hearts.

The Arab stands by the vast inland sea and joy lights his face. Our fathers were slain by the invaders, and to-day an invader's steel strikes down our enemy upon his own sod.

In the east are great multitudes calling. We remember! We remember! We rebelled, and they came and slew and tied our men to the cannon's mouth. And low the cannon cut them down as the knife cuts the fodder for the cattle. To the north men call gleefully, The Cossack! The Cossack! They who beat and tortured[,] themselves fall under the rod.

And on Thy most lovely island in the western ocean, men and women sit by their scarred hill, and remember the palms and the song and the gay dance, and weep for the multitudes who died that the greed of the Teuton might flourish. But anon they rise and give praise that the string is broken and the feet are still in the house of their enemy.

Then the Lord of Hosts moved out of the temple and looked down upon the earth.

As they have sowed
So shall they reap.
Let it go on,
He said.

New York Times, 15 October
ERNST LISSAUER

A CHANT OF HATE
AGAINST ENGLAND

Translated by Barbara Henderson

French and Russian, they matter not,
A blow for a blow and a shot for a shot;
We love them not, we hate them not,
We hold the Weichsel and Vosges-gate,
We have but one and only hate,
We love as one, we hate as one,
We have one foe and one alone.

He is known to you all, he is known to you all,
He crouches behind the dark gray flood,
Full of envy, of rage, of craft, of gall,
Cut off by waves that are thicker than blood.
Come let us stand at the Judgment place,
An oath to swear to, face to face,
An oath of bronze no wind can shake,
An oath for our sons and their sons to take.
Come hear the word, repeat the word,
Throughout the Fatherland make it heard.
We will never forego our hate,
We have all but a single hate,
We love as one, we hate as one,
We have one foe and one alone—
    ENGLAND!

In the Captain's Mess, in the banquet-hall,
Sat feasting the officers, one and all,
Like a sabre-blow, like the swing of a sail,
One seized his glass held high to hail;
Sharp-snapped like the stroke of a rudder's play,
Spoke three words only: "To the Day!"

Whose glass this fate?
They had all but a single hate.

64

Who was thus known?
They had one foe and one alone—
   ENGLAND!

Take you the folk of the Earth in pay,
With bars of gold your ramparts lay,
Bedeck the ocean with bow on bow,
Ye reckon well, but not well enough now.
French and Russian they matter not,
A blow for a blow, a shot for a shot,
We fight the battle with bronze and steel,
And the time that is coming Peace will seal.
You will we hate with a lasting hate,
We will never forego our hate,
Hate by water and hate by land,
Hate of the head and hate of the hand,
Hate of the hammer and hate of the crown,
Hate of seventy millions, choking down.
We love as one, we hate as one,
We have one foe and one alone—
   ENGLAND!

New York Times, 21 October
McLandburgh Wilson

MOTHERHOOD'S CHANT

French or Russian, they matter not,
German or English, as one begot.
We bore them all and we bore them well,
We went for them to the gates of hell,
We are the makers of flesh and bone,
We have one foe, one hate alone—
   WAR!

He is known to you all, he has called to you all,
He crouches behind each boundary wall,
He rides on the waves of a crimson flood,

He rides on the tides of our children's blood,
He lies of glory and sacrifice,
Of honor and fame and pomp he lies—
  WAR!

Come, let us stand in the Judgment Place
And take an oath for the human race,
An oath our daughters, and theirs, shall take,
An oath no trumpet or drum can shake.
We hate no sinner, we hate the sin,
Not those who lose, not those who win.
We, the makers of flesh and bone,
We have one foe, one hate alone—
  WAR!

You take the folk of our pain to slay,
That gold nor steel can ever repay.
You shall we hate with a lasting hate.
We will never forego our hate—
Hate of the heart and hate of the womb,
Hate of the cradle and hate of the tomb.
And you shall answer and make reply,
For we are partners of God on high.
What will you say before that Throne
To Us, the makers of flesh and bone,
  WAR?

Solidarity, 31 October
CHARLES ASHLEIGH

THE ANTI-MILITARIST

Out of the deeps of toil am I born
And am faithful to my clan.
I seek no wider marts to trade
For I have naught.

The thrill of a myriad war lusts beats upon me;
The churning of a million passions is abroad.
I will not cast myself into this frenzy.

66

I will be a rock of irony.
I will be a rain of pity.
I will be a wind of scorn.

My arm is strong to destroy, but I withhould it;
I will destroy only that which stands in the way of our red redemption.

Poetry, November
LOUISE DRISCOLL

THE METAL CHECKS

[*The scene is a bare room, with two shaded windows at the back, and a fireplace between them with a fire burning low. The room is furnished scantily with a few plain chairs, and a rough wooden table on which are piled a great many small wooden trays.* The Counter, *who is Death, sits at the table. He wears a loose gray robe, and his face is partly concealed by a gray veil. He does not look at* The Bearer, *but works mechanically and speaks in a monotonous tone.* The Bearer *is the World, that bears the burden of War. He wears a soiled robe of brown and green and he carries on his back a gunny-bag filled with the little metal disks that have been used for the identification of the slain common soldiers.*]

The Bearer
  Here is a sack, a gunny sack,
    A heavy sack I bring.
  Here is toll of many a soul—
    But not the soul of a king.

  This is the toll of common men,
    Who lived in the common way;
  Lived upon bread and wine and love,
    In the light of the common day.

  This is the toll of working men,
    Blood and brawn and brain.
  Who shall render us again
    The worth of all the slain?

  [*As* The Counter *speaks,* The Bearer *pours out the disks on the table.* The
    Bearer *obeys* The Counter.]

67

The Counter

   Pour them out on the table here.
      C l i c k e t y—c l i c k e t y—c l a c k !
   For every button a man went out,
   And who shall call him back?
      C l i c k e t y—c l i c k e t y—c l a c k !

   One—two—three—four—
     Every disk a soul!
   Three score—four score—
   So many boys went out to war.
   Pick up that one that fell on the floor—
     Didn't you see it roll?
   That was a man a month ago.
   This was a man. Row upon row—
   Pile them in tens and count them so.

The Bearer

   I have an empty sack.
     It is not large. Would you have said
   That I could carry on my back
     So great an army—and all dead?

[*As* The Counter *speaks* The Bearer *lays the sack over his arm and helps count.*]

The Counter

   Put a hundred in each tray—
   We can tally them best that way.
   Careful—do you understand
   You have ten men in your hand?
   There's another fallen—there—
   Under that chair.

[The Bearer *finds it and restores it.*]

   That was a man a month ago;
   He could see and feel and know.
   Then, into his throat there sped
   A bit of lead.
   Blood was salt in his mouth; he fell
   And lay amid the battle wreck.
   Nothing was left but this metal check—
   And a wife and child, perhaps.

[The Bearer *finds the bag on his arm troublesome. He holds it up, inspecting it.*]

The Bearer
　What can one do with a thing like this?
　Neither of life nor death it is!
　For the dead serve not, though it served the dead.
　The wounds it carried were wide and red,
　Yet they stained it not. Can a man put food,
　Potatoes or wheat, or even wood
　That is kind and burns with a flame to warm
　Living men who are comforted—
　In a thing that has served so many dead?
　There is no thrift in a graveyard dress,
　It's been shroud for too many men.
　I'll burn it and let the dead bless.

　　　[*He crosses himself and throws it into the fire. He watches it burn. The*
　　Counter *continues to pile up the metal checks, and drop them by hundreds*
　　into the trays, which he piles one upon another. The Bearer *turns from the*
　　fire and speaks more slowly than he has before. He indicates the metal
　　checks.]

　Would not the blood of these make a great sea
　For men to sail their ships on? It may be
　No fish would swim in it, and the foul smell
　Would make the sailors sick. Perhaps in Hell
　There's some such lake for men who rush to war
　Prating of glory, and upon the shore
　Will stand the wives and children and old men
　Bereft, to drive them back again
　When they seek haven. Some such thing
　I thought the while I bore it on my back
　And heard the metal pieces clattering.

The Counter
　Four score—five score—
　These and as many more.
　Forward—march!—into the tray!
　No bugles blow today,
　No captains lead the way;
　But mothers and wives,
　Fathers, sisters, little sons,
　Count the cost
　Of the lost;
　And we count the unlived lives,

The forever unborn ones
Who might have been your sons.

The Bearer
Could not the hands of these rebuild
That which has been destroyed?
Oh, the poor hands! that once were strong and filled
With implements of labor whereby they
Served home and country through the peaceful day.
When those who made the war stand face to face
With these slain soldiers in that unknown place
Whither the dead go, what will be the word
By dead lips spoken and by dead ears heard?
Will souls say King or Kaiser? Will souls prate
Of earthly glory in that new estate?

The Counter
One hundred thousand—
One hundred and fifty thousand—
Two hundred—

The Bearer
Can this check plough?
Can it sow? can it reap?
Can we arouse it?
Is it asleep?

Can it hear when a child cries?—
Comfort a wife?
This little metal disk
Stands for a life.

Can this check build,
Laying stone upon stone?
Once it was warm flesh
Folded on bone.

Sinew and muscle firm,
Look at it—can
This little metal check
Stand for a man?

The Counter
One—two—three—four—

Poetry, November
MAXWELL BODENHEIM

THE CAMP FOLLOWER

We spoke, the camp-follower and I.
About us was a cold, pungent odor—
Gun-powder, stale wine, wet earth, and the smell of thousands of men.
She said it reminded her of the scent
In the house of prostitutes she had lived in.
About us were soldiers—hordes of scarlet women, stupidly, smilingly giving
    up their bodies
To a putrid-lipped, chuckling lover—Death;
While their mistresses in tinsel whipped them on. . . .
She spoke of a woman she had known in Odessa,
Owner of a huge band of girls,
Who had pocketed their earnings for years,
Only to be used, swindled and killed by some nobleman. . . .
She said she thought of this grinning woman
Whenever she saw an officer brought back from battle, dead. . . .
And I sat beside her and wondered.

Poetry, November
WALLACE STEVENS

PHASES

I.
There's a little square in Paris,
Waiting until we pass.
They sit idly there,
They sip the glass.

There's a cab-horse at the corner,
There's rain. The season grieves.
It was silver once,
And green with leaves.

There's a parrot in a window,
Will see us on parade,
Hear the loud drums roll—
And serenade.

II.

This was the salty taste of glory,
That it was not
Like Agamemnon's story.
Only, an eyeball in the mud,
And Hopkins,
Flat and pale and gory!

III.

But the bugles, in the night,
Were wings that bore
To where our comfort was;

Arabesques of candle beams,
Winding
Through our heavy dreams;

Winds that blew
Where the bending iris grew;

Birds of intermitted bliss,
Singing in the night's abyss;

Vines with yellow fruit,
That fell
Along the walls
That bordered Hell.

IV.

Death's nobility again
Beautified the simplest men.
Fallen Winkle felt the pride
Of Agamemnon
When he died.

What could London's
Work and waste
Give him—
To that salty, sacrificial taste?

What could London's
Sorrow bring—
To that short, triumphant sting?

Poetry, November
KARLE WILSON BAKER

UNSER GOTT

They held a great prayer-service in Berlin,
And augured German triumph from some words
Said to be spoken by the Jewish God
To Gideon, which signified that He
Was staunchly partial to the Israelites.
The aisles were thronged; and in the royal box
(I had it from a tourist who was there,
Clutching her passport, anxious, like the rest,)
There sat the Kaiser, looking "very sad."
And then they sang; she said it shook the heart.
The women sobbed; tears salted bearded lips
Unheeded; and my friend looked back and saw
A young girl crumple in her mother's arms.
They carried out a score of them, she said,
While German hearts, through bursting German throats
Poured out, *Ein Feste Burg Ist Unser Gott!*

(Yea, "Unser Gott! Our strength is *Unser* Gott!
Not that light-minded Bon Dieu of France!")

I think we all have made our God too small.
There was a young man, a good while ago
Who taught that doctrine . . . . but they murdered him
Because he wished to share the Jewish God
With other folk.
　　　They are long-lived, these fierce
Old hating Gods of nations; but at last
There surely will be spilled enough of blood
To drown them all! The deeps of sea and air,
Of old the seat of gods, no more are safe,
For mines and monoplanes. The Germans, now,

Can surely find and rout the God of France
With Zeppelins, or some slim mother's son
Of Paris, or of Tours, or Brittany,
Can drop a bomb into the *Feste Burg,*
And, having crushed the source of German strength,
Die happy in his blazing monoplane.

Sad jesting! If there be no God at all,
Save in the heart of man, why, even so—
Yea, all the more,—since we must make our God,
Oh, let us make Him large enough for all,
Or cease to prate of Him! If kings must fight,
Let them fight for their glory, openly,
And plain men for their lands and for their homes,
And heady youths, who go to see the fun,
Blaspheme not God. True, maybe we might leave
The God of Germany to some poor frau
Who cannot go, who can but wait and mourn,
Except that she will teach Him to her sons—
A God quite scornful of the Slavic soul,
And much concerned to keep Alsace-Lorraine.
They should go godless, too—the poor, benumbed,
Crushed, anguished women, till their hearts can hold
A greater Comforter!

      (Yet it is hard
To make Him big enough! For me, I like
The English and the Germans and the French,
The Russians, too; and Servians, I should think,
Might well be very interesting to God.
But, do the best I may, my God is white,
And hardly takes a nigger seriously
This side of Africa. Not those, at least
Who steal my wood, and of a summer night
Keep me awake with shouting, where they sit
With monkey-like fidelity and glee
Grinding through their well-oiled sausage-mill—
The dead machinery of the white man's church—
Raw jungle-fervor, mixed with scraps sucked dry
Of Israel's old sublimities: not those.
And when they threaten us, the Higher Race,

Think you, which side is God's? Oh, let us pray
Lest blood yet spurt to wash that black skin white,
As now it flows because a German hates
A Cossack, and an Austrian a Serb!)

What was it that he said so long ago,
The young man who outgrew the Jewish God—
"Not a sparrow falleth—?" Ah, God, God,
And there shall fall a million murdered men!

Columbia Jester, November
MORRIE

[TEN THOUSAND TOMMY ATKINSES WENT FORTH INTO THE FRAY]

> London, Sept. 3.—England, ready for a staggering blow on pub-
> lication of the government casualty list, heaved a sigh of relief
> when it was found that so few of the noble families had been
> affected.
> —*The Mail,* Sept. 3.

Ten thousand Tommy Atkinses went forth into the fray;
Ten thousand stalwart Tommies who gave Death their lives for pay.
But still we sing: "God Save the King," and thank the Fates of War:
For Viscount What-the-Who's-This hasn't even got a scar.

Ten thousand Tommy Atkinses, courageous, clear-eyed, brave,
Went boldly into battle—and the battlefield's their grave.
Their souls God rest! He knows what's best: Good news, bad news shall
    match:
The Duke of What-You-Call-It hasn't even got a scratch.

Ten thousand Tommy Atkinses that faced the German hordes;
Ten thousand Tommy Atkinses cut down by guns and swords.
In peace they sleep—why do ye weep, ye girls they left behind?
Lord So-and-So is safe and sound—the others never mind!

Outlook, 4 November
Civis Americanus

A SCRAP OF PAPER

> "Will you go to war just for a scrap of paper?"
>
> —Question of the German Chancellor to the British Ambassador,
> August 5, 1914.

A mocking question! Britain's answer came
Swift as the light and searching as the flame.

"Yes, for a scrap of paper we will fight
Till our last breath, and God defend the right!

"A scrap of paper where a name is set
Is strong as duty's pledge and honor's debt.

"A scrap of paper holds for man and wife
The sacrament of love, the bond of life.

"A scrap of paper may be Holy Writ
With God's eternal word to hallow it.

"A scrap of paper binds us both to stand
Defenders of a neutral neighbor land.

"By God, by faith, by honor, yes! We fight
To keep our name upon that paper white."

Masses, December
Charles W. Wood

KING OF THE MAGICAL PUMP

Words by Charles W. Wood. Music Omitted by Request.

1.

Oh, the loyalest Gink with the Royalest wink
  Is the King of the Magical Pump;
  Of the magical, tragical pump:

The latest and greatest and right-up-to-datest
And finest, divinest old I-am-the-State-ist
Who ever held sway for a year and a day
    In the Kingdom of Chumpetty-Chump.

2.

And the magical pump in His Majesty's dump,
    That, too, is a wonderful thing,
    A wonderful, thunderful thing.
  It's wonderful, blunderful, thunderful, plunderful,
  Cranky and yanky and get-out-and-under-ful:
And what do you s'pose (if there's no one who knows)
    What it pumpetty-pumped for the King!

3.

It pumped up his prunes and his new pantaloons
    And it pumped up his bibles and beer;
    His tribal old bibles and beer:
  For palaces, chalices, garters or galluses,
  Or jeans for his queens or his Julias and Alices,
The King of the Chumps, he just went to the pumps
    And whatever he wished would appear.

4.

And the Chumpetty-Chumps who were pumping the pumps
    Which pumped up these thing-a-mum bobs,
    These thing-a-mum, jing-a-mum bobs,
  They humped it and jumped it and pumpetty-pumped it
  And fearfully, tearfully liked it or lumped it;
While the King in his glee hollered: "Bully for Me!
    Ain't you glad that I gave you your jobs?"

5.

Oh, the Chumpetty-Chumps were a wise lot o' gumps
    And they said a religious "Amen,"
    A prodigious, religious "Amen."
  For ages these sages had had (it's outrageous)
  One jing-a-mum thing-a-mum each as their wages:
And pray, who could say, if he cut off their pay,
    What on earth would become of them then?

6.

But the King of the Chumps was a kindly old Umps
    And he paid them as much as he durst

(As much as all such as he durst)
For humping and jumping and pumpty-pump-pumping
Anything that a king could imagine their dumping:
Till he said: "Go to roost, we have over-produced
And we've got to get rid of this first."

7.

Then the Chumpetty-Chumps went to bumping the bumps
    In a tragic and thingum-less plight;
    In a thingum-less, jingum-less plight:
  They blubbered and lubbered and went to the cupboard—
  "No pumpee, no Chumpee," they said as they rubbered—
Till the loving old King caught a thought on the wing
    Which was sure to set everything right.

8.

Said the King of the Pumps to the Chumpetty-Chumps:
    "It is plain as the face on your nose,
    As the face on the base of your nose,
  The lesson this session of business depression
  Points out beyond doubt is that foreign aggression
Has caused a big slump in the work of the pump—
    So up, men, and after your foes!"

9.

Then in joy and in laughter, they upped and went after
    To fight for their country and King;
    For their pumpty old country and King:
  And dashing in, crashing in, bravely they're smashing in;
  (One jingum per dingum they get while they're cashing in)
Until the Big Umps wants to start up the Pumps:
    When they'll work for one thingum per ding.

10.

Oh, the loyalest Gink with the royalest wink
    Is the King of the Magical Pump;
    Of the magical, tragical pump:
  An oodle of boodle he's got by his noodle
  And umpty-nine Chumpties he's fed with flapdoodle—
For we live for a thingum and die for a jingum
    In the Kingdom of Chumpetty-Chump.

PART 3
1915

Notice!

Travellers intending to embark on the Atlantic voyage are reminded
that a state of war exists between Germany and her allies and Great
Britain and her allies; that the zone of war includes the waters adjacent
to the British Isles; that, in accordance with formal notice given by the
Imperial German Government, vessels flying the flag of Great Britain,
or of any of her allies, are liable to destruction in those waters and that
travellers sailing in the war zone on ships of Great Britain or her allies
do so at their own risk.

—Imperial Germany Embassy, *New York Times,* 1 May

The example of America must be a special example. The example of
America must be the example not merely of peace because it will not
fight, but of peace because peace is the healing and elevating influence
of the world and strife is not. There is such a thing as a man being too
proud to fight. There is such a thing as a nation being so right that it
does not need to convince others by force that it is right.

—Woodrow Wilson, "Address to Several Thousand Foreign-Born
  Citizens, after Naturalization Ceremonies, at Philadelphia, May 10,
  1915"

In 1915, Americans' responses to the war may be fairly summed up by
the stories of two ships: the *Lusitania* and the *Oscar II.* On 30 April the
Cunard Line announced the sailing on the following day of the *Lusita-
nia,* the largest ship in the world at its christening and the fastest liner
then in commercial service. On 1 May the German government placed
its own notice in the *New York Times,* just below the Cunard Line's ad-
vertisement of that day, warning that U.S. citizens planning to travel on
the ships of "Great Britain or her allies" could not depend on U.S. neu-
trality to shield them from attack. On 7 May, approaching the coast of
Ireland, the *Lusitania* was torpedoed by *Unterseeboot 20* and sank in
about twenty minutes; of over 1,900 passengers and crew, almost 1,200

were killed, 128 of them Americans. Condemnations in the American press were rampant, and in retrospect the event appeared to mark the dividing line between fairly strict U.S. neutrality and open sympathy with Great Britain and its allies. With the sinking of the *Lusitania*, the political and moral arguments that would eventually lead to U.S. intervention found embodiment. By the middle of the year, most peace organizations formed prior to the war, though still against warfare "in principle," ceased to oppose U.S. participation in this particular conflict. In July leaders of the New York Peace Society founded the League to Enforce Peace, stating categorically that this new organization did "*not* seek to end the present war" but rather sought to prevent *future* wars. The group's chief organizer, Henry Holt, also gained control of the then-inactive World Peace Federation, orchestrating the transfer of a $10,000 yearly stipend from its coffers to the league's (Marchand 155, 157).

Yet 1915 was also a year of genuine peace activism. In its first three months Alfred Bryan and Al Piantadosi's song "I Didn't Raise My Boy to Be a Soldier" sold 650,000 copies, and it went on to become one of the year's best-selling songs (Slonimsky 249). After the *Lusitania* disaster, most Americans continued to support Wilson's determination to stay clear of the European hostilities and embraced his declaration that the nation was "too proud to fight" (Wilson 1:117). Meanwhile, new and assertive organizations moved to the vanguard of the peace movement. In January activist women, including many involved in the New York City peace march the previous August, founded the Woman's Peace party and drafted Jane Addams as its national chair. Its Co-operating Council, composed of leaders of seventeen other organizations dedicated to supporting peace activism, included a bewildering cross-section of activist women: Carrie Chapman Catt, the president of the National American Woman Suffrage Association, Daisy Allen Story, president of the Daughters of the American Revolution, Anna Gordon, president of the National Woman's Temperance Union, Mary McDowell, president of the National Federation of Settlements, and Belle Van Doren Harbert, president of the International Congress of Farm Women ("WPP Preamble"). When in April a delegation from the party traveled to The Hague for the International Congress of Women, not only was the group the most visible, active, and ambitious of the U.S. peace organizations but also it could fairly claim to represent the majority of American women's organizations.

During the summer, international delegations formed at The Hague conference fanned out across Europe, visiting combatant and neutral nations alike, seeking and usually gaining audience with the national

Fred Spear. "Enlist." Color poster. *1915*. (From original at the Museum of the
City of New York.)

ministers of state, and gathering information about wartime conditions and local sentiments (Addams, Balch, and Hamilton). They returned to the United States with a plan: to establish a conference of neutral nations offering continuous mediation. In August and again in November, Jane Addams and other women from the congress petitioned Woodrow Wilson to sponsor such a conference. Rebuffed, Addams and others in the peace movement, notably the Hungarian activist Rosika Schwimmer, subsequently sought to organize a conference of private citizens from neutral countries. About the same time, automaker and multimillionaire Henry Ford reportedly pledged half his wealth to "shorten the war by a single day" (qtd. Sullivan 5:145–46); Schwimmer, in Detroit to attend a peace rally, met with Ford and gained his financial backing for the unofficial conference of neutrals. Apparently regarding the war as a minor glitch in the assembly line of Western civilization, Ford then commissioned an entire ship, the *Oscar II*, to transport the U.S. delegation and signed a press release pledging, "We'll get the boys out of the trenches by Christmas" (5:169–70). William Jennings Bryan, who had resigned as Wilson's secretary of state because he saw the president's response to the *Lusitania* as biased against Germany, was at dockside when the *Oscar II* weighed anchor on 4 December, but had refused to go aboard as a delegate. Soon the members of the large press corps Ford had invited were dispatching reports of the disorganization and infighting among the (supposedly) pacifist delegates. Bud Fisher even portrayed his comic strip characters Mutt and Jeff as peace delegates aboard the *Oscar II*. The ship's voyage, which should have culminated the party's constructive, year-long campaign for peace, proved a colossal embarrassment. By Christmas Eve Ford was on his way home nursing a cold. Later Addams reported that after the debacle "the newspapers were, of course, closed to us so far as seriously advocating . . . a conference" (Addams, *Peace* 27).

Similar mixtures of high idealism and tough realism—either of which could become self-parody, if ill managed—abound in the following selection of poems. Sometimes the two tendencies were actually complementary: idealism, even pushed to the brink of absurdity, could have tangible effects in the real world of politics and social opinion. Joyce Kilmer's "The White Ships and the Red," for one, transforms the most material of facts—the drownings of some twelve hundred passengers and crew—into a bizarre abstraction: a personification of the *Lusitania* that brushes aside the pathos of debris, fuel oil, and entombed, drowning civilians in favor of a *bloody ship:*

> The pale green waves about her
>   Were swiftly, strangely dyed,
> By the great scarlet stream that flowed
>   From out her wounded side.

Thus a scene of specific human suffering becomes a moral abstraction: a ship stained red, sunk among the white. Yet this was the *Lusitania* poem reprinted more often than any other, and the sinking was to become precisely the high, moral abstraction that Kilmer had hoped. We might even say that it *had* to become a cause—crying out for vengeance—and a symbol—of German menace to American security—for it to become an effective rallying cry for U.S. intervention. So, too, some of the most idealized and overdrawn caricatures in pacifist poems apparently mobilized their constituency quite effectively. Angela Morgan's "Battle Cry of the Mothers," for instance, addresses the world's leaders on behalf of the world's mothers, who are regarded as essentially pacifistic:

> You have bargained our milk, you have bargained our blood,
> Nor counted us more than the forest brutes;
> *By the shameful traffic of motherhood*
> *Have you settled the world's disputes.*

These assumptions about women's solidarity did not even reflect the diversity of views among women in the Woman's Peace party, let alone in the United States. But the poem and its ideology did function effectively as political and social mythology. It illustrates the logic whereby so many organizations—in spite of difference—could be quickly brought together. Morgan's idealizing and essentializing apparently did not hurt the poem's reception, for she performed "Battle Cry" and two other poems at a series of Detroit rallies that helped persuade Henry Ford to bankroll the U.S. delegation to Oslo. As part of the subsequent effort to enlist Wilson's support, twelve thousand telegrams from women across the country—paid for by Clara Bryant Ford, the wife of Henry Ford—bore words that could serve as a gloss for Morgan's poem: "We work for peace. The mothers of America pray for it" (Degen 124).

Almost equal measures of close analysis of wartime politics and of idealization virtually unencumbered by real-world considerations are put on display in the most grandiose of all American war poems published in 1915, Lincoln Colcord's book-length epic *Vision of War*. In the cantos of his *Vision* included in this section, Colcord's recognition of Belgian guilt over the colonization of the Congo and his ironic commentary on the hollowness of British patriotism are salient and concrete—making precisely the kinds of critiques of European imperialism and class politics that British propaganda was so eager to conceal and that admirers of "brave little Belgium" and noble England were eager to overlook. The larger movement of Colcord's poem, however, seeks to rationalize the death and destruction of the war as a necessary step in the evolution of an overarching World Spirit, as Colcord seeks to blend Hegelianism and Walt Whitman. So runs part of canto XXVI:

> I have been trying to say what human nature is, and where it
>   stands;
> I have been trying to say that the trouble with life lies in
>   convention which makes it imperative to be selfish, in
>   order to eat and live;
> (The root strikes deep into the soil of human nature—it is
>   bound to retain its hold for many centuries to come;)
> I have been trying to say that if each of us would attend to his
>   spirit, we could bring about the millennium in any social
>   order, and in any day;
> (The social order is servant, not master, of the average man;)
> I have been trying to say that nothing ails our day, but the
>   growing evil of individual selfishness;
> (We need one thing alone—salvation of the soul.)
>
> (ll. 1–7)

Such idealism—in what seems a peculiarly American analysis, imagining modern warfare, that most complex and irrational of social problems, to be amenable to straightforward, rational, and individual solution—is remarkably common in 1915 poetry. But lest this observation seem an indictment, it must be noted that American idealisms could serve both as powerful political motivators and as important yardsticks for national and personal ethics. To Americans, history did not yet appear to be an unstoppable flood of inscrutable events, as it had to Europeans since July 1914. And if Americans' convictions about the malleability of their history led to ridiculous overestimates of the powers of an ethical and scientific intellect, this conviction contributed to an authentic reckoning between American ideals and actions. In the year of American pacifism, ideals at least *seemed* to dictate events. To be sure, preferences to stay clear of the European war did not generally lead to an active role in mediation. The political challenge of preparing for a war in which the United States had no unequivocal material interest— no direct threat to national boundaries, for instance—was solidly reinforced by the practical difficulty of mobilizing a diverse population that counted German Americans and Irish Americans as major ethnic groups. Yet the maternal pacifism of Bryan and Piantadosi's hit song "I Didn't Raise My Boy to Be a Soldier," published in January, may have defined the dominant tenor of the year, even if the limits of American pacifism were all too well revealed by the tragedy of the *Lusitania* and the farce of the *Oscar*.

Leo Feist, January
Alfred Bryan

I DIDN'T RAISE MY BOY
TO BE A SOLDIER

Lyrics by Alfred Bryan. Music by Al Piantadosi.

Ten million soldiers to the war have gone,
Who may never return again.
Ten million mothers' hearts must break
For the ones who died in vain.
Head bowed down in sorrow
In her lowly years,
I heard a mother murmur thro' her tears:

(Chorus)
"I didn't raise my boy to be a soldier,
I brought him up to be my pride and joy,
Who dares to place a musket on his shoulder,
To shoot some other mother's darling boy?
Let nations arbitrate their future troubles,
It's time to lay the sword and gun away,
There'd be no war today,
If mothers all would say,
[']I didn't raise my boy to be a soldier.[']" (repeat)

What victory can cheer a mother's heart,
When she looks at her blighted home?
What victory can bring her back
All she cared to call her own.
Let each mother answer
In the years to be,
Remember that my boy belongs to me!

Scribner's, January
OLIVE TILFORD DARGAN

FROM THIS WAR

III.
O, Brothers of the lyre and reed,
   Lend not a note to this wild fray,
   Where Christ still cries in agony
"They know not, Father, *thou* dost bleed!"
   Cast here no song, like flower prest
      To Slaughter's seething breast.

But be the minstrel breath of Peace;
   For her alone lift up your lyre,
   Mad with the old celestial fire,
Or on our earth let music cease,
   While keep we day and night the long
      Dumb funeral of song.

And if among ye one should rise,
   Blind garlander of armored crime,
   Trailing the jungle in a rhyme,
Let him be set 'neath blackened skies
   By mourning doors, and there begin
      The last chant of our sin.

Long gone the warrior's dancing plume
   That played o'er battle's early day;
   Now must his song be laid away,

Child-relic, that was glory's bloom;
　And Man who cannot sing his scars,
　　Is he not done with wars?

Ay, hearts deny the feet of haste,
　And as they muster, oh, they break!
　Hate's loudest fife no more can wake
In them the lust to kill and waste,
　And madly perish, fool on fool,
　　That Might, the brute, may rule.

We hope! Love walks thee yet, O Earth!
　Through thy untunable days she glows
　A bowed but yet untrampled rose,
Wearing the fearless flush of birth,—
　Yea, in our songless shame doth see
　　Thyself her harp to be!

Ye ages turning men to mould,
　The past be thine, the future ours!
　God hear us! There are infant powers
Stronger than giant sins of old!
　To all the hells that are and were
　　Man rises challenger.

Tho' now at final Autumn seem
　Our world with blood and ashes wound,
　Unfaltering Spring shall choose her ground;
Man shall rebuild with bolder dream,
　The god astir in every limb,
　　And earth be green for him.

And Peace shall cast afar her seed,
　Shall set the fields where skulls have lain
　With altar herb for every pain,
With myrtle and with tunèd reed,
　Till stars that watch have sign to sing
　　A sister's flowering.

Masses, January
LOUIS UNTERMEYER

TO A WAR POET

You sang the battle—
Boldly you called for the muskets to rattle,
You, in your slippered ease.
And bade the bugles lift to the breeze.
Glory you sang—from your couch—
With a weak and sagging pouch
You uttered your militant prattle—
You sang the battle!

What was your singing for,
With its two-penny craving for gore;
With its blatant and shoddy glamor
False to the core?
Evil enough is the poisonous clamor—
Why should you yammer
Of war?

Safe in your club or your den
You watch them go past you again;
Other than when you first sung them,
(Thankful that you're not among them)
Soldiers no longer, but men.
Men—and young boys—who were hot with the breath
Of your ardor and noisy ferment—
Look at them now; they are broken and spent. . . .
Are you not glad that your doggerel sent
Hundreds of these to their death?

Go now—stop clearing your throat;
Drop those fat hands that smote
Your twanging and trumpery lute.
Go now—and learn from the battered recruit
Of his jubilant sixty days!
Of the horror that crowded the dawn;
Of a fragrant and peace-breathing lawn
Turned to a roaring blaze;
Of frantic drums that blustered and beat

A nightmare retreat;
Of the sickness, the death-dealing stenches;
Of the blundering fight through the sleet
Waist-high in the water-filled trenches.
Of women ravished in a gust
Of horrible, hasty lust;
And children conceived with the crippling weight
Of frenzied and cancerous hate. . . .
The dusk settling down like a blight,
Screening unnamable hordes;
Searchlights stabbing the night
With blinding and bodiless swords;
Of a sudden welter of cries
And death dropping down from the skies. . . .
What was your singing for?
This music that dared to enamor
The crowd with the clamor
It could not ignore. . . .
Go—with your falsetto roar;
Go—with your ready-made glamor.
Why should you stay here to gurgle and stammer
Of war?

Masses, February
CARL SANDBURG

BUTTONS

I have been watching the war map slammed up for advertising in front of the
    newspaper office.
Buttons—red and yellow buttons—blue and black buttons—are shoved back
    and forth across the map.

A laughing young man, sunny with freckles,
Climbs a ladder, yells a joke to somebody in the crowd
And then fixes a yellow button one inch west
And follows the yellow button with a black button one inch west.

(Ten thousand men and boys twist on their bodies in a red soak along a river
    edge,

Gasping of wounds, calling for water, some rattling death in their throats.)
Who by Christ would guess what it cost to move two buttons one inch on the
war map here in front of the newspaper office where the freckle-faced
young man is laughing to us?

Independent, 1 February

ANGELA MORGAN

BATTLE CRY OF THE MOTHERS

Bone of our bone, flesh of our flesh,
Fruit of our age-long mother pain,
They have caught your life in the nations' mesh,
They have bargained you out for their paltry gain
And they build their hope on the shattered breast
Of the child we sang to rest.
On the shattered breast and the wounded cheek—
O, God! If the mothers could only speak!—
Blossom of centuries trampled down
For the moment's red renown.

   Pulse of our pulse, breath of our breath,
   Hope of the pang that brought to birth,
   They have flung you forth to the fiends of death,
   They have cast your flesh to the cruel earth,
   Field upon field, tier upon tier
   Till the darkness writhes in fear.
   And they plan to marshal you more and more—
   Oh, our minds are numb and our hearts are sore!—
   They are killing the thing we cherish most,
   They are driving you forth in a blinding host,
   They are storming the world with your eager strength—
   But the judgment comes at length.

Emperors! Kings! On your heedless throne,
Do you hear the cry that the mothers make?
The blood you shed is our own, our own,
You shall answer, for our sake.
When you pierce his side, you have pierced our side—
O, mothers! The ages we have cried!—

And the shell that sunders his flesh apart
Enters our bleeding heart.
'Tis over our bodies you shout your way,
Our bodies that nourished him, day by day
In the long dim hours of our sacred bliss,
Fated to end in this!

Governors! Ministers! You who prate
That war and ravage and wreck must be
To save the nation, avenge the state,
To right men's wrongs and set them free—
You who have said
Blood must be shed
Nor reckoned the cost of our agony—
Answer us now! Down the ages long
Who has righted the mother's wrong?
You have bargained our milk, you have bargained our blood,
Nor counted us more than the forest brutes;
By the shameful traffic of motherhood
Have you settled the world's disputes.
Did you think to barter the perfect bloom,
Bodies shaped in our patient womb
And never to face the judgment day
When you and your kind should pay?

Flesh of our flesh, bone of our bone,
Hope of the pang we bore alone,
Sinew and strength of the midnight hour
When our dream had come to flower.

O, women! You who are spared our wo,
You who have felt the mother throe
Yet cannot know the stark despair
Of coffins you shall never bear—
Are you asleep that you do not care,
Afraid, that you do not dare?
Will you dumbly stand
In your own safe land
While our sons are slaughtered and torn?
Bravely thru centuries we have borne
And suffered and wept in our secret place,
But now our silence and shame are past,
The reckoning day has come at last—

We must rise! We must plead for the race!
You who behold the mothers' plight,
Will you join our battle cry with might,
Will you fight the mothers' fight?
We who have given the soldiers birth,
Let us fling our cry to the ends of earth,
To the ends of Time let our voice be hurled
Till it waken the sleeping world.
Flesh of our flesh, bone of our bone,
Toil of the centuries come to speech,
As far as the human voice can reach
We will shout, we will plead for our own!

Warriors! Counsellors! Men at arms!
You who have gloried in war's alarms,
When the great rebellion comes
You shall hear the beat
Of our marching feet
And the sound of our million drums.
You shall know that the world is at last awake—
You shall hear the cry that the mothers make—
You shall yield—for the mothers' sake!

Clayton F. Summy (March)
W. N. Ewer

FIVE SOULS

As Sung by the Fuller Sisters

I was a peasant of the Polish plain;
I left my plow because the message ran,
Russia, in danger, needed ev'ry man
To save her from the Teuton: and was slain.
I gave my life for freedom, this I know:
For those who bade me fight had told me so.

I was a Tyrolese, a mountaineer.
I gladly left my mountain home to fight
Against the brutal treach'rous Muscovite;

And died in Poland on a Cossack spear.
I gave my life for freedom, this I know
For those who bade me fight had told me so.

I worked in Lyons at my weaver's loom,
When suddenly the Prussian despot hurled
His felon blow at France and at the world;
Then I went forth to Belgium and my doom.
I gave my life for freedom, this I know.
For those who bade me fight had told me so.

I owned a vineyard by the wooded Main
Until the Fatherland, begirt by foes
Lusting her downfall, Called me, and I rose
Swift to the call and died in fair Lorraine.
I gave my life for freedom, this I know
For those who bade me fight had told me so.

I worked in a shipyard by the Clyde.
There came a sudden word of wars declared,
Of Belgium, peaceful, helpless, unprepared,
Asking our aid: I joined the ranks and died.
I gave my life for freedom, this I know
For those who bade me fight had told me so.

Everybody's Magazine, April
CHARLES HANSON TOWNE

TO MY COUNTRY

One told me he had heard it whispered: "Lo!
   The hour has come when Europe, desperate
   With sudden war and terrible swift hate,
Rocks like a reed beneath the mighty blow.
Therefore shall we, in this her time of woe,
   Profit and prosper, since her ships of state
   Go down in darkness. Kind, thrice kind is Fate,
Leaving our land secure, our grain to grow!"

America! They blaspheme and they lie
   Who say these are the voices of your sons!

In this foul night, when nations sink and die,
    No thought is here save for the fallen ones
    Who, underneath the ruin of old thrones,
Suffer and bleed, and tell the world good-by!

Atlanta Constitution, 2 May
FRANK L. STANTON

MISSIONARY AND HOTTENTOT

A world at war, and the thunder-guns,
And never a river but reddened runs
To the storm-black sea where the secret foe
Hurls death to the ships from the depths below—
Waves of terror and winds of woe!
Glitter of steel in the hands of Hate,
Wolves of War that in darkness wait
On the wreck of a world made desolate!
And the Cross of Christ in the crimson thrall
With its holy shadow over all;
And far away on the heathen sod
Men with the Word of the living God
Pointing the dusky tribes of Night
To paths that lead to Stars of Light!

Said the Missionary to the Hottentot:
"Be Light thy guide and Love thy lot,
This breathing world God's garden spot!
Behold Love's broad and beauteous plan—
Thy holy Brotherhood of Man!
We are our brother's keepers—we,
From sunlit land to wave-high sea,
Spirits of hate to darkness hurled;
Love rules and reigns o'er all the world!"

Then the Hottentot—he caught the gleam
Of a wild drama in a dream;
He saw Earth's green fields splashed with red,
With never room to hide Love's head,
While women wailed, uncomforted,

And children—they of the Kingdom sweet
Trampled under War's iron feet,
Houseless—homeless! grief-stricken lands
Lifting to Heaven imploring hands;
And he heard the whole creation sigh
As the ghosts of a million slain marched by,
Souls to the wild, brute battle given,
Uncalled of God, yet storming Heaven,
To wait where the worlds at last shall meet
Till the War Kings come to the Judgment Seat!

Said the Hottentot to the Missionary:
"Go preach to graves where your dead you bury!
Praise human love with all your art
Over your brother's bleeding heart!
Raise altars, seen from Heaven's high domes,
Over the ashes of ruined homes;
Preach brother-love, of light-born years,
To a war-rent world of blood and tears;
Or pray in battle's crimson rain
To bring these dead to life again!
You are your brother's keeper—you,
With light that shines the centuries through;
Your brother fares on War's wild quest—
His sword is at his brother's breast!
Save him from darkness of the fight—
Lift your lost brother to the Light!"

Said the Hottentot on his savage sod
As the souls of the slain went up to God!

New York Times Magazine, 16 May
JOYCE KILMER

THE WHITE SHIPS AND THE RED

With drooping sail and pennant
    That never a wind may reach,
They float in sunless waters
    Beside a sunless beach.

Their mighty masts and funnels
  Are white as driven snow,
And with a pallid radiance
  Their ghostly bulwarks glow.

Here is a Spanish galleon
  That once with gold was gay,
Here is a Roman trireme
  Whose hues outshone the day.
But Tyrian dyes have faded
  And prows that once were bright
With rainbow stains wear only
  Death's livid, dreadful white.

White as the ice that clove her
  That unforgotten day,
Among her pallid sisters
  The grim Titanic lay.
And through the leagues above her
  She looked, aghast, and said:
"What is this living ship that comes
  Where every ship is dead?"

The ghostly vessels trembled
  From ruined stern to prow;
What was this thing of terror
  That broke their vigil now?
Down through the startled ocean
  A mighty vessel came,
Not white, as all dead ships must be,
  But red, like living flame!

The pale green waves about her
  Were swiftly, strangely dyed,
By the great scarlet stream that flowed
  From out her wounded side.
And all her decks were scarlet
  And all her shattered crew.
She sank among the white ghost ships
  And stained them through and through.

The grim Titanic greeted her
  "And who art thou?" she said;

"Why dost thou join our ghostly fleet
   Arrayed in living red?
We are the ships of sorrow
   Who spend the weary night,
Until the dawn of Judgment Day,
   Obscure and still and white."

"Nay," said the scarlet visitor,
   "Though I sink through the sea
A ruined thing that was a ship
   I sink not as did ye.
For ye met with your destiny
   By storm or rock or fight,
So through the lagging centuries
   Ye wear your robes of white.

"But never crashing iceberg
   Nor honest shot of foe,
Nor hidden reef has sent me
   The way that I must go.
My wound that stains the waters,
   My blood that is like flame,
Bear witness to a loathly deed,
   A deed without a name.

"I went not forth to battle,
   I carried friendly men,
The children played about my decks,
   The women sang—and then—
And then—the sun blushed scarlet
   And Heaven hid its face,
That world that God created
   Became a shameful place!

"My wrong cries out for vengeance,
   The blow that sent me here
Was aimed in Hell. My dying scream
   Has reached Jehovah's ear.
Not all the seven oceans
   Shall wash away the stain;
Upon a brow that wears a crown
   I am the brand of Cain."

When God's great voice assembles
  The fleet on Judgment Day,
The ghosts of ruined ships will rise
  In sea and strait and bay.
Though they have lain for ages
  Beneath the changeless flood,
They shall be white as silver.
  But one—shall be like blood.

San Francisco Bulletin, 5 June
GERALD G. LIVELY

'TWAS YOU WHO RAISED YOUR BOY TO BE A SOLDIER

Answer to the Popular Song, "I Didn't Raise My Boy to Be a Soldier"

O! Mothers of the world I hear you weeping,
  My heart has caught the echo of your pain;
The fruit of what you sowed you now are reaping
  When you read your loved one's name among the slain.
'Twas you who taught your boy to be a soldier,
  You lifted him when soldiers passed your way.
You first gave him a gun—I know 'twas only fun—
  But it trained his baby fingers for the fray.

Take down the general's picture in the parlor,
  Tear down the gaudy butchers from the wall,
'Tis time to teach your boy life's wider meaning
  That he may understand a brother's call.
Don't give your boy a toy-gun for a plaything—
  'Twill only teach the little hands to slay;
Hide away the screeching fife that whistles for your life,
  Burn the drum and throw the wretched sword away.

'Twas you who gave the boy a book of "heroes,"
  That showed in gaudy tints the soldier's life;
You thrilled the baby-mind with empty "glory"
  That tinsel's lie which is the soul of strife.

'Twas you who gave the box of wooden soldiers,
  'Twas you who gave the little sword of tin;
'Twas you who raised your boy to be a soldier,
  And mothers, you are paying for your sin.

Detroit Saturday Night
ANONYMOUS

M. O. R. C.

They didn't raise their boy to be a soldier;
They much preferred to raise him as a pet,
They didn't want him taught
How these naughty wars are fought,
And the using of a gun and bayonet.

They figure if you never talked of warfare,
Abolished patriotic songs complete,
And have histories redone,
Ousting Yorktown and Bull Run,
He would think that wars are something people eat.

If the army and navy were unmentioned,
Just ignoring that they ever did exist,
All the uniforms eschewed,
Brass bands utterly tabooed,
Then he'd certainly grow up a pacifist.

So he lived a life of peaceful vegetation
On a ladylike, inconsequential plan,
Full of happiness and joy,
Mamma's perfect little boy
Till the guns commenced to shoot and war began.

Fatherland: Fair Play for Germany and Austria-Hungary,
   7 July
GEORGE SYLVESTER VIERECK

THE NEUTRAL

Thou who canst stop this slaughter if thou wilt,
   Lo, how with death we freight the unwilling sea!
   Lift up thy voice to end this infamy:
Hands may be blood-stained that no blood have spilt.
Into a people's heart, yea to the hilt,
   Is plunged the sword of thy Neutrality.
   Though each wave bring some golden argosy,
Each on our soul heaps a new load of guilt.

Curses for us commingle with the tears
Of anguished mothers. Man, hast thou no ears?
   Upon thy White House falls a streak of red
From Europe's carnage. In the long night-tide
Canst thou not see them marching side by side,
   The mute accusing army of the dead?

Little Review, August
AMY LOWELL

PATTERNS

I walk down the garden paths,
And all the daffodils
Are blowing, and the bright blue squills.
I walk down the patterned garden paths
In my stiff, brocaded gown.
With my powdered hair and jewelled fan,
I too am a rare
Pattern. As I wander down
The garden paths.

My dress is richly figured,
And the train
Makes a pink and silver stain
On the gravel, and the thrift
Of the borders.
Just a plate of current fashion,
Tripping by in high-heeled, ribboned shoes.
Not a softness anywhere about me,
Only whale-bone and brocade.
And I sink on a seat in the shade
Of a lime tree. For my passion
Wars against the stiff brocade.
The daffodils and squills
Flutter in the breeze
As they please.
And I weep;
For the lime tree is in blossom
And one small flower has dropped upon my bosom.

And the splashing of waterdrops
In the marble fountain
Comes down the garden paths.
The dripping never stops.
Underneath my stiffened gown
Is the softness of a woman bathing in a marble basin,
A basin in the midst of hedges grown
So thick, she cannot see her lover hiding,
But she guesses he is near,
And the sliding of the water
Seems the stroking of a dear
Hand upon her.
What is Summer in a fine brocaded gown!
I should like to see it lying in a heap upon the ground.
All the pink and silver crumpled up on the ground.

I would be the pink and silver as I ran along the paths,
And he would stumble after,
Bewildered by my laughter.
I should see the sun flashing from his sword hilt and the buckles on his shoes.
I would choose
To lead him in a maze along the patterned paths,
A bright and laughing maze for my heavy-booted lover,

Till he caught me in the shade,
And the buttons of his waistcoat bruised my body as he clasped me,
Aching, melting, unafraid.
With the shadows of the leaves and the sundrops,
And the plopping of the waterdrops,
All about us in the open afternoon—
I am very like to swoon
With the weight of this brocade,
For the sun sifts through the shade.

Underneath the fallen blossom
In my bosom,
Is a letter I have hid.
It was brought to me this morning by a rider from the Duke.
"Madam, we regret to inform you that Lord Hartwell
Died in action Thursday sen'night."
As I read it in the white, morning sunlight,
The letters squirmed like snakes.
"Any answer, Madam?" said my footman.
"No," I told him.
"See that the messenger takes some refreshment.
No, no answer."
And I walked into the garden,
Up and down the patterned paths,
In my stiff, correct brocade.
The blue and yellow flowers stood up proudly in the sun,
Each one.
I stood upright too,
Held rigid to the pattern
By the stiffness of my gown.
Up and down I walked,
Up and down.

In a month he would have been my husband.
In a month, here, underneath this lime,
We would have broke the pattern;
He for me, and I for him,
He as Colonel, I as Lady,
On this shady seat.
He had a whim
That sunlight carried blessing.
And I answered, "It shall be as you have said."
Now he is dead.

In Summer and in Winter I shall walk
Up and down
The patterned garden paths
In my stiff, brocaded gown.
The squills and daffodils
Will give place to pillared roses, and to asters, and to snow.
I shall go
Up and down,
In my gown.
Gorgeously arrayed,
Boned and stayed.
And the softness of my body will be guarded from embrace
By each button, hook, and lace.
For the man who should loose me is dead,
Fighting with the Duke in Flanders,
In a pattern called a war.
Christ! What are patterns for?

Independent, 9 August
PERCY MACKAYE

THE RETURN OF AUGUST

Darkly a mortal age has come and gone
And man grown ancient in a single year.
August! The summer month is blasted sere
With memories earth bleeds to dream upon.

To dream upon! Ah, were we dreaming then
Ere Europe, blindfold, lulled in holiday,
Harkened the sudden thunder thru her play
And fumbling held her breath to hark again,

Or is this blighted year our dream?—How swift
The blackening tempest fell! How vast, thru fire
And cloud of Belgium's rape, a planet's ire
Flared on that pall of shame, while thru the rift

The livid sorrows racked our sympathies!
For still thought burned unclouded: Right and wrong

Strove for the palm as in epic song;
And so we poured our succor overseas,

Neutral in act but never in our souls,
Yet guarding the brave goal of peace. Till soon—
Slow-warping to the waning year's blind moon—
The tide ebbed back, and in the freezing shoals

We stared upon the dead—the dead, whose mothers
Suckled them still in dreams. Stark mid the stench
And yellow choke that reeked from shell and trench
They lay together there—mere boys, and brothers.

Were *these* the epic hosts of Wrong and Right
Whose clash had whirled us in their spirits' war?
These silent boys! What had they battled for
To lie such still bedfellows in the night?

Must breath of dying brothers wake the brass
That thrills the call to arms? Shall ghostly lips
Summon the living to the dark eclipse
And all their dearest shout to see them pass

Merely for this: That these who might have shared
A simple handclasp share a bloodied sod?—
So for a while we gazed and questioned God:
A haunted while: for dimly as we stared

Far off we heard the multitudinous cry
Of mangled Poland like a cry in sleep,
And Serbia fever-panting, and the deep
Half-breathed self-doubt of prisoned Germany,

And still far tidings blew, but that first spark
Of August splendor burned in them no more;
Pity and sorrow palled, and custom wore
A deeper callus and a blur more dark,

Till sudden—the "Lusitania"! Lightnings shot
The unhallowed message, and a shuddering fire
Leapt from our long-charred hearts—a glowing spire,
And Europe's sword swung nearer to the knot

That ties the bond of peace. And now—And now
The summer steals again toward winter's sleep.

The reaping time draws near—ah, *what* to reap?
And spring, that lurks beyond, comes hither—how?

Still, O my Country, while we may, look back!
The blighted year cries from the charnel grass:
Must breath of dying brothers wake the brass
That thrills the call to arms?—A blood-sered track

Leads backward to that other August day
Prowled by the still unglutted Minotaur;
But we, who watch to slay that beast of War,
Shall we hunt *him* or those he mangles?—Say:

For reason has its ire more just than hate;
Imagination has its master hour,
And pity its foil, and mother-love its power
Mightier than blood-lust and more obdurate.

My Country! poised in forward visioning,
With pity, love and reason let us pray
Our lives shall serve to cleanse this August day!—

      ❦ ❦ ❦

The summer wanes: the ploughman comes with spring.

Poems (September)
DANA BURNET

THE RETURN

Home across the clover
When the war was over
Came the young men slowly with an air of being old,
On a morning blue and gold
Through the weed-grown meadow-places
Marched young soldiers with old faces,
Marched the columns of the Emperor with dull, bewildered eyes,
And the day was like a rose upon the skies;
But they feared both light and life,
Feared the aftermath of strife.

Slow they came—
   Now that it was over—
Silent and sick and lame,
   Home across the clover.

A woman knelt in a garden by the road,
   Patting a little mound of earth
With aimless hands. Along the highway flowed
   The gray tide, while the day was at its birth.
She heard the drums, looked up, half smiled:
   "Why do you march," she said, "and play at soldiers?"
There's none to laugh at you—no little child!
   Not one. They've all gone back to sleeping."
   She fell to awful weeping.
   "Why do you play at soldiers?"
Then dropped down
To pat the little grave. The line went on and on into the town.

They saw it first in the city's eyes,
   Old men grouped by their fright, ran here and there
In startled herds, with shrill unmeaning cries.
   And there was white in every woman's hair,
And when a window yielded them a face
   'Twas like a flower blasted by the sun;
   Children there were none.
The world seemed robbed of joyousness and grace,
   A young girl with a head of snow
Sat weaving garlands in the market-place
   With hands unearthly slow,
As though her toil must be
The very measure of eternity.
A boy ran from the ranks, stooped, touched her brow;
"Margot, Margot! Is it thou?"
She did not glance up at the white-faced lad.
   Deep in the gray line rang a sudden shout:
"They're mad! They're mad!"
   "Silence, you dogs, until you're mustered out.
Forward, to greet the Emperor!"

        The line
Wavered and moaned and stumbled through the town
   Like some dark serpent with a broken spine.

Before the palace gate, in cloak and crown,
A shriveled figure sat with shaking hands,
Forming toy soldiers into various bands.
A figure in a jeweled diadem,
   Who as the swords leaped with a ringing noise,
Lifted his wasted eyes and looked at them.
   "Ah!" said the Emperor, and smiled:
     "More toys!"

(September)
LINCOLN COLCORD
From *Vision of War*

XIV

I

Tell me, was Belgium heroically true in times of peace?
Was the spirit of Belgium exalted in times of peace, as it is in times of war?

(Above the dark, secret continent,
On the tropic air, in the deathly solitudes of hidden, horrible places,
Where childlike souls have lost their only hope,
Lingers a mournful cry.)

Ivory, and gold, and human greed!
Do you think the only evil is, that a few men forgot themselves on the
    Congo—that a few men at home turned their faces aside?
Do you think these few will suffer for their crimes, here or hereafter, and pay
    off the score?
Is not the money that they made, spread broadcast, part of the wealth of
    western civilization?

Is not the idea that lay behind the making of this money, the idea of
    convention?
Will not this money, turning over and over, serve to confirm and strengthen
    this idea?
I tell you, out of the mouth of the Congo issued a far-permeating stream of
    evil,
Tainting the spirit of the whole world.

2

What, give up a share of profits, to make some savages happier?
Give all the profits up?—consider the profits held in trust for savages?
They could not have made the money, without our trade:
(But I was not thinking so much of the savages' money, as of the state of your
    soul.)

What, would you place the savage above the civilized man?—would you place
    the savage on an equality, even, with the civilized man?
He is not worthy of our condition—he cannot grasp our relations and
    purposes—he is not able to comprehend our political, social, ethical ideas:
(But he can suffer, and be unhappy, and die.)

3

What of the land?
Shall the savage retain his ample sovereignties, while the civilized man pants
    in confinement?
Has not the land ever belonged to the power that could seize and hold it?

(Profound, elusive contradiction:
Truth in a falsehood—right in wrong:
The spirit advancing over the bodies of the slain!)

4

Bow down in the twilight, bare the head:
Hour of the War! Belgium, thy sad, immortal hour.

We may not see again the lands of home;
We may not see the faces that we loved;
For the best truth we know, we fight and die;
Our country calls! Our country, and our King!

XV

1

Ah, England, England, England!
What works are these, in times of peace?

I suppose that, by keeping Turkey alive beyond her day, for your designs,
You thought to balance off dead Christians in Turkey against live Christians
    at home;
So many massacred in Turkey, to pay the price of a more profitable peace for
    greater numbers of the happy living, in another place;
Claiming that all of them would die some day.

(*Compromise! Compromise! Compromise!*
The world's weak, time-worn, easy argument,
While it rakes in the profits with both hands.)

2

I tell you, there are not lives enough in all England, to pay the price of one
    Armenian killed for England's benefit, through England's agency;
I tell you, when you arranged this matter, you were thinking of peoples'
    bodies, bodily happiness, material possessions;
I tell you, you were disregarding altogether the spirits both of those you
    sheltered and those you sacrificed;
I tell you, those you thought to save shall be lost, and those you thought to
    abandon shall be saved.

3

But what of China's opium trade?
No shadow there, no subtle shift—nothing but bitter fact;
Nothing but gold, nothing but greed of gain;
These Chinamen were powerless to resist;
A people had no right to be so powerless;
A people so powerless, had no right;
So you imposed the curse, and pocketed the proceeds,
Sending out missionaries to teach them love of Christ.

(You have mended that matter of the opium trade?
I know all that—compromise!—compromise!—compromise!
You have had your money, and used it as you pleased;
Nothing shall be forgotten in the final settlement.)

4

You slackened this slow torture of the yellow millions, when you were
    brought to it by material considerations, and not before;
You let up on the screws, when it paid you better to let up, than to give them
    another turn;
Only when China was making other friends, and when your friends were
    making friends with China;
Only when you saw that it would pay you better in other directions, to keep
    friends with China;
(And only when this great people, roused at last to the insidious danger,
Was throwing off the evil, in times of peace, in the face of every obstacle
    raised by you, by the assembled efforts of individual strong wills;)
Only then, did you consent to remove the terrible ban.

(Take thought upon that act and issue:
This is the people keeping its lands constantly fertile for forty centuries;
This is the people holding its strain pure and productive;
This is the people cleaving to fundamentals, deep and wise;
This is the people moored for long in a sheltered harbor, watching storms go
    by outside;
This is the people now calmly and confidently weighing anchor and setting
    sail, bound on a long momentous voyage.)

5

Hour of the War!
England, I see you hiding still among the shadows.

Tell me, what is the difference between the right to hold previous conquests,
    and the right to make new conquests?
Tell me, have you ever been seen fighting the fight of a smaller nation, when
    it did not serve your own ends?
Tell me, have you religiously, consistently respected all treaties, neutralities,
    obligations?

(I have been reading some queer Eastern tales;
Stories of Persia, India, Africa—they are full of human nature;
Strange, how human nature is everywhere the same!)

6

Come, England, face about, and take an honest stand;
God knows, there is good reason for you to fight.
Empire in danger! Sound the trumpets! Give alarm!
Flash it beneath the sea, and through the sky, to your outlying realms!

The mother-land in danger!—see them rise!
See, on the distant sky-line, the banners waving!
See, on the far horizon, the great ships sailing on!
See all your children arming, marching, coming home!
(Our country calls! Our country, and our King!)

7

You say that you are fighting a battle, too, for my America?
Perhaps—but I say, it is no kindness to her, either intentional or consequent;
She must fight her own battles some day, win or lose.

8

I think democracy is in greater danger from your untrue alliance, and from
    your arbitrary censorship, than from anything that I have seen;

I think the autocracy of Germany is but another step farther removed from
    truth itself, than your democracy, or than the democracy of my America;
I think there is the same long road for all of us ahead;
(We may be overtaken and passed on the road.)

9

England, fight well! Be glad to show yourself, and prove yourself;
Be glad of courage reaffirmed, and grace reborn.

(But no more talk of broken faith, thou faithless!
But no more talk of wrong of conquest, thou born arch-conqueror!)

North American Review, October
ALAN SEEGER

CHAMPAGNE, 1914–15

In the glad revels, in the happy fêtes,
    When cheeks are flushed, and glasses gilt and pearled
With the sweet wine of France that concentrates
    The sunshine and the beauty of the world,

Drink sometimes, you whose footsteps yet may tread
    The undisturbed, delightful paths of Earth,
To those whose blood, in pious duty shed,
    Hallows the soil where that same wine had birth.

Here, by devoted comrades laid away,
    Along our lines they slumber where they fell,
Beside the crater at the Ferme d'Alger
    And up the bloody slopes of La Pompelle,

And round the city whose cathedral towers
    The enemies of Beauty dared profane,
And in the mat of multicolored flowers
    That clothe the sunny chalk-fields of Champagne.

Under the little crosses where they rise
    The soldier rests. Now round him undismayed
The cannon thunders, and at night he lies
    At peace beneath the eternal fusillade...

That other generations might possess—
    From shame and menace free in years to come—
A richer heritage of happiness,
    He marched to that heroic martyrdom.

Esteeming less the forfeit that he paid
    Than undishonored that his flag might float
Over the towers of liberty, he made
    His breast the bulwark and his blood the moat.

Obscurely sacrificed, his nameless tomb,
    Bare of the sculptor's art, the poet's lines,
Summer shall flush with poppy-fields in bloom,
    And Autumn yellow with maturing vines.

There the grape-pickers at their harvesting
    Shall lightly tread and load their wicker trays,
Blessing his memory as they toil and sing
    In the slant sunshine of October days. . .

I love to think that if my blood should be
    So privileged to sink where his has sunk,
I shall not pass from Earth entirely
    But when the banquet rings, when healths are drunk,

And faces that the joys of living fill
    Glow radiant with laughter and good cheer,
In beaming cups some spark of me shall still
    Brim toward the lips that once I held so dear.

So shall one coveting no higher plane
    Than nature clothes in color and flesh and tone,
Even from the grave put upward to attain
    The dreams youth cherished and missed and might have known;

And that strong need that strove unsatisfied
    Toward earthly beauty in all forms it wore,
Not death itself shall utterly divide
    From the belovéd shapes it thirsted for.

Alas, how many an adept for whose arms
    Life held delicious offerings perished here,
How many in the prime of all that charms,
    Crowned with all gifts that conquer and endear!

Honor them not so much with tears and flowers,
  But you with whom the sweet fulfilment lies,
Where in the anguish of atrocious hours
  Turned their last thoughts and closed their dying eyes,

Rather when music or bright gathering lays
  Its tender spell, and joy is uppermost,
Be mindful of the men they were, and raise
  Your glasses to them in one silent toast.

Drink to them—amorous of dear Earth as well,
  They asked no tribute lovelier than this—
And in the wine that ripened where they fell,
  Oh, frame your lips as though it were a kiss.

Deuxième Régiment Étranger
Champagne, France, July, 1915

Solidarity, 16 October
J. F. KENDRICK

WHAT FOR?

Now the simple folks are praying
And the dogs of war are baying,
For the chauvinists are braying,
Braying, bellowing for war.
And the youngsters, green and willing,
Undertake the dusty drilling,
Getting ready for the milling
And the grilling that's in store;
For the shibboleth that lures them
To the killing that's in store
Is the jingo's
  "ON TO WAR!"

But amid the blow and blunder
Of the armies bent on plunder
There are men evincing wonder,
Wonder at the red furore.
As they see the corpses falling,

As they hear the stricken calling,
While they help the wounded, sprawling,
In their sticky, drippy gore,
They are asking why men wallow
In their smeary, drippy gore—
"All this slaughter:
    WHAT'S IT FOR?"

In the wholesale-murder season
Common sense is rabid treason.
And it's rash to seek the reason,
Reason back of every war:
For behind the raping raider
And the bellicose crusader
Comes the calculating trader
Using methods we deplore.
If his ledger shows a profit
Through the methods we deplore,
It's a righteous
    HOLY WAR.

While the tariff sharks are plotting,
Pools of youthful blood are clotting,
Shed because a system's rotting,
Rotting to its very core.
Let us hope the day is nearing,
When all workingmen, cohering,
Will prohibit buccaneering
With its butchery galore;
And the howl for licensed rapine
And for butchery galore
Shall be uttered
    NEVERMORE.

Chicago, October 5, 1915

New York Times, 24 October
ROBERT UNDERWOOD JOHNSON

EDITH CAVELL

Room mid the martyrs for a deathless name!
  Till yesterday, in her how few could know
  Black War's white angel, succoring friend and foe—
Whose pure heart harbored neither hate nor blame
When Need or Pity made its sovereign claim.
  Today she is the world's! Its poignant woe,
  We thought had been outwept, again doth flow
In tenderest tears that multiply her fame.

Oh, something there is in us yet, more bright
  Than Rouen's hungry flames—that could consume
Jeanne's slender limbs but not her spirit's might.
  Fate still has noble colors in her loom.
One lonely woman's courage in the night
  Has sealed the savage Hohenzollerns' doom!

Solidarity, 4 December
JOHN F. KENDRICK

[ONWARD, CHRISTIAN SOLDIERS!]

Onward, Christian soldiers!
Duty's way is plain:
Slay your Christian neighbors,
Or by them be slain.
Pulpiteers are spouting
Effervescent swill,
God above is calling you
To rob and rape and kill.
All your acts are sanctified
By The Lamb on high;
If you love The Holy Ghost,
Go murder, pray and die.

Onward, Christian soldiers,
Rip and tear and smite!
Let the gentle Jesus
Bless your dynamite.
Splinter skulls with shrapnel,
Fertilize the sod:
Folks who do not speak your tongue
Deserve the curse of God.
Smash the doors of every home,
Pretty maidens seize;
Use your might and sacred right
To treat them as you please.

Onward, Christian soldiers!
Eat and drink your fill;
Rob with bloody fingers,
Christ O. K.'s the bill.
Steal the farmers' savings,
Take their grain and meat;
Even though the children starve,
The Saviour's bums must eat.
Burn the peasants' cottages,
Orphans leave bereft;
In Jehovah's holy name
Wreak ruin right and left.

Onward, Christian soldiers!
Drench the land with gore;
Mercy is a weakness
All the gods abhor.
Bayonet the babies,
Jab the mothers, too;
Hoist The Cross of Calvary
To hallow all you do.
File your bullets' noses flat,
Poison every well;
God decrees your "enemies"
Must all go plumb to hell.

Onward, Christian soldiers!
Blighting all you meet,
Trampling human freedom
Under pious feet.
Praise The Lord whose dollar-sign
Dupes his favored race!
Make the foreign trash respect
Your bullion brand of grace.
Trust in mock salvation,
Serve as pirates' tools;
History will say of you:
"That pack of g—— d—— fools."

Public, December
GRACE ISABEL COLBRON

THE BALLAD OF BETHLEHEM STEEL
OR
THE NEED FOR "PREPAREDNESS"

A TALE OF THE TICKER

A fort is taken, the papers say,
    Five thousand dead in the murderous deal.
A victory? No, just another grim day.
    But—up to five hundred goes Bethlehem Steel.

A whisper, a rumor, one knows not where;
    A sign, a prayer from a torn heart rent;
A murmur of Peace on the death-laden air,
    But—Bethlehem Steel drops thirty per cent.

"We'll fight to the death," the diplomats cry.
    "We'll fight to the death," sigh the weary men.
As the battle roars to the shuddering sky,
    And—Bethlehem Steel has a rise of ten.

What matters the loss of a million men?
  What matters the waste of blossoming lands?
The children's cry or the women's pain?
  If Bethlehem Steel at six hundred stands?

And so *we* must join in the slaughter-mill,
  We must arm ourselves for a senseless hate,
We must waste our youths in the murder drill—
  That Bethlehem Steel may hold its state.

PART 4
1916

While poetic merit has been, of course, the paramount consideration, I have endeavored to exercise a catholic judgment, and to give fair representation to various schools of thought and expression as well as to various phases of the War. If undue prominence seems to be given to what may be called its more personal aspects—the spirit of sacrifice and devotion which inspired men and women to give themselves and those dearest to them to a great cause—I must plead in excuse that during much of the time of the preparation of this volume my mind was full of the memory of my friend Lieut.-Col. G. H. Baker of the 5th Canadian Mounted Rifles, who fell in command of his battalion during the third battle of Ypres on June 2, 1916.

—J. W. Cunliffe, Preface to *Poems of the Great War,* November 1916

In January 1916, Britain began conscripting soldiers, finally joining the rest of the principal European combatants with the passage of its Military Service Act. By summer many men taken in this first draft had been trained and were stationed on the Western Front; they comprised the larger part of the 20,000 dead and 40,000 wounded on 1 July, the first day of the Battle of the Somme (Fussell, *Great War* 13). Renewed attacks failed to reach any but the closest objectives and resulted in terrible death tolls: nearly 200,000 French soldiers, some 400,000 German, and well over 400,000 British troops by the end of September (Ferro 80–81). Verdun, where the German army took the offensive and the French the defensive, was little better: between February and September 350,000 French soldiers were killed as were a like number of Germans (76, 78). The ebb and flow of the battle lines were dutifully recorded in U.S. newspapers, but only the least careful readers could be fooled by these maps' greatly magnified scale: the Somme offensive was making little progress toward liberating Belgium, and outside Verdun even less ground was being traded back and forth. Of course, true casualty figures were revealed only after the war, but that many thousands were being killed on both sides was clear enough.

Ralph H. Chaplin. "Beware: Sabotage." Color stickerette. [Cleveland:] IWW, [*1916.*]
(From original at the Washington State Historical Society, Tacoma. EPH/*331.886.*)

In this context, it is no surprise that Democrats seized on the slogan "He kept us out of war" for Woodrow Wilson's reelection campaign and not much surprise either that it helped give him a second term. It was, however, a remarkably awkward expression for a campaign slogan, especially for a president famous for his rhetorical gifts. Foremost, "He kept us out of war" implies passivity: a negation of action. Wilson is said to have been uncomfortable with running on it precisely because his successes in averting war had depended heavily on the German government's actions, which he knew were out of his control (Baker 257–58). The slogan came, in fact, from a plank of the Democratic party platform that was added virtually as an afterthought by an unknown author: "In particular we commend to the American people the splendid diplomatic victories of our great President, who has preserved the vital interests of our Government and its citizens, and kept us out of war" (257). These "diplomatic victories" were not altogether insubstantial. In the summer and fall of 1915 Wilson extracted German assurances, initially, that unarmed passenger ships would be warned prior to attack and, later, that merchant vessels and armed passenger ships would be similarly warned. These promises effectively brought a halt to the submarine blockade of Great Britain and ended, for the time being, the immediate threat of war to the United States (D. Smith 61–62, 64–66). Yet if there was substance behind the platform, the slogan spells out an especially reactive form of pacifism. Just as significantly, it made no promises whatsoever about the president's future policy.

Indeed, other features of the campaign presaged war. Whereas Wilson had been indifferent about the pacifist convention plank, he had insisted on another devoted to "Americanism": a commendation of absolute loyalty to the nation—and warning against disloyalty—that was directed particularly toward "hyphenated" Americans, recent immigrants whom Wilson and many other leaders suspected of being overly sympathetic toward the countries of their birth. Wilson's focus on "hyphenates," as opposed to any American biased toward one combatant, effectively cast suspicion on German Americans in the Midwest and on Irish Americans in the Northeast. These groups had a significant proportion of recent immigrants and were, of course, inclined to sympathy toward Germany and antipathy toward Britain; established immigrant groups, dominated by WASPs but rarely thought of as anything but "native" Americans, tended to identify with the Belgians, French, and British. Thus, Wilson's version of Americanism not only promoted the national unity presumed necessary to fight a major war but also indicated unmistakably which alliance Wilson and virtually all other national leaders assumed the United States would join.

Going hand in hand with Americanism was the other political catch-phrase of the moment: preparedness. Preparedness meant, most obviously, the material readiness of the armed forces. In the summer of 1916 Congress passed large appropriations for naval shipbuilding, formed the unified Council for National Defense, nationalized the state guard units, and expanded the standing army (Finnegan 154). The U.S. Army was still less than one-quarter the size of the armies of Germany or France in 1913—U.S. representatives favoring a bigger build-up had in fact been forced to compromise—but a broader foundation for later expansion of the navy and army was laid. The army also found practical opportunities to prepare for war in Europe. Punitive expeditions into Mexico were first launched in March and continued until February 1917. While their purpose was to locate and capture the rebel leader Pancho Villa, whose forces had several times crossed the U.S. border and raided U.S. towns, the ventures were also a proving ground for the American army and its commander, General John Pershing. When on 21 June U.S. soldiers confronted loyalist Mexican troops at Carrizal and were defeated badly, national guard units were mobilized and placed on the border (Baker 76). They did not see combat but did get additional training.

More broadly, however, preparedness was ideological and involved all sectors of U.S. society. It meant the general inculcation of military virtues: physical fitness, mental alacrity, efficiency, patriotic devotion, respect for authority. The outward signs of this broader preparedness abounded: Summer paramilitary camps were set up in Plattsburg, New York, and elsewhere around the country; military training courses were proposed for the public schools; the Boy Scouts came into their own. By 1916, just five years after the organization's founding, Scoutmaster James E. West could count 42,000 adult males who served as volunteer leaders and 190,000 boys enrolled in Boy Scout programs (807). Indeed, West argued that scouting for boys and girls alike (Girl Scouts of America had been founded in 1912) should supersede "purely technical military training." More important was moral character: "Those things which make for discipline, obedience, loyalty, endurance, initiative, alertness, good health, knowledge of how to care for oneself, etc., should not be considered distinctive military training, but should be given to all boys and girls in order properly to prepare them for their later responsibilities as home-makers, wage-earners, and citizens" (806). It was a useful coincidence, at least, that the kind of modern, mass war that the United States would be called upon to fight—that Europe was already plainly fighting—demanded the loyalty, labor, and strength of civilians as well as soldiers.

In 1916, with the United States assuming a more belligerent posture but still officially committed to neutrality, opponents of war attempted to shore up their position by renewing their previously successful arguments. In December 1915, Grace Isabel Colbron's "Ballad of Bethlehem Steel; or, The Need for 'Preparedness'" had commented sardonically on the issue of military preparedness. As congressional debate on preparedness measures proceeded in summer 1916, opponents reprinted the ballad in the political leaflet *Seven Congressmen on Preparedness*, so that antipreparedness views were preceded by Colbron's tangy verses charging that U.S. arms manufacturers, already profiting handsomely from European demand, would be the main beneficiaries of an American arms buildup. That year the book trade began to catch up with the periodical press in the publication of war poetry, and editors and poets took the opportunity to reprint and repackage poems written earlier. J. W. Cunliffe's *Poems of the Great War,* the first major-press anthology published in the United States, offered a particularly compendious review of the poems of 1914, 1915, and 1916. George Sylvester Viereck persisted in editing and publishing his weekly journal *Fatherland: Fair Play for Germany and Austria-Hungary* and collected many of his verses originally published there in *Songs of Armageddon.* Thus he brought back into print "The Neutral," originally written in 1915 to criticize Wilson's less-than-complete neutrality in the wake of the *Lusitania* tragedy. Also reprinted was "The German American to His Adopted Country," originally published in August 1914, in which Viereck hoped to stir the kind of close identification between Americans and Germans that had so far been cultivated mostly between Americans and the Allies:

> We catch a mother's smile. We seize
> > In thought a father's hand again.
> We see the house and, through the trees,
> > A girl's face in the window pane.

Viereck was attempting to attack war preparedness not so much on the level of military and industrial production as on the level of ideological production. His aim was no less than to reconfigure the identifications, the loyalties, even the very "character" of U.S. citizens, and in this project he was both resisting powerful cultural currents favoring the Allies and competing with other poets seeking to influence American attitudes. The contest was less over formal pro- and antipreparedness arguments and more over how American identities were to be defined, a process which often came down to *who* was permitted to speak, *for whom,* and *to whom.* For example, Charles T. Dazey, a white writer whose stereotypical black characters were well known through his play *In Old Kentucky,* then in its twenty-fourth year of continuous production, seized the opportunity to write of the heroic black soldiers who fought in the Carrizal debacle. Dazey's poem published in the *New York Times* is, as it happens, celebratory. Yet if Dazey's poem is taken as an accurate reflection of black heroism and of African Americans' celebration of its young men in uniform, what are the consequences? It would appear the poem worked to encourage military aggressiveness among at least two audiences: African Americans, by modeling black patriotic self-sacrifice, and white elites, by reassuring them that blacks would follow if they led the nation into war.

Attempting to speak for recent immigrants was Lurana Sheldon, a frequent contributor to the *New York Times.* In "The Naturalized Alien," appearing on the *Times* editorial page of 5 July, Sheldon impersonates the voice of the immigrant while, not so subtly, offering a civics lesson: "The land I claim claims me! / It holds me sacredly its own, and I / For its best welfare will both fight and die." Ralph H. Chaplin's poem "Preparedness" likewise assumes identification between the speaker of the poem and the have-nots of American society: "For freedom die? but we were never free / Save but to drudge and starve or strike and feel / The bite of bullets and the thrust of steel." But Chaplin offers a radically different interpretation of the life experiences of recent arrivals who continually filled out the ranks of the lowest of the working classes, even while using the same terms and touching on the same preparedness debate.

That Viereck did not persuade many pro-Entente readers had less to do with his skill as a publisher and poet than with the hostile context in which readers received his work: the anti-German newspaper editorials and poems that Viereck rails against, and, it must be added, the arrogant hypocrisy of the German military leadership reflected in Viereck's own verses with phrases like "Teutons strike for liberty." In other words, Viereck, Chaplin, Sheldon, and the rest could not simply weave their visions of American identity and ideology out of whole cloth; they had to persuade real, independent, prejudiced, more or less autonomous people and confront historical knowledge accepted widely as given (whether true or not). Viereck had to counter conventional wisdom that condemned the German army's invasion of Belgium and the German navy's submarine warfare, both of which had accepted the killing of civilians as collateral damage. Moreover, if in the confused opening days of the war Germany could somewhat plausibly claim a threat to its national security—with Russia rapidly advancing into East Prussia—it could hardly do so credibly in 1916, with Russia beaten back and its own army entrenched in northern France.

The contingencies of history would presently lay an even heavier hand on American war poets, particularly those who persisted in raging against the rising tide of patriotism. In 1916, to judge by the falling off of active pacifism and the passive disconnection from the war suggested by Wilson's campaign slogan, the United States became less closely engaged with the tragedy in Europe; accordingly, fewer war poems were published in 1916 than in any other year of the hostilities. But in the midst of this psychological weariness and political disengagement, a historical snare was, in effect, being set. In 1916 the United States became ever more deeply involved with economic trade and financial support for Britain, France, and Russia, and so the American economic stake in the success of those countries grew. By 1916 American companies were exporting over $1 billion in munitions, virtually all to the Allies and next to none, because of the British blockade, to the Central Powers (C. Wright 921). This expansion led to a tighter labor market and, consequently, a stronger bargaining position for most U.S. unions. Among these, ironically enough, was the antimilitarist and antinationalist IWW, whose farm workers' local alone, the Agricultural Workers Organization, grew from a few hundred members in 1914 to 20,000 in 1916. The IWW overall was to swell from about 40,000 in 1916 to some 100,000 members in 1917 (Dubofsky 316, 349). Represented in the previous section by John F. Kendrick's poems and in this section by Chaplin's "Preparedness" and Harry McClintock's version of the "Hymn of Hate," the IWW's poetry and songs had always been brash, but now they were on the lips of many more discontented workers in some of the very industries most crucial to the war economy: agriculture, coal, copper, forestry, textiles. Buoyed by the organizing successes of the war years, IWW leaders including Chaplin, the new editor of *Solidarity* in 1917, felt themselves most powerful at nearly the time it would become most imperative to the government that they submit to its authority. Similar historical traps awaited other Americans: pacifists who felt vindicated by Woodrow Wilson's victory on an antiwar platform; black Americans who hoped that further self-sacrifice for the nation would bring respect and equal rights; even perhaps a president who believed that "preparedness" and "Americanism" were terms he understood, whose meanings he could control by his own considerable eloquence.

Solidarity, 1 January
HARRY MCCLINTOCK

HYMN OF HATE

For the sailors that drown when your ill found ships go crashing on the
    shore,
For the mangled men of your railroads, ten thousand a year or more.
For the roasted men in your steel mills, and the starving men on your roads,
For the miners buried by hundreds, when the fire damp explodes,
For our brothers maimed and slaughtered for your profits every day,
While your priests chant the chorus "God giveth—and God hath taken
    away."
For a thousand times that you drove back when we struck for a living wage,
For the dungeons and jails our men have filled because of your devilish rage.
For Homestead and for Chicago, Coeur D'Alene and Telluride,
For your bloody shambles at Ludlow, where the women and babies died,
For our heroes you hanged on the gallows high to fill your slaves with awe,
While your Judges stood in a sable row and croaked, "Thus saith the law."
For all of the wrongs we have suffered from you, and for each of the wrongs
    we hate,
With a hate that is black as the deepest pit, that is steadfast and sure as fate.
We hate you with hand, and heart, and head, body, and mind, and brain.
We hate at the forge, in the mine and mill, in the field of golden grain.
We curse your name in the market place as the workman talks with his mate,
And when you dine in your gay cafe the waiter spits on your plate.
We hate you! D'amnyou! hate you! we hate your rotten breed.
We hate your slave religion with submission for its creed.
We hate your judges. We hate your courts, we hate that living lie,
That you call "Justice" and we hate with a hate that shall never die.

We shall keep our hate and cherish our hate and our hate shall ever grow.
We shall spread our hate and scatter our hate 'till all of the workers know.
And The Day shall come with a red, red dawn; and you in your gilded halls,
Shall taste the wrath and the vengeance of the men in overalls.
The riches you heaped in your selfish pride we shall snatch with our naked
    hands,
And the house ye reared to protect you shall fall like a castle of sand.
For ours are the hands that govern in factory, mine and mill,
And we need only to fold our arms and the whole wide world stands still!
SO GO YE AND STUDY THE BEEHIVE, and do not quite forget,
That we are the WORKERS of the world and we have not spoken—yet.

The Book of the Homeless (January)
EDITH WHARTON

THE TRYST

I said to the woman: Whence do you come,
With your bundle in your hand?
She said: In the North I made my home,
Where slow streams fatten the fruitful loam,
And the endless wheat-fields run like foam
To the edge of the endless sand.

I said: What look have your houses there,
And the rivers that glass your sky?
Do the steeples that call your people to prayer
Lift fretted fronts to the silver air,
And the stones of your streets, are they washed and fair
When the Sunday folk go by?

My house is ill to find, she said,
For it has no roof but the sky;
The tongue is torn from the steeple-head,
The streets are foul with the slime of the dead,
And all the rivers run poison-red
With the bodies drifting by.

I said: Is there none to come at your call
In all this throng astray?

They shot my husband against a wall,
And my child (she said), too little to crawl,
Held up its hands to catch the ball
When the gun-muzzle turned its way.

I said: There are countries far from here
Where the friendly church-bells call,
And fields where the rivers run cool and clear,
And streets where the weary may walk without fear,
And a quiet bed, with a green tree near,
To sleep at the end of it all.

She answered: Your land is too remote,
And what if I chanced to roam
When the bells fly back to the steeples' throat,
And the sky with banners is all afloat,
And the streets of my city rock like a boat
With the tramp of her men come home?

I shall crouch by the door till the bolt is down,
And then go in to my dead.
Where my husband fell I will put a stone,
And mother a child instead of my own,
And stand and laugh on my bare hearth-stone
When the king rides by, she said.

Paris, August 27th, 1915

Songs and Satires (March)
EDGAR LEE MASTERS

O GLORIOUS FRANCE

You have become a forge of snow white fire,
A crucible of molten steel, O France!
Your sons are stars who cluster to a dawn
And fade in light for you, O glorious France!
They pass through meteor changes with a song
Which to all islands and all continents
Says life is neither comfort, wealth, nor fame,
Nor quiet hearthstones, friendship, wife nor child

131

Nor love, nor youth's delight, nor manhood's power,
Nor many days spent in a chosen work,
Nor honored merit, nor the patterned theme
Of daily labor, nor the crowns nor wreaths
Of seventy years.

      These are not all of life,
O France, whose sons amid the rolling thunder
Of cannon stand in trenches where the dead
Clog the ensanguined ice. But life to these
Prophetic and enraptured souls is vision,
And the keen ecstasy of fated strife,
And divination of the loss as gain,
And reading mysteries with brightened eyes
In fiery shock and dazzling pain before
The orient splendor of the face of Death,
As a great light beside the shadowy sea;
And in a high will's strenuous exercise,
Where the warmed spirit finds its fullest strength
And is no more afraid. And in the stroke
Of azure lightning when the hidden essence
And shifting meaning of man's spiritual worth
And mystical significance in time
Are instantly distilled to one clear drop
Which mirrors earth and heaven.

      This is life
Flaming to heaven in a minute's span
When the breath of battle blows the smoldering spark.
And across these seas
We who cry Peace and treasure life and cling
To cities, happiness, or daily toil
For daily bread, or trail the long routine
Of seventy years, taste not the terrible wine
Whereof you drink, who drain and toss the cup
Empty and ringing by the finished feast;
Or have it shaken from your hand by sight
Of God against the olive woods.

As Joan of Arc amid the apple trees
With sacred joy first heard the voices, then
Obeying plunged at Orleans in a field
Of spears and lived her dream and died in fire,

Thou, France, hast heard the voices and hast lived
The dream and known the meaning of the dream,
And read its riddle: How the soul of man
May to one greatest purpose make itself
A lens of clearness, how it loves the cup
Of deepest truth, and how its bitterest gall
Turns sweet to soul's surrender.

      And you say:
Take days for repetition, stretch your hands
For mocked renewal of familiar things:
The beaten path, the chair beside the window,
The crowded street, the task, the accustomed sleep,
And waking to the task, or many springs
Of lifted cloud, blue water, flowering fields—
The prison house grows close no less, the feast
A place of memory sick for senses dulled
Down to the dusty end where pitiful Time
Grown weary cries Enough!

Masses, April
MARY CAROLYN DAVIES

TO THE WOMEN OF ENGLAND

While you weep
For your men, blind, legless, broken
Or only dead perhaps—
While you despair—

We dance and shop
And feel annoyance when upon the street
They hold a box for pennies in our faces
And beg for food for little children
And bandages and socks
For soldiers somewhere.

And you raise your heads
Eyes dull with tears and peer across the sea
In wonder at our callousness.

We women have a right to dance and shop
And to refuse your pennies.
We have never—
Yet—
Pinned a feather on a boy and killed him.

Masses, June
CHARLES W. WOOD

NATIONAL ANTHEM

I love my country, yes I do,
  I love my Uncle Sam.
I also love my steak and eggs,
  And beer and beans and ham.
If I went dead, I couldn't eat,
  And though I'd not be missed,
I'd miss my feed—oh, yes, indeed—
  I guess I won't enlist.

I love the flag, I do, I do,
  Which floats upon the breeze:
I also love my arms and legs
  And neck and nose and knees.
One little shell might spoil 'em all
  Or give 'em such a twist
They wouldn't be no use to me—
  I guess I won't enlist.

I love my country, yes I do,
  I hope her folks stay well:
Without no arms or legs or things,
  I think they'd look like hell.
Young men with faces shot away
  Ain't fitten to be kissed:
I've read in books it spoils their looks—
  I guess I won't enlist.

Solidarity, 24 June
RALPH H. CHAPLIN

PREPAREDNESS

For freedom die? but we were never free
   Save but to drudge and starve or strike and feel
   The bite of bullets and the thrust of steel.
For freedom die, while all the land can see
   How strikers writhe beneath thy crushing heel
And mothers shudder at the thought of thee!
   For freedom die . . . . . . ?

Defend the flag? beneath whose reeking fold
   The gun-men of our masters always came
   To burn and rape and murder in thy name!
Defend the flag whose honor has been sold
   And soiled until it is a thing of shame—
The brazen paramour of Greed and Gold—
   Defend the flag . . . . . . ?

Protect our land? we, who are dispossessed,
   And own not space to sleep in when we die!
   The continent is held by thieves on high—
The brood of vipers sheltered at thy breast.
   Your "liberty" is but a loathsome lie;
We have no homes nor any place to rest—
   Defend our land . . . . . . ?

Resist the foe, we shall! from sea to sea
   The lewd invaders battle-line is thrown;
   Here is our enemy and here alone—
The Parasite of world-wide industry!
   His wealth is red with mangled flesh and bone.
Resist the foe, ah, crush him utterly—;
   Resist the foe . . . . . . ?

New York Times, 30 June
CHARLES T. DAZEY

AT CARRIZAL

("Captain Morey says his negro troops faced death singing.")

By day the sky of Mexico
   Stares, brazen, overhead;
By night the light of alien stars
   Keeps watch above the dead.

How did they die in that far land,
   How did they face the grave—
Those men whose fathers bore the brand
   That marked the southland slave?

Did they, like recreant cowards, weep,
   Or vainly seek to fly?
Ah, no, upon that bloody field
   They showed how men should die!

Betrayed, outnumbered, still they fought
   To their heroic end,
And smiled at death, and bravely sang,
   As welcoming a friend.

The strange, wild music of their race
   With mellow, low refrain,
From cabin homes, from rice-land swamps,
   In memory swells again.

But never such a song rang out
   As when they faced the foe,
And, singing, charged from trench to trench,
   And gave him blow for blow!

And in the annals of our land,
   Long as our flag shall wave,
That song will show that men are men,
   Though children of the slave.

New York Times, 5 July
LURANA SHELDON

THE NATURALIZED ALIEN

The land I claim claims me!
  It holds me sacredly its own, and I
  For its best welfare will both fight and die
If such a sacrifice shall be
Part of the great necessity.

The land I claim has made
  My chance for victory, for strong success.
  In other climes my triumph would be less,
For here has freedom truly laid
Each open path of honest trade.

The land I claim has left
  My hands unbound, my will at peace.
  Rich are the blessings, precious the release
From chains whose links were cleft
Ere hope my soul bereft.

The land I claim claims me,
  And she shall find her foster-soldier true
  To this her flag, the red, the white, the blue,
Though kith and kin shall cross the sea
To call me back to loyalty.

Masses, August
ARTURO GIOVANNITTI

THE DAY OF WAR

Madison Square, June 20th

A hawk-faced youth with rapacious eyes, standing on a shaky chair,
Speaks stridulously in the roar of the crossways, under the tower that
    challenges the skies, terrible like a brandished sword.

A thin crowd, idle, yawning, many-hungered, beggarly, rich with the
    inexhaustible treasures of endless hours of dreaming and scheming.
Imperial ruins of the Mob.
Listens to him, wondering why he speaks and why they listen.
The fierce incandescence of noon quivers and drones with the echoes
Of distant clamors, grumbling of voices, blaring of speed-mad fanfares;
But as the roar reaches the group, it turns and recoils and deviates, and runs
    around it,
As a stream runs around a great rock,
And his voice alone is heard in this little island of silence.
His arms go up as he speaks; his white teeth fight savagely with his black eyes,
His red tie flows tempestuously in the wind, the unfurled banner of his heart
    amidst the musketry of his young words.
He has been speaking since dawn; he has emerged from the night, and the
    night alone shall submerge him.
They listen to him and wonder, and grope blindly in the maze of his words,
They fear his youth and they pity it,
But the sunlight is strong on his head,
And his shadow is heavy and hard upon their faces.

Suddenly, like a flash of yellow flame
The blast of a trumpet shoots by, its notes ramming like bullets against the
    white tower.
The soldiers march up the Avenue. The crowd breaks, scatters, and runs away,
    and only six listeners remain:
A girl, a newsboy, a drunken man, a Greek who sells rugs, an old man, and
    the stranger I know.
But he speaks on, louder, with the certainty of the thunder that only speaks
    after the bolt.
"Workers of America, we alone can rehabilitate this generation before history.
    We must and shall stop this war."
The Greek vendor moves on; wearily the old man turns towards a seat, far away.
But he speaks on.
"The great voice of Labor shall rise fearlessly today, and the world shall listen,
    and eternity shall record its words."
The drunken man grumbles, stares at his open hands and lurches away
    towards the approaching tramway.
But he speaks on.
"Our protest and our anger will be like a cloudburst, and the masters shall
    tremble. Brothers, don't you see it? The Revolution is at the threshold."
The newsboy swings his bag over his shoulder and dashes away through the
    park.

But he speaks on.

"As sure as this sun shall set, so will injustice and tyranny go down. Men and
women of America, I know that this is the great day."

The stranger I know shrinks in the hollow places of himself; he fades; and
vanishes, molten in the white heat of that young faith.

But the girl stands still and immobile, her upturned face glowing before the
brazier of his soul,

As from the tower one by one drop at his feet the twelve tolls of the clock that
marks time, the time that knows and flows on until his day comes.

And the girl, and the tower, and he

Are the only three things that stand straight and rigid and inexpugnable

Amidst the red omens of war,

In the fulness of the day,

In the whiteness of the noonlight

In the city of dread and uproar.

Crisis, August

IDA B. LUCKIE

RETRIBUTION

"Alas, My Country! Thou wilt have no need
Of enemy to bring thee to thy doom
If these be they on whom we must rely
To prove the right and honor of our arms."

Thus spake Abdullah, gazing, with sad eyes
And heart fear-stricken, on the motley horde
Of Turks now gathered in with feverish haste
To meet the dread, on-coming Bulgar host.
Truly he spake, for scarce the foes had met
When the wild flight began, the vengeful sword
Of the Bulgarian taking fearful toll
As fleeing thousands fall to rise no more.
Surely the years bring on the fatal day
To that dark land, from whose unhallowed ground
The blood of countless innocents so long
Has cried to God, no longer cries in vain.

But not alone by war a nation falls.
Tho' she be fair, serene as radiant morn,
Tho' girt by seas, secure in armament,
Let her but spurn the Vision of the Cross;
Tread with contemptuous feet on its command
Of Mercy, Love and Human Brotherhood,
And she, some fateful day, shall have no need
Of enemy to bring her to the dust.
Some day, tho' distant it may be—with God
A thousand years are but as yesterday—
The germs of hate, injustice, violence,
Like an insidious canker in the blood,
Shall eat the nation's vitals. She shall see
Break forth the blood-red tide of anarchy,
Sweeping her plains, laying her cities low,
And bearing on its seething, crimson flood
The wreck of government, of home, and all
The nation's pride, its splendor and its power;
On, with relentless flow, into the sea
Of God's eternal vengeance wide and deep,
But for God's grace! Oh, may it hold thee fast,
My Country, until justice shall prevail
O'er wrong and o'er oppression's cruel power,
And all that makes humanity to mourn.

Scribner's, September
CHARLOTTE HOLMES CRAWFORD

VIVE LA FRANCE!

Franceline rose in the dawning gray,
And her heart would dance though she knelt to pray,
For her man Michel had holiday,
    Fighting for France.

She offered her prayer by the cradle-side,
And with baby palms folded in hers she cried:
"If I have but one prayer, dear, crucified
    Christ—save France!

"But if I have two, then, by Mary's grace,
Carry me safe to the meeting-place,
Let me look once again on my dear love's face,
    Save him for France!"

She crooned to her boy: "Oh, how glad he'll be,
Little three-months old, to set eyes on thee!
For, 'Rather than gold, would I give,' wrote he,
    'A son to France.'

"Come, now, be good, little stray *sauterelle*,
For we're going by-by to thy papa Michel,
But I'll not say where for fear thou wilt tell,
    Little Pigeon of France!

"Six days' leave and a year between!
But what would you have? In six days clean,
Heaven was made," said Franceline,
    "Heaven and France."

She came to the town of the nameless name,
To the marching troops in the street she came,
And she held high her boy like a taper flame
    Burning for France.

Fresh from the trenches and gray with grime,
Silent they march like a pantomime;
"But what need of music? My heart beats time—
    Vive la France!"

His regiment comes. Oh, then where is he?
"There is dust in my eyes, for I cannot see,—
Is that my Michel to the right of thee,
    Soldier of France?"

Then out of the ranks a comrade fell,—
"Yesterday—'twas a splinter of shell—
And he whispered thy name, did thy poor Michel,
    Dying for France."

The tread of the troops on the pavement throbbed
Like a woman's heart of its last joy robbed,
As she lifted her boy to the flag, and sobbed:
    "Vive la France!"

North American Review, October
ALAN SEEGER

I HAVE A RENDEZVOUS
WITH DEATH

I have a rendezvous with Death
At some disputed barricade,
When Spring comes round with rustling shade
And apple blossoms fill the air.
I have a rendezvous with Death
When Spring brings back blue days and fair.

It may be he shall take my hand
And lead me into his dark land
And close my eyes and quench my breath;
It may be I shall pass him still.
I have a rendezvous with Death
On some scarred slope of battered hill,
When Spring comes round again this year
And the first meadow flowers appear.

God knows 'twere better to be deep
Pillowed in silk and scented down,
Where love throbs out in blissful sleep,
Pulse nigh to pulse, and breath to breath,
Where hushed awakenings are dear.
But I've a rendezvous with Death
At midnight in some flaming town,
When Spring trips north again this year,
And I to my pledged word am true,
I shall not fail that rendezvous.

                    (*Killed in battle at Belloy-en-Santerre, July, 1916.*)

Poems of the Great War (November)

JOHN McRAE

IN FLANDERS FIELDS

(Reprinted by the special permission of the proprietors of <u>Punch</u>)

In Flanders fields the poppies blow
Between the crosses, row on row,
   That mark our place, and in the sky,
   The larks, still bravely singing, fly,
Scarce heard amid the guns below.

We are the dead; short days ago
   We lived, felt dawn, saw sunset glow,
Loved and were loved, and now we lie
      In Flanders fields.

Take up our quarrel with the foe!
To you from failing hands we throw
   The torch; be yours to hold it high!
   If ye break faith with us who die
We shall not sleep, though poppies grow
      In Flanders fields.

Century, December

JOHN GOULD FLETCHER

THE LAST RALLY

(Under England's new Conscription Act, the last of the married men joined her colors on June 24, 1916.)

In the midnight, in the rain,
That drenches every sooty roof and licks each window-pane,
The bugles blow for the last rally
Once again.

Through the horror of the night,
Where glimmers yet northwestward one ghostly strip of white,
Squelching with heavy boots through the untrodden plowlands,
The troops set out. Eyes right!

These are the last who go because they must,
Who toiled for years at something leveled now in dust;
Men of thirty, married, settled, who had built up walls of comfort
That crumbled at a thrust.

Now they have naked steel,
And the heavy, sopping rain that the clammy skin can feel,
And the leaden weight of rifle and the pack that grinds the entrails,
Wrestling with a half-cooked meal.

And there are oaths and blows,
The mud that sticks and flows,
The bad and smoky billet, and the aching legs at morning,
And the frost that numbs the toes;

And the senseless, changeless grind,
And the pettifogging mass of orders muddling every mind,
And the dull-red smudge of mutiny half rising up and burning,
Till they choke and stagger blind.

But for them no bugle flares;
No bright flags leap, no gay horizon glares;
They are conscripts, middle-aged, rheumatic, cautious, weary,
With slowly thinning hairs;

Only for one to-night
A woman weeps and moans and tries to smite
Her head against a table, and another rocks a cradle,
And another laughs with flashing eyes, sitting bolt upright.

PART 5

1917

We are now about to accept gage of battle with this natural foe to liberty and shall, if necessary, spend the whole force of the Nation to check and nullify its pretensions and its power. We are glad, now that we see the facts with no veil of false pretense about them, to fight thus for the ultimate peace of the world and for the liberation of its peoples, the German peoples included: for the rights of nations great and small and the privilege of men everywhere to choose their way of life and of obedience. The world must be made safe for democracy. Its peace must be planted upon the tested foundations of political liberty. We have no selfish ends to serve. We desire no conquest, no dominion. We seek no indemnities for ourselves, no material compensation for the sacrifices we shall freely make. We are but one of the champions of the rights of mankind. We shall be satisfied when those rights have been made as secure as the faith and the freedom of nations can make them.

—Woodrow Wilson, "Address to Congress Advising that Germany's Course Be Declared War against the United States (Delivered in Joint Session, April 2)"

And the intellectuals are not content with confirming our belligerent gesture. They are now complacently asserting that it was they who effectively willed it, against the hesitation and dim perceptions of the American democratic masses. A war made deliberately by the intellectuals! A calm moral verdict, arrived at after a penetrating study of inexorable facts! Sluggish masses, too remote from the world-conflict to be stirred, too lacking in intellect to perceive their danger! An alert intellectual class, saving the people in spite of themselves, biding their time with Fabian strategy until the nation could be moved into war without serious resistance! An intellectual class, gently guiding a nation through sheer force of ideas into what the other nations entered only through predatory craft or popular hysteria or militarist madness! A war free from any taint of self-seeking, a war that will secure the triumph of democracy and internationalize the world! This is the picture which the more self-conscious intellectuals have formed of themselves, and which they are slowly impressing upon a population which is being led no man knows whither by an indubitably intellectualized President.

—Randolph Bourne, "War and the Intellectuals," *Seven Arts,* June

When asking Congress for a declaration of war on 2 April 1917, Woodrow Wilson cast the United States as a uniquely idealistic champion of justice and equality. His address emphasized the country's role as an impartial defender of the nations imperiled by Germany's aggression, not its possible material gain from intervening. As a just and disinterested participant, the United States acted out of no particular animus against the people of Germany, only against their autocratic, militarist government. Thus Wilson admonished his audience, "We must put excited feeling away. Our motive will not be revenge or the victorious assertion of the physical might of the nation, but only the vindication of right, of human right, of which we are only a single champion" (1:373). To be sure, Wilson urged that the United States be unstinting in its war effort, offering financial credit and war materiel for the Allies and increasing the U.S. Army to half a million troops (1:377). Yet even while Wilson was demanding an end to neutrality, he sought to reassert his country's role as an impartial power broker. His administration professed a similar idealism on the home front—and sent similarly mixed messages about its dual aims to win the war and to promote democracy. George Creel, head of the Committee on Public Information, maintained in 1920 that the most rigorous American standards of free speech were adhered to during the war. Even though U.S. guarantees on freedom of speech resulted, Creel felt, in irresponsible criticism of the government—"No other right guaranteed by democracy has been more abused"—he maintained that "even these abuses are preferable to the deadening evil of autocratic control" (17). As Creel recalled it, the Committee on Public Information had actually encouraged the voices of "the weak and the powerless" (17). Repressive "autocratic control" was the European way; democratic free expression was the American way, even if this threatened the efficiency of the American military machine. At the beginning of the winter of 1917–18, U.S. Food Administration chair Herbert Hoover wrote that this was "the period when there will be tested in this great free country of ours the question as to whether or not our people are capable of voluntary individual self-sacrifice to save the world" (U.S. Food 8). Organized in May 1917, the Food Administration sought to increase the supply of foodstuffs to the U.S. military and the Allies while maintaining an adequate supply to the U.S. homefront. To bring about greater food conservation, volunteers went door to door to secure pledges from American homemakers to follow the Food Administration's directives. Ten million households were enrolled by the end of 1917 and 13–14 million participated by the end of the war. Besides following "the gospel of the

George F. Griffin. "Enlist." Color poster. Chicago: National Printing and Engraving, 1917.
(From original at the Joseph M. Bruccoli Great War Collection, Special Collections
Library, University of Virginia Library.)

clean plate," homemakers were to limit sugar consumption to three pounds per person per month and to observe Meatless Tuesdays, Wheatless Wednesdays, and Porkless Saturdays.

Given that the United States had kept clear of the war so long and that Wilson's democratic ideals and principles of fair play were so often and loudly proclaimed, the kind of war that the United States would wage in Europe and on the home front did in fact seem up for grabs in 1917. The poetry of the year reflects this, in at least two senses: by the intensity with which poets entered the public debate, operating under the assumption that their work might well significantly shape public attitudes and even policy, and by the amazing openness of expression, as not only supporters of intervention but also dissenters appear to have believed that a war for world democracy would entail, as a logical precondition, freedom of speech at home. Yet Hoover's appeals to democracy and voluntarism were not subtle about demanding "sacrificial" limits on individual autonomy and threatening involuntary procedures if citizens did not choose sacrifice. Hoover's principle of voluntarism meant that patriotic conformity was expressly demanded by state edict and maintained by community leaders denouncing disloyal "elements" and by neighbors spying on one another. Creel's book *How We Advertised America* amounts to an apologia for some of the worst abuses of free speech rights in U.S. history. Wilson's declarations of even-handedness were belied by his own campaigns for preparedness and 100 percent Americanism that had branded recent immigrants as "foreigners" and nonconformist ideas as "alien." Indeed, Wilson's idealism may well have catalyzed the depth and mendacity of American repression: a war of material expansion or national defense might be fought largely on the battlefield; a war of ideals must be waged in every publication, every political demonstration, and every public utterance.

As bold as any group in its assertion of free-speech rights was the National Woman's party, which placed a pro-suffrage picket line outside the White House. The picketers began their vigil in January, before Germany announced the resumption of unrestricted submarine warfare, but even after U.S. intervention they remained determined that they would not let any man's war get in the way of women's votes. Their favorite strategy, which Wilson reportedly found "insulting" but could hardly form the basis for treason charges, was to quote the president's statements word for word, including lines from the conclusion of his request for a war declaration: "We shall fight for the things we have always carried nearest our hearts, for democracy, for the right of those who submit to authority to have a voice in their own governments" (Wilson 1:382–83). Even while the National American Woman Suffrage

Association pledged to help mobilize American women for the war and to suspend its public campaign for the vote, the National Woman's party continued its stand-off with the White House throughout the summer and fall. By midsummer, bystanders regularly jeered at picketers as unpatriotic and even attacked them; around the same time the District of Columbia police began arresting them for loitering; by the fall dozens of woman's rights advocates had been sent to the Occoquan Work House in Virginia. But when the press reported that the women were beaten and force-fed by prison guards, Wilson ordered their release. In January 1918 he proffered his support for the suffrage amendment. Meanwhile, the *Suffragist*, the organ of the National Woman's party, had been printing articles and poetry charging that America's war ideals remained a sham until women were granted votes. The parodic song "We Worried Woody-Wood," for example, chronicled the suffrage picketers' confrontation with Wilson.

Few other dissenting groups and publications were able to traverse the abyss of disloyalty so skillfully—or so fortunately. Many asserted their free speech rights just as vigorously but were silenced, either by direct government action or by indirect pressures. The Espionage Act, passed in June, was outwardly modest in its requirements; its main provision outlawed "willful" promotion in print or speech of "insubordination, disloyalty, mutiny, or refusal of duty in the military or naval forces of the United States" (qtd. in Peterson and Fite 17). In fact, the federal judiciary prosecuted only a small number of cases based on its provisions. It was, rather, Postmaster General Albert Burleson, acting on provisions that allowed second-class mailing privileges to be denied any publication deemed disloyal, who interpreted the bill broadly to proscribe any public speech or publication that criticized U.S. war intervention. Burleson ran amok, using his authority to harass the American Left, though his mandate did have its limits. Newspapers were particularly resistant to post office censorship, as they could continue to be distributed locally by carriers (with, of course, the risk that at a later day the federal judiciary would also find the publication seditious). This enabled socialist papers such as the *Milwaukee Leader*, which lost its mailing privileges in September, and the *New York Call*, which reported post office interference in December, to be published and then distributed locally throughout the war (Peterson and Fite 47; "Subscribers"). The postmaster's exertions were more deadly to national and international publications. The *Masses* was denied the mails from August 1917 onward. The *International Socialist Review*, harassed from the summer of 1917, published its last issue in February 1918. Yet even the national magazines were not fully thwarted by the post office. In

December 1917 the staff of the *Masses* produced the last issue of a magazine that since August had been deemed undeliverable by mail, but in February 1918 virtually the same staff commenced publication of the *Liberator,* a magazine that adopted much of the same critical attitude toward American society and government and, especially via coverage of the IWW trial in Chicago, managed to mount some of the same criticism of the war mobilization as before.

Direct suppression of presses was, however, just one of several ways in which dissent was limited and punished in 1917. The forty-five periodicals said to have been denied use of the mails by May 1918, when the Espionage Act was strengthened by the Sedition Act (Wynn 50), was not a large number relative to the thousands of newspapers and magazines published in the country. But additional publishers modified editorial policies to avoid losing their mailing rights, in effect practicing self-censorship. For them, the postmaster held the power of economic ruin; with livelihoods and jobs on the line, it was a matter of economic necessity to abandon direct questioning of the war effort. Journalistic consciences could be assuaged by the fact that the national emergency demanded sacrifice and compromise of many citizens. Also helpful was the widespread assumption, carefully cultivated by journalists and politicians who had favored American intervention all along and seemingly confirmed by the Germans' submarine warfare, that Germany was an autocratic militarist state that would threaten world security into perpetuity—unless crushed once and for all.

Even little magazines, usually considered forums for the avant-garde in politics as well as literature, became casualties of unofficial censorship. Most, however radical their editorial policies, depended upon patronage, which gave wealthy and almost invariably more conservative benefactors an effective power of private censorship. *Four Lights,* the little magazine launched by the most active of the Women's Peace party affiliates, the New York branch, was amply supported by patron donations in January 1917 when the president was extolling "Peace without Victory" (Wilson 1:352). By the fall, the managing editor reported, "Not one of the women who gave us money this past year, have offered to renew their pledges," and the board voted to discontinue publication (Davidson).

Roughly the same fate met a little magazine today well known for its cutting-edge status, *Seven Arts.* Founded in November 1916, *Seven Arts* was edited by James Oppenheim and funded entirely by A. K. Rankine, at that time eager to support a journal of arts and criticism, even one purporting to be "radical." This was, however, prior to the U.S. declaration of war and prior to Oppenheim's decision to make

Randolph Bourne the primary oracle of the magazine's views on in-
tervention; Bourne contributed major articles on the subject in five
consecutive issues, June–October 1917. Even while the *New Republic* and
the *Dial* blackballed Bourne (Schaffer 119, 123), *Seven Arts* gave him free
rein to critique the supposedly rational, moral, and disinterested mo-
tives for U.S. war involvement put forward by the government and the
liberal intelligentsia. Rankine severed her connection with *Seven Arts*
and before the year was out committed suicide, apparently driven by
remorse over supporting those she believed to be anti-American trai-
tors (Schaffer 123). In fact, *Seven Arts* was also wracked by dissension
on its editorial board. Associate editor Van Wyck Brooks was critical
of Oppenheim's continued publication of Bourne. Robert Frost assert-
ed by limerick the folly of discussing politics at all in a journal dedi-
cated to the arts:

> In the Dawn of Creation that morning
> I remember I gave you fair warning:
> The Arts are but Six!
> You add politics
> And the Seven will all die a-Bourneing.

(qtd. in Schaffer 122)

Amy Lowell, whose appearances in the journal and independent wealth
made her a natural candidate to take up where Rankine had left off,
conditioned her support on Oppenheim's severing the journal's con-
nection with Bourne (Untermeyer 95–96). This Oppenheim would not
do, as he argued: "If . . . Bourne writes about the breakdown of prag-
matism and the need of the poetic vision instead, it is necessary for him
to show the moment of breakdown; namely, the application of prag-
matism to the war technique" (qtd. in Untermeyer 96). But Lowell was
steadfast, and the October 1917 issue was the last of *Seven Arts*. Her
explanation, like Frost's, stressed the necessity of separating poetry
from politics: "If you believe, as I do . . . in the saving grace of the arts,
and poetry in particular, you will not allow any desire to express your
personal opinions upon subjects outside of this scope to interfere with
your mission of keeping alive the spirit of poetry and of beauty in this
sorely tried country" (qtd. in Untermeyer 96).

In Lowell's peculiar formulation, an aesthetically pure poetry is of
the utmost importance to the national mobilization, but this poetry,
mediated via culture, is not itself "political." Only poetry critical of the
mobilization is debased by that label. This distinction, logically sophis-
tical, utterly dissolves when we recall that in 1917 Lowell allowed her
name to be associated with the most partisan and instrumental orga-

nization of writers to be formed in the United States during the war, the Vigilantes. The dedication of art to the cause of nationalism, and special pleading on behalf of this alliance by poets and critics who otherwise (or simultaneously) claimed the separation between poetry and politics, became commonplace in 1917. Evidence that American poets were keen to make their craft serviceable to Uncle Sam may be found in the patriotic verse that appeared day after day in virtually all American newspapers and found in the scores of collections of such poetry that were published privately as well as commercially.

Lowell's comments are characteristic of the poetry of American mobilization in another respect as well. The nation, in Lowell's view, faced such innumerable and powerful threats to its national integrity that its defenders were cast as beleaguered, individualistic, even solitary heroes. Thus, even while the U.S. government and civilian war enthusiasts were working to suppress dissent, poets writing in league with this suppression were themselves posing as prophetic voices crying in the wilderness. This persona was cultivated with particular assiduousness by the Vigilantes, though the organization was as centralized and bureaucratic as any pro-war group—and remarkably so for a writers' collective. Porter Emerson Browne, the group's cofounder, asserted that the United States was confronting a German propaganda juggernaut, which "has beaten Russia from a great and powerful nation to a helpless, writhing pulp" and "is daily confusing and rendering difficult the best efforts of America to win the war; encouraging treason; aiding and abetting sedition; cultivating depression; tainting honest criticism with the innuendo of treachery; fanning the fires of Bolshevikism, disunion, disorganization, anarchy, and disaster." In contrast, he portrays Vigilantes writers as individualistic, virtually starving artists:

> The Vigilantes, single-handed, under the wearing handicaps of lack of money and the painful necessity of making their several and individual livings, with the wolf ever at the door and occasionally poking his lean snout even into the vestibule, have been doing everything in their power to fight as best they could this great and terrible engine of German destruction. [F]or Germany long ago mobilized her artists and writers. But she made the mistake of immediately denaturing them into Government servants—a sort of His Master's Voice. We Vigilantes have, and we think wisely, remained independent and non-partisan. (68–69)

It may be safely ventured that the Vigilantes and the U.S. mobilization succeeded primarily because, behind the facade of want, disorder, and autonomy, they were in fact financed generously, organized with businesslike (if not Prussian) efficiency, and capable of considerable coercive leverage. And yet the facade also mattered, for it was crucial for Americans to believe that the ideals prompting intervention were distinctive from, and superior to, the European powers' motivations in 1914; that American citizens felt they had freely chosen their roles in the war effort and the sacrifices entailed by those; that patriotic American poets—however pedestrian or utilitarian their verse became—gave expression not to a partisan position but to a transcendent national purpose. These illusions were valuable not only because they generated enthusiastic participation in the war effort among poets and other common folk but also because the conjured figure of the embattled artist and citizen made it seem credible that the relatively small but more ideologically collectivist organizations to which many dissenters belonged would actually threaten to derail the state's war machine. That dissenting voices were heard for a time in 1917 testifies in part to inconsistencies in the U.S. mobilization and in part to a limited democratic heterogeneity—the modicum of debate necessary to lay claim to the ideals of free speech and democracy. But as 1917 wore on, the U.S. war effort became both less tolerant of dissent and more efficient in suppressing it.

Yale Review, January
ROBERT FROST

NOT TO KEEP

They sent him back to her. The letter came
Saying . . . and she could have him. And before
She could be sure there was no hidden ill
Under the formal writing, he was in her sight—
Living.—They gave him back to her alive—
How else? They are not known to send the dead—
And not disfigured visibly. His face?—
His hands? She had to look—to ask
"What was it, dear?" And she had given all
And still she had all—*they* had—they the lucky!
Wasn't she glad now? Everything seemed won,
And all the rest for them permissible ease.
She had to ask "What was it, dear?"
                                                        "Enough,
Yet not enough. A bullet through and through,
High in the breast. Nothing but what good care
And medicine and rest—and you a week,
Can cure me of to go again." The same
Grim giving to do over for them both.
She dared no more than ask him with her eyes
How was it with him for a second trial.
And with his eyes he asked her not to ask.
They had given him back to her, but not to keep.

New York Times, 19 March
KATHARINE LEE BATES

SOLDIERS TO PACIFISTS

Not ours to clamor shame on you,
Nor fling a bitter blame on you,
Nor brand a cruel name on you—
    That evil name of treason—
You who have heard the ivory flutes,
Who float white banners, brave recruits
Of Peace, seeking to pluck her fruits
    In bud and blossom season.

A sterner bugle calls to us;
More direful duty falls to us;
God grants no garden-walls to us
    Till the scarred waste be delivered
From dragon passions that destroy
All sanctitudes of faith and joy;
We, too, are on divine employ;
    By sword shall sword be shivered.

Cherish your bud, star-eyed of bloom,
Dawn-flower of hope, belied of gloom,
While, surges of the tide of doom,
    The gathering nations thunder
Against a red colossal throne;
Cherish it, that the seed be sown
At last, even where that monstrous stone
    Crushes life's roots asunder.

Follow your flutes the fairy way;
Wing-sandaled, climb the airy way,
The wonderful, unwary way,
    Too lovely for derision;
While we, your comrades at the goal,
Step to the drum-beat and unroll
The flag of Freedom, every soul
    Obedient to its vision.

Seven Arts, April
AMY LOWELL

ORANGE OF MIDSUMMER

You came to me in the pale starting of Spring,
And I could not see the world
For the blue mist of wonder before my eyes.
You beckoned me over a rainbow bridge,
And I set foot upon it, trembling.
Through pearl and saffron I followed you,
Through heliotrope and rose,
Iridescence after iridescence,
And to me it was all one
Because of the blue mist that held my eyes.

You came again, and it was red-hearted Summer.
You called to me across a field of poppies and wheat,
With a narrow path slicing through it
Straight to an outer boundary of trees.
And I ran along the path,
Brushing over the yellow wheat beside it,
And came upon you under a maple-tree, plaiting poppies for a girdle.
"Are you thirsty?" said you,
And held out a cup.
But the water in the cup was scarlet and crimson,
Like the poppies in your hands.
"It looks like blood," I said.
"Like blood," you said,
"Does it?
But drink it, my Beloved."

War Flames (April)
JOHN CURTIS UNDERWOOD

ESSEN

More than seven score thousand men are toiling there at Essen,
Working day and night in double shifts in haste infuriate,
Round blast furnaces roaring flare and stab the air with fear at midnight.
Tilting crucibles are pouring molten steel like hydra's hair to sear the
    shadows.
Fiery serpents fall and flame along the moulds and slowly lapse to torpor.

Where they toil in desperation they are shaping sorrow there at Essen.
While they cast shell casings, drill truncated cylinders for monster mortars
    that they put together;
While they prime time fuses, file machine gun gears and rake their bores with
    circling rifling;
They are welding will to chains of steel that only steel as strong shall ever
    sever.
Into bullets and to shrapnel they are crystallizing ruin.

They are casting loss and havoc. Huge steel billets are the devil's dice of death
    at Essen.
And their crucibles devouring are his ladles that all Germany have gutted.
Into them they cast the riches of their mines and the steel strength of cities,
Casting faster all their cattle, all the growth of grain and earth's abundance;
All the frenzied flesh of soldiers, old men, boys, defectives, weaklings,
    maniacs marched to battle.

They have cast the hearts and hopes and long despairs of women there at
    Essen.
These they crushed to crimson welter, flayed and shredded where
    triphammers tirelessly are falling clanging.
There they fuse their prayers and tears and fears that stab them as the pangs
    of child birth stab them.
There they cast the glorious years of all that Germany for music won and
    science.
There they cast their mutilated sanctities that frightfulness and force might
    triumph.

They cast honor there disowned, and all the lies that wasted, wait to wound
    them there at Essen.

Toiling to uproot the earth and righteousness and freedom with a madman's ammunition,

Seeking to o'ershadow sunlight with their Zeppelins and turn back tides with submarine torpedoes.

All that suns and tides have wrought since earth was fire must war against them.

Maddened, reeling, Germany is whirling east and west and north and south as armies eat her substance.

And the vortex of her ruin is this town of soot and steel where naked workmen

Fight with fire and fail, as fail the gun crews in the turret of a Dreadnaught mined and sinking.

June 12, 1915

War Flames (April)

THE LAVOIR

Two years ago ten women washed a town's stained linen on these stones.

And they beat its grayness white in running water flashing bright, and flowing to the Loire and to the Ocean.

The March winds shook snow flurries out like suds, and whipped gray skies that dried to fluttering, white, curling clouds at last.

April wrung out the sap through the gray boughs of apple trees that blossomed white above the bleaching linen.

And the petals fell and floated down on girls' dark hair and laughing faces looking up, and on the lights and shadows gliding through the sliding water.

And the apple petals were rosy as the wind-whipped faces of the girls; and some were tainted in their April beauty with a blight as old as earth.

Claire, the most competent, laundered indifferently, lace of her Countess by birth, and the latest Tours prostitute leasing the villa at Dol for the season.

And the borders of one bore a coronet, of the others a cypher such as one sees interlacing initials of kings on the Louvre.

Between the loud lavishness and intricate luxury of their webs of white waste there, Claire could find little to choose.

With her cold fingertips coolly she touched the lost lives of these women, the
last of their lovers, and brought back one whiteness that blindly all
women must worship.

And the touch of white lace like a kiss on warm flesh came closer to her as
she worked toward the end of her task by the river.

And the river called and flowed by the road, and the wind in the trees
beckoned, and the drying lace teased her as a trailing skirt may tease a
kitten.

Little Angêle was washing the broad brassières trimmed with Bruges, of the
bourgeoises who cringed to the countess and envied the other.

Little Angêle with her one shift a week dreamed dully how happy such
wonderful women must be.

Dreamed as a child will of red wine and strawberries and huge glossy plums
of the Midi that went with their white table cloths.

Margot the hunchback beat savagely camisoles sheer as the seven pairs of
high clocked silk stockings a week, worn by Lucile the tall midinette,
flaunting her hat shop from Paris.

Older and coarser women who did the coarser work of the town, slaved at
their task as they laved its stains away.

And their hands and their faces took a color from the grime ground into them.

Those too old for all but scandal and lies and covetousness, told stories that
small Angêle had lost the grace to blush to.

And Margot's sneer wore towards a fixed mask of hate, and Claire grew ever
wearier of the torment of her task and intolerable longing for a lover she
could love, who never came.

Then War the great lover came like the bridegroom in the night to the wise
virgins and the foolish ones and made full trial of them.

And Margot began to smile from watching other women weep, till tears
untied at last the black knots of hate in her face and heart, in tenderness
she never knew before.

And little Angêle was aware that all her women's wasted linen was white to
make bandages for France and the wounded soldiers of France,

And Claire who had always worked for herself and planned for herself, forgot
her phantom lover, in her love for all the men of France that marched
and died and were maimed and mangled for her.

The older women went away one by one to men's tasks in the town and the
fields.

But the three girls still toiled by the river day by day, washing the bed clothes
and the bandages black with blood and red with blood still bright on
their whiteness.

For the countess had given her chateau for a hospital, and the prostitute had
    given her jewels and her motor and herself to the service.
And Claire and Margot and Angêle toiled and were stifled in the steam of its
    cellars through the winter.
And the spring came again, and again they beat their linen white by the river
    on stones that felt the falling petals and the swaying apple trees.

The stones and the river felt her tears that fell as Angêle knelt there in endless
    litanies of service for her dead who died for France and her.
And time that stains and whitens all at last, washed the color from her face,
    purged dull pain from Margot's, and pride of youth that stands
    demanding all from Claire their fairer sister.
And the three girls washed their hands and their souls as they knelt, in the
    river that flashed to the sea taking all the stains and pains of war along
    with it.
Day by day they went their way heaping their baskets high with whiter petals
    of passion and prayer than ever fell there from their apple trees on them.

And they said little, but they sang and whispered softly to the murmur of the
    river, for time and pain had made them women as they knelt there.
Woman who stains the mind of man with little lies, who wraps herself in
    lace-like webs of lust and waste around his pilgrim passions;
Woman whose fingers wring all clinging taints from life; who makes herself a
    still cool bandage and white bed of rest for all the wounds and sufferings
    of souls;
Woman who kneels wherever rivers flow and fruit trees bloom and clouds
    come white, waiting in light till war brings back its heroes' hearts made
    white to worship her.

March 11, 1916

War Flames (April)

THE MACHINE

A British commissariat clerk looked out of a shattered window at
    Amentieres,
Weary of the endless monotony of counting and checking and issuing
    rations,
Thousands of boxes of Peek and Frean's assorted biscuits for officers' tea,

Millions of bars of Fry's and Cadbury's and Nestle's milk and haz[el]nut
    chocolate,
Myriads of glasses of Cross and Blackwell's red raspberry jam, and Andrew
    Kieler's Dundee orange marmalade in its little white porcelain jars,
Turned to suppurating wounds and blood that caked as it oozed in the sepsis
    of trench fever and intermittent typhoid.

He grew utterly weary of the immense agony and futility of the seamy side of
    the war as it was shown to him,
Sick of the unending procession of hospital trains and ships from England to
    the front,
And the interminable scavenging in motor cars of broken bodies from third
    line trenches and huge shell holes in little French towns ten miles behind
    the lines,
Sick of the insufferable organization and standardization of suffering,
In huge base hospitals and clearing houses of horror like the one behind him
    where the longest trains went,
Where deadly wounds were as much a matter of routine as his own red jars
    of raspberry jam were,
And amputations were as simple and essential as the tearing of a printed
    form out of his own red backed order book.

He grew utterly weary of the thought of the ammunition trains rolling back
    and forth as regularly as a machine gun shifts its spray of death;
And the munition factories working day and night in double and triple shifts;
And the soft hands of women grown hard like their lips and their hearts from
    handling lead bullets and copper shell cases.
And he gazed out of his glassless window at a gray street and the roofless
    rafters of a house ten yards away.
And he wondered what was the use and the reason and the sufficient cause
    for anyone in the world going on living and seeing and hearing it all an
    hour or a second longer.

He got up from his seat on an empty packing case and leaned away out of the
    window again,
And he saw a string of British troopers riding their tall gray horses back from
    the river where they went to water them.
And every one of the ten men had a French child laughing and crying aloud
    astride of the gray back in front of him.
And his thoughts went back suddenly twenty years to the time when he first
    rode his father's horse to the blacksmith's to be shod in Rottingdean.
And his thoughts went forward suddenly twenty years and more to a time to
    come,

That all the agony and the monotony and the huge and wholesale blundering
  of the war was working and waiting for.
And he went back to his store room again as the last tall trooper turned the
  corner.
And he went on handling his boxes and his bales and his invoices and his
  checking lists,
As Joffre and Cordona are handling batteries and battalions and *corps
  d'armée* and conquering armies.

September 26, 1916

Four Lights, 21 April
A. B. CURTIS

A STUDY IN EVOLUTION:
FROM MR. ASQUITH AND THE
BRITISH GOVERNMENT

And for your service and your sacrifice,
Your heroism, self-denial, skill,
Endurance, strength,
Your nimble fingers shaping things that kill,
We grant you votes.
You speak the language that we understand,
In these, our days of war.
You have defended us
From death,
England will honor thus
Her warrior women and herself,
And grant them votes.

We had no eyes to see
The patient service of the days of peace,
The steady building of each human life.
The clash of steel,
The trenches and the fumes
Taught us to feel
Your worth,
And so we grant you votes.

You have translated thus
Yourselves to us,
And for your service and your sacrifice,
Your heroism, self-denial, skill,
Endurance, strength,
Your nimble fingers shaping things that kill,
We grant you votes.

New York Call, 1 June
BERTON BRALEY

THE TRAITOR

He hangs out a flag from his home and his office[,]
    He always stands up at "The Star-Spangled Banner,"
In talks and discussions he rails at the Prussians
    And handles the kaiser in a virulent manner;
He always is present at loyalty meetings,
    And up on the platform he pays for a seat,
(The price doesn't matter, his profits are fatter
    Since war gave him chances for cornering wheat.)

He talks with emotion of "brave soldier laddies"
    Or "noble young jackies who sail on the foam,"
Then shoots up the price on potatoes and rice
    And other things needed abroad and at home;
He praises brave mothers who give their sons freely
    Then soaks those same mothers for clothing and food,
But if you cry "traitor," this smooth speculator
    Will think you are one of a lunatic brood.

Yet Benedict Arnold was only a piker
    Compared to the man who, amid all the strife,
Will seize on the chances to force huge advances
    In things that a nation depends on for life;
He did his foul work in the war of secession[,]
    He poisoned our boys in the conflict with Spain—
High up on a gibbet we ought to exhibit
    The traitor who holds up a nation for gain!

New York Times, 8 June
C. Arthur Coan

THE CONSEQUENTIOUS OBJECTOR

Be you int'rested in this here War?
  Wall, settin' round in rainy weather
  An' thinkin' hard, I dunno whether
I scurcesly guess I know what-all it's for!
You hear about them Belgians in Louvain?
  But they ain't kith nor kin of mine,
  An' if their shot that ain't no sign
I gotta jump in too, with nothin' to gain?

What's Poles to me—'nless they're poles for beans?
  An' what if Reems Cathedral does fall?
  It ain't a-goin' to shake no wall
In Hermitville, you'll find, by any means!
Then there's them Serbs! Now, listen! What d' I know
  About such folks? Be they white?
  I hear they started in to fight
Somewheres in Eurup. Let 'em have it so!

A submurine I dunno much about,
  Nor all this highfalutin talk
  Of "rights" at Sea. A man can walk
Most anywhere's wuth goin', I've found out!
Home cookin's best, and to my notion
  No fella 'd ought to go away
  From where they raised him, and I say
'Tain't good sense to try to sail the Ocean!

An' now they come and tell me danger's near
  While Uncle Sam's a-goin' to raise
  A lot of men in ninety days
To go to War! I betcha I keep clear!
This plan for draftin' men's a nawful shame—
  I'd most get married, only now
  They tell me such a new-made vow
Won't make 'em scratch a solitary name!

I hoped they'd make the limit twenty-eight,
　So's to leave me safe and sound!
　But now they turn around
And make the dead-line thirty! Ain't that fate?
Ther's gotta be some way of keepin' free—
　I'm far too good to lose my life
　A-mixin' in that furrin strife
To help some critters I ain't never see!

I'm big and got my stren'th an' appetite—
　Never sick sence I was born—
　Not a soul to leave forlorn—
But I *won't* go! You get that right?
'N' I hear I only gotta join a League
　Where the consciences of all the men objecks
　To the riskin' of their valuable necks
　　To marchin' in the rain
　　Or standin' any pain
　　Or bein' much subjected to fatigue
Sure, I'll join that League!

New York Call, 13 June
An English Schoolgirl

THE CONSCIENTIOUS OBJECTOR

(After "The Five Souls," by W. N. Ewer)

　I was a soldier of the Prince of Peace;
"Thou shalt not kill" is writ among His laws;
So I refused to fight, and for this cause
　Myself was slain. 'Twas thus I gained release.
I gave my life for freedom, this I know:
For He for whom I fought has told me so.

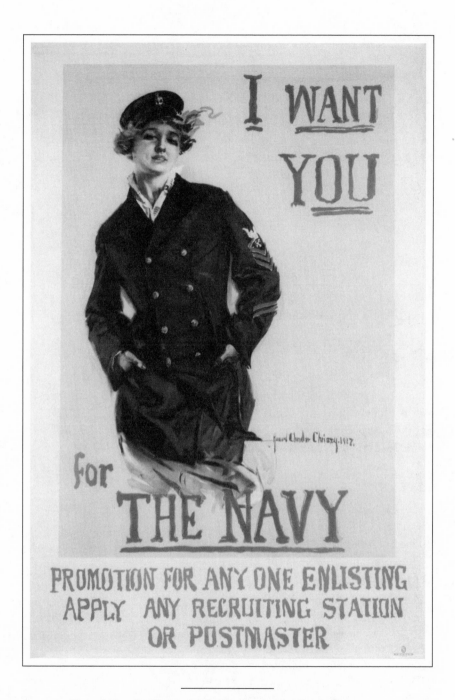

Howard Chandler Christy. "I Want You for the Navy." Color Poster. *1917.*
(From original at the Library of Virginia.)

New York Call, 13 June
ELLEN WINSOR

THE AMERICAN CONSCRIPT, 1917

My country gave the cry; it needed me,
But sent me to the European strife;
I gave my blood and took another's life,
  'Twas thus, they said, I'd set the whole world free.
I spent my life in poverty and woe;
I died to please my Masters, now I know.

Century, July
MARION PATTON WALDRON

VICTORY

Many and many are weeping for their lovers;
For the shallow graves in Flanders they are weeping,
For the lovers heaped with earth who cannot come to them,
While I—I have my lover back again!

First, word that he lay upon a narrow bed
As in a grave without the grave's release.
Death had despoiled his body, claimed his soul;
Yet those who tended would not give him up
To the earth's rest, and I who waited could not.
By that brave magic which proves man a god
Only less cunning than a modern gun
The surgeons mended bit by broken bit;
Patiently blew to spark the reluctant ashes,
Built with their will upon his power of anguish,
While I compelled his spirit with my spirit
Moment by moment, holding, drawing him back.
They wrote at last that he was coming home!

It was at dusk they brought him back to me
And laid him gently down and covered him;

Lingered, wanting to speak, yet silent, troubled,
Till awkwardly they left me with my living.

He lay so still, so still beneath the covers,
It was as if they had said, "Your soldier's dead."
But when I laid my hand on him I felt
The warm blood beating, and he spoke. His voice—
His voice it was—and he was calling me!

All night I crouched with my head against his arm
To feel its warmth. It was as if I doubted
The miracle. I dared not lift his shroud,
But watched beside him as a wife beside
Her husband laid in death—a wife who, turning
As in old griefs to her old comforter,
Longing to cower against him, and yet fearing
Lest he should shut her from him, *he* be cold
When most she needs him, *he* be stone to her,
Suddenly hears his answers fill her silence,
Feels the touch of the dead healing her pain.
Such was my miracle.

O lover's body with its man's grave beauty,
O lover's eyes in which I launched my soul!
I shall be hands and feet to him, and eyes!
And he can never see me if I falter;
No, and he cannot see me. God forgive me
If I shrink and sicken when I look at him
Before I learn to bear it! There will be years,
There will be years and years to learn. Even now
I can laugh when he makes jests about the fingers
He left to fight for him while he ran home!

Through the long, useless hours what are his thoughts?
What is he thinking all the idle days?
Sometimes he hides his marred face close against me
Like a tired child. That's easier, almost sweet,
Till I mind me of the old times when I teased him
Because he was so big, and called him little,
Half vexed, half pleased him calling him my baby,
He who planned always how he'd care for me
With his great strength, how he would always spare me.
My man, my man that's turned a poor stale joke;

But I can't think of any other now,
So I keep silent, thinking out my thoughts.

They say the lame child is his mother's dearest.
He *is* my child now, yes, *our* child, *our* child.
Not like the son we dreamed of long ago;
No, but the child of our renunciation,
Born of his beautiful body that went away,
Born of my spirit that sent him forth and waited.

What though the fruit of us be blighted and broken?
We have fought with death, the odds against us, and conquered!
(Hush! What was that echo of terrible laughter?
Who laughed? I fancied a far-off, cynical mocking.)

Many and many are weeping for their lovers;
For the shallow graves in Flanders they are weeping,
For the lovers heaped with earth who cannot come to them,
While I—I have my lover back again!

New York Times, 25 July
Edith M. Thomas

AQUILA
(A WAR CHANGE)

I trimmed a pen wherewith to write
A fragile lyric, swift and light,
That from on high—yet not too far—
Might send below a rippling bar
An idle moment's space to fill,
Perchance a balm to passing ill.

But oh, it was not to my will!
My pen—it was an Eagle's quill
That once the savage crags had known
And all the clamors that have blown
Through every land, in every age—
I set my pen along the page.

But now, but now—past all presage!—
Arose a vorticed legion-rage.
The pen became a bristling quill
And did with roar of tempest fill;
And, as it thrust along the line,
It seemed a thing of wrath divine.
From stormy word to word it ranged,
Then, to an Eagle's wing it changed;
A hundred barbed quills it bore
To write the high impassioned score.
What, what! *World-Freedom* was its theme,
And every patriot's dying dream—
And chastisement condign for those
That for the Despot hurl their blows!

The Eagle's namesake-wind arose
And every heaven-born air that knows
And loves the nidus where 'twas fledged.
The script it was with lightnings edged;
But, all at once, as on it ranged,
The Wing into an Eagle changed—
The Eagle of the Fiery Eye.
It shot at me the accusing cry:
   "I am of War—I was not thine,
   Weak thing, but I have made thee mine,
   For thou dids't trim an Eagle's quill!
   So, write thou must as I shall will.
   No softling lyric henceforth raise,
   But the wild Hymn of Unmatched Days!
   Now, circle with me o'er the fight,
   Thy glance divide the smoky light—
   Thou from the strife a soul upcatch!
   Watch how my talons Victory snatch—
   Victory with Freedom set on high,
   Most beautiful to every eye. . . .
   Do this; and, after, thou mayst try
   The Requiem for Those Who Die."

Four Lights, 28 July
FLORENCE GUERTIN TUTTLE

IF.

A MOTHER TO HER DAUGHTER.

(After Rudyard Kipling.)
If you can lose your head when all about you
    Are losing theirs and saying false is true;
If you can feel that Might alone is Mighty—
    Reverse your creed in all you say and do;
If you can cast aside your private ethics,
    And claim another law holds for the pack;
If you can join in race annihilation
    And never pause to question or look back;

If you can call yourself a Christ disciple
    Yet incense burn before the God of war;
If you can chant with saints the sixth commandment,
    Then plan to kill and kill—and kill some more;
If you can keep your tender woman's spirit
    And dull the charge of murder on your soul,
If you can ease your conscience with a bandage
    And daily sit and dumbly roll and roll;

If you can sing "My Country first" and never
    Observe that lands melt freely into one;
If you can prove mankind is not united,
    Led by one hope as by one rising sun;
If you can doubt that greed of State must perish,
    And God, the King, One Sovereignty unfurl,
You'll be a "loyal patriot" my darling,
    And which is more—a thing of stone, my girl.

Portraits and Protests (August)
SARAH NORCLIFFE CLEGHORN

PEACE HATH HER BELGIUMS

There is a Belgium in the bedrooms dark,
Tiny dark bedrooms, feeders to the grave.
Hark how the besieged Belgians cough and gasp
Where those tall Uhlans, Profits, have cut off
Their sunlight and their air!

       And there was news,
Bad news from Belgium, in the morning paper:
A mine caved in: the Belgians were entombed
By twenty thousand tons of fallen rock.
In what dim corner of the farthest workings,
As evening of the second day draws near,
Huddle they now, to share their final candle?

There is a Belgium in the red-light street,
Where all the habitations of the heart,
And all the fair cathedrals of the soul
Go up in flame, in shrapnel fire of hell.

And every city every winter hath
Her homemade Belgium of the unemployed.

Seven Arts, August
JAMES OPPENHEIM

EDITORIAL

In the pause of ominous foreboding days,
In the strange darkening silence,
I listen . . . I listen to myself . . .
I hear what is larger than myself, what is gigantic and terrible in strength,
The approaching reverberations of footsteps and tongues quivering on the
    air, gathering and drawing close,
The confused murmur of assembling voices,

The guttural animal rumble of growing crowds,
The suffocating, the inarticulate groans of peoples.

The air grows sultry, the skies thicken, the shrill birds beat against the wind . . .
When shall the clear thunder speak?
When shall the lightning of holy revolt cleave asunder the prisons?
When shall there sweep the envenomed earth and sky in shouted blasts the
    music of the storm?

Where are you lagging, Isaiah of the factories?
Where, O Joan of the slums?
Where, O prophet of the proletariat?
O masters, come forth from the side-street or the mill-town
And sweep into a divine symphony
The dark mute music of multitude:
Gather the heavy drops of rain—this man and that—this woman, that child—
Into the releasing storm, into the clear-voiced storm, into the storm that lets
    our hearts out, our souls out, thunder-trumpeting what we feel.

Bright archangel of battle
Ride on the northern winds of Revolution,
Ride the blast from arisen Russia
And girdle the world like a typhoon sucking the peoples into a column of war,
A war against the war,
A war against the swindling glory of war,
A war against the divine rights of kings and states, of heroes and of
    presidents,
A war against hate and holiness:
A war for life, for the laughter of children and the love of women and men.

How long, O how long, beloved race,
How long, beloved multitudes,
Shall you be drugged with the damned, the opiate fake of military music,
And slay one another like beasts to make a blood-spectacle for the old men,
To fatten with your deaths the Egoists who send you out to die?
Seven million of our young are murdered dead in Europe,
And the numbers of a great people are broken for the days of their life . . .
How long shall you feed the cannon you do not own,
And the States you do not run?
How long shall you taste dumb agony for a myth and a creed and a lie?

O the hope of the world were dead, and we were doomed to the undoing of
    man,
Were it not for thee, Russia, holy Russia,

Thou glimpse of the splendid sun in the black battle-smoke,
Thou shining health, thou virtue in the insane death-shambles!
To thee, the leadership has passed.
From America to thee has been handed the torch of freedom,
Thou art the hope of the world, the asylum of the oppressed,
The manger of the Future.

Rise, ever higher, more splendid,
Be as the divine dawn sending the rays of thy promised joy into the
    wilderness of madness,
Call us with thy clear lips,
Call us to the Day of Man, to the Planet of Humanity,
Call us into thy triumphing Revolution . . .
Call up the magnificent storm which shall be a throat and a tongue for our
    dumb thick anguish,
Which shall be a flaying terror to the thrones of the kingdoms and republics,
Which shall be a word of love in a world of hate,
A sanity in madness.

We march over the invisible edge of the precipice,
We drop thousand by thousand into the abyss,
We walk dumbly, like driven beasts, in lonely separation, in inarticulate rage—
Under us rolls a growing murmur, an ascending rumble, an ominous
    groaning . . .
We wait the Voice . . . we wait the Storm . . .

Poetry, September
SCHARMEL IRIS

WAR-TIME CRADLE SONG

The king sent out your father to war
As once he sent my father before.
My wedding ring and the gold on my ear
Today have I bartered for bread, my dear.
The moon is dying, her throat is red,
The wind is crying, "Your father's dead."

The holy priest for saying a mass
Will take our gentle ox and our ass,

And we must give our cow away
To a man who digs the grave today.
The king has given us a reward—
A medal of bronze, and your father's sword.

Grain there is none on the granary floor.
The lean wolf, Misery, howls at our door—
Until I wake and cut off my hair.
My son, I will keep you strong and fair,
For soon you shall take your father's sword
And bring me the king's head for reward.

Scribner's, September
ARTHUR DAVISON FICKE

TO THE BELOVED OF ONE DEAD

The sunlight shall not easily seem fair
To you again,
Knowing the hand that once amid your hair
Did stray so maddeningly
Now listlessly
Is beaten into mire by summer rain.

The spirit has its sanctities in death—
But the bright clay
Knows naught of recompense. And the swift breath
That in some darkened place
Once swept your face—
What shall sublime that memory away?

He died amid the thunders of the great war;
His glory cries
Even now across the lands; perhaps his star
Shall shine forever. . . .
But for you, never
His wild white body and his thirsting eyes.

Masses, September
LOUIS UNTERMEYER

BATTLE HYMN OF THE RUSSIAN REPUBLIC

God, give us strength these days—
  Burn us with one desire;
To smother this murderous blaze,
  Beat back these flames with fire.

Let us not weaken and fail
  Or spend ourselves in a shout;
Let our white passion prevail
  Till the terror is driven out.

Give us the power to fling
  Ourselves and our fury, employed
To blast and destroy this thing
  Lest Life itself be destroyed.

Friends in all lands, arise—
  Turn all these fires to shake
Against their refuge of lies;
  Force it to crumble and break.

Rise, ere it grow too late
  And we have not strength enough.
Sweep it down with our hate!
  Trample it with our love!

Cover. *International Socialist Review,* Aug. *1917.* (From original
at the University of Minnesota, Twin Cities.)

Solidarity, 27 September
ARTURO GIOVANNITTI

WHEN THE COCK CROWS

To the Memory of Frank Little,
Hanged at Midnight.

I.

Six men drove up to his house at midnight, and woke the poor woman who
  kept it,
And asked her: "Where is the man who spoke against war and insulted the
  army?"
And the old woman took fear of the men and the hour, and showed them the
  room where he slept,
And when they made sure it was he whom they wanted, they dragged him
  out of his bed with blows, tho' he was willing to walk,
And they fastened his hands on his back, and they drove him across the black
  night.
And there was no moon and no stars and not any visible thing, and even the
  faces of the men were eaten with the leprosy of the dark, for they were
  masked with black shame,
And nothing showed in the gloom save the glow of his eyes and the flame of
  his soul that scorched the face of Death.

II.

No one gave witness of what they did to him, after they took him away, until
  a dog barked at his corpse,
But, I know, for I have seen masked men with the rope, and the eyeless things
  that howl against the sun, and I have ridden beside the hangman at
  midnight.
They kicked him, they cursed him, they pushed him, they spat on his cheeks
  and his brow,
They stabbed his ears with foul oaths, they smeared his clean face with the
  pus of their ulcerous words,
And nobody saw or heard them. But I call you to witness John Brown, I call
  you to witness, you Molly Macguires,
And you, Albert Parson, George Engel, Adolph Fischer, August Spies,
And you, Leo Frank, kinsman of Jesus, and you, Joe Hill, twice my germane
  in the rage of the song and the fray,

And all of you, sun-dark brothers, and all of you harriers of torpid faiths,
    hasteners of the great day, propitiators of the holy deed,
I call you all to the bar of the dawn to give witness if this is not what they do
    in America when they wake up men at midnight to hang them until
    they're dead.

III.

Under a railroad trestle, under the heart-rib of Progress, they circled his neck
    with the noose, but never a word he spoke.
Never a word he uttered, and they grew weak from his silence,
For the terror of death is strongest upon the men with the rope,
When he who must hang breathes neither a prayer nor a curse,
Nor speaks any word, nor looks around, nor does anything save to chew his
    bit of tobacco and yawn with unsated sleep.
They grew afraid of the hidden moon and the stars, they grew afraid of the
    wind that held its breath, and of the living things that never stirred in
    their sleep.
And they gurgled a bargain to him from under their masks.
I know what they promised to him, for I have heard thrice the bargains that
    hounds yelp to the trapped lion:
They asked him to promise that he would turn back from his road, that he
    would eat carrion as they, that he would lap the leash for the sake of the
    offals, as they—and thus he would save his life.
But not one lone word he answered—he only chewed his bit of tobacco in
    silent contempt.

IV.

Now black as their faces become whatever had been white inside of the six
    men, even to their mothers' milk,
And they inflicted on him the final shame, and ordered that he should kiss
    the flag.
They always make bounden men kiss the flag in America, where men never
    kiss men, not even when they march forth to die.
But tho' to him all flags are holy that men fight for and death hallows,
He did not kiss it—I swear it by the one that shall wrap my body.
He did not kiss it, and they trampled upon him in their frenzy that had no
    retreat save the rope.
And to him who was ready to die for a light he would never see shine, they
    said: "You are a coward."
To him who would not barter a meaningless word for his life, they said: "You
    are a traitor."

And they drew the noose round his neck, and they pulled him up to the
trestle, and they watched him until he was dead.

Six masked men whose faces were eaten with the cancer of the dark.

One for each steeple of thy temple, O Labor.

V.

Now he is dead, but now that he is dead is the door of your dungeon faster, O
money changers and scribes, and priests and masters of slaves?

Are men now readier to die for you without asking the wherefore of the
slaughter?

Shall now the pent up spirit no longer connive with the sun against your
midnight?

And are we now all reconciled to your rule, and are you safer and we
humbler, and is the night eternal and the day forever blotted out of the
skies,

And all blind yesterdays risen, and all tomorrows entombed,

Because of six faceless men and ten feet of rope and one corpse dangling
unseen in the blackness under a railroad trestle?

No, I say, no. It swings like a terrible pendulum that shall soon ring out a
mad tocsin and call the red cock to crowing.

No, I say, no, for someone will bear witness of this to the dawn,

Someone will stand straight and fearless tomorrow between the armed hosts
of your slaves, and shout to them the challenge of that silence you could
not break.

VI.

"Brothers["]—he will shout to them—["]are you then, the Godborn,
reduced to a mute of dogs

That you will rush to the hunt of your kin at the blowing of a horn?

Brothers, have then the centuries that created new suns in the heavens,
gouged out the eyes of your soul,

That you should wallow in your blood like swine,

That you should squirm like rats in carrion,

That you, who astonished the eagles, should beat blindly about the night of
murder like bats?

Are you, Brothers, who were meant to scale the stars, to crouch forever before
a footstool,

And listen forever to one word of shame and subjection,

And leave the plough in the furrow, the trowel on the wall, the hammer on
the anvil, and the heart of the race on the knees of screaming women,
and the future of the race in the hands of babbling children,

And yoke on your shoulders the halter of hatred and fury,

And dash head-down against the bastions of folly,

Because a colored cloth waves in the air, because a drum beats in the street,

Because six men have promised you a piece of ribbon on your coat, a carved tablet on a wall and your name in a list bordered with black?

Shall you, then, be forever the stewards of death, when life waits for you like a bride?

Ah no, Brothers, not for this did our mothers shriek with pain and delight when we tore their flanks with our first cry;

Not for this were we given command of the beasts,

Not with blood but with sweat were we bidden to achieve our salvation.

Behold! I announce now to you a great tiding of joy,

For if your hands that are gathered in sheaves for the sickle of war unite as a bouquet of flowers between the warm breasts of peace,

Freedom will come without any blows save the hammers on the chains of your wrists, and the picks on the walls of your jails!

Arise, and against every hand jeweled with the rubies of murder,

Against every mouth that sneers at the tears of mercy,

Against every foul smell of the earth,

Against every head that a footstool raises over your head,

Against every word that was written before this was said,

Against every happiness that never knew sorrow,

And every glory that never knew love and sweat,

Against silence and death, and fear

Arise with a mighty roar!

Arise and declare your war;

For the wind of the dawn is blowing,

For the eyes of the East are glowing,

For the lark is up and the cock is crowing,

And the day of judgment is here!"

VII.

Thus shall he speak to the great parliament of the dawn, the witness of this murderous midnight,

And even if none listens to him, I shall be there and acclaim,

And even if they tear him to shreds, I shall be there to confess him before your guns and your gallows, O Monsters!

And even tho' you smite me with your bludgeon upon my head,

And curse me and call me foul names, and spit on my face and on my bare hands,

I swear that when the cock crows I shall not deny him.

And even if the power of your lie be so strong that my own mother curse me
    as a traitor with her hands clutched over her old breasts,

And my daughters with the almighty names, turn their faces from me and
    call me coward,

And the One whose love for me is a battleflag in the storm, scream for the
    shame of me and adjure my name,

I swear that when the cock crows I shall not deny him.

And if you chain me and drag me before the Beast that guards the seals of
    your power, and the caitiff that conspires against the daylight demand
    my death,

And your hangman throw a black cowl over my head and tie a noose around
    my neck,

And the black ghoul that pastures on the graves of the saints dig its snout
    into my soul and howl the terrors of the everlasting beyond in my ears,

Even then, when the cock crows, I swear I shall not deny him.

And if you spring the trap under my feet and hurl me into the gloom, and in
    the revelation of that instant eternal a voice shriek madly to me

That the rope is forever unbreakable,

That the dawn is never to blaze,

That the night is forever invincible,

Even then, even then, I shall not deny him.

New York Call, 30 September
BERNICE EVANS

THE SAYINGS OF PATSY

As Recorded by Bernice Evans

SAYS PATSY:
You can't pick up
A magazine
These days
Without reading
A column about
The American sin
Of extravagance,
And feeding
The allies

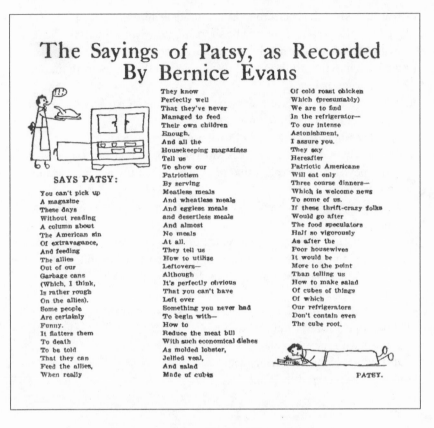

Bernice Evans. "The Sayings of Patsy." Illustrated poem.
(*New York Call*, 30 Sept. 1917, magazine sec.)

Out of our
Garbage cans
(Which, I think,
Is rather rough
On the allies).
Some people
Are certainly
Funny.
It flatters them
To death
To be told
That they can
Feed the allies,
When really

They know
Perfectly well
That they've never
Managed to feed
Their own children
Enough.
And all the
Housekeeping magazines
Tell us
To show our
Patriotism
By serving
Meatless meals
And wheatless meals
And eggless meals
[A]nd des[s]ertless meals
And almost
No meals
At all.
They tell us
How to utilize
Leftovers—
Although
It's perfectly obvious
That you can't have
Left over
Something you never had
To begin with—
How to
Reduce the meat bill
With such economical dishes
As molded lobster,
Jellied veal,
And salad
Made of cubes
Of cold roast chicken
Which (presumably)
We are to find
In the refrigerator—
To our intense
Astonishment,
I assure you.

They say
Hereafter
Patriotic Americans
Will eat only
Three course dinners—
Which is welcome news
To some of us.
If these thrift-crazy folks
Would go after
The food speculators
Half so vigorously
As after the
Poor housewives
It would be
More to the point
Than telling us
How to make salad
Of cubes of things
Of which
Our refrigerators
Don't contain even
The cube root.

Poetry, October
Vachel Lindsay

THE SOAP-BOX

"This my song is made for Kerensky."

O market square, O slattern place,
Is glory in your slack disgrace?
Plump quack doctors sell their pills,
Gentle grafters sell brass watches,
Silly anarchists yell their ills.
Shall we be as weird as these—
In the breezes nod and wheeze?

Heaven's mass is sung,
Tomorrow's mass is sung
In a spirit tongue
By wind and dust and birds;
The high mass of liberty,
While wave the banners red,
Sung round the soap-box—
A mass for soldiers dead.

When you leave your faction in the once-loved hall,
Like a true American tongue-lash them all;
Stand then on the corner under starry skies,
And get you a gang of the worn and the wise.
The soldiers of the Lord may be squeaky when they rally,
The soldiers of the Lord are a queer little army;
But the soldiers of the Lord, before the year is through,
Will gather the whole nation, recruit all creation,
To smite the hosts abhorred and all the heavens renew;
Enforcing with the bayonet the thing the ages teach—
Free speech!
Free speech!

Down with the Prussians, and all their works!
Down with the Turks!
Down with every army that fights against the soap-box—
The Pericles, Socrates, Diogenes soap-box,
The old-Elijah, Jeremiah, John-the-Baptist soap-box,
The Rousseau, Mirabeau, Danton soap-box,
The Karl-Marx, Henry-George, Woodrow-Wilson soap-box.
We will make the wide earth safe for the soap-box,
The everlasting foe of beastliness and tyranny,
Platform of liberty—Magna Charta liberty,
Andrew Jackson liberty, bleeding-Kansas liberty,
New-born Russian liberty:
Battleship of thought, the round world over,
Loved by the red-hearted,
Loved by the broken-hearted,
Fair young amazon or proud tough rover;
Loved by the lion,
Loved by the lion,
Loved by the lion!—
Feared by the fox.

Death at the bedstead of every Kaiser knocks.
The Hohenzollern army shall be felled like the ox.
The fatal hour is striking in all the doomsday clocks;
The while, by freedom's alchemy,
Beauty is born.

Ring every sleigh-bell, ring every church bell,
Blow the clear trumpet and listen for the answer—
The blast from the sky of the Gabriel horn.
Hail the Russian picture around the little box:
Exiles,
Troops in files,
Generals in uniform,
Mujiks in their smocks,
And holy maiden soldiers who have cut away their locks.

All the people of the world, little folk and great,
Are tramping through the Russian Soul as through a city gate,
As though it were a street of stars that paves the shadowy deep;
And mighty Tolstoi leads the van along the stairway steep.

    But now the people shout:
"Hail to Kerensky—he hurled the tyrants out!"
And this my song is made for Kerensky,
Prophet of the world-wide intolerable hope—
There on the soap-box, seasoned, dauntless,
There amid the Russian celestial kaleidoscope,
Flags of liberty, rags and battlesmoke.

Moscow!—Chicago!
Come let us praise battling Kerensky!
Bravo! bravo!—
Comrade Kerensky, thunderstorm and rainbow,
Comrade Kerensky, bravo, bravo!

Atlantic Monthly, October
KATHARINE LEE BATES

THE RETINUE

Archduke Francis Ferdinand, Austrian Heir-Apparent,
Rideth through the Shadow Land, not a lone knight errant,
But captain of a mighty train, millions upon millions,
Armies of the battle-slain, hordes of dim civilians;

German ghosts who see their works with tortured eyes, the sorry
Spectres of scared tyrants, Turks hunted by their quarry,
Liars, plotters red of hand—like waves of poisonous gases
Sweeping through the Shadow Land the host of horror passes;

Spirits bright as broken blades drawn for truth and honor,
Sons of Belgium, pallid maids, martyrs who have won her
Love eternal, bleeding breasts of the French defiance,
Russians on enraptured quests, Freedom's proud alliance.

Through that hollow hush of doom, vast, unvisioned regions,
Led by Kitchener of Khartoum, march the English legions:
Kilt and shamrock, maple-leaf, dreaming Hindoo faces,
Brows of glory, eyes of grief, arms of lost embraces.

Like a moaning tide of woe, midst those pale battalions
From the Danube and the Po, Arabs and Australians,
Pours a ghastly multitude that breaks the heart of pity,
Wreckage of some shell-bestrewed waste that was a city;

Flocking from the murderous seas, from the famished lowland,
From the blazing villages of Serbia and Poland,
Woman phantoms, baby wraiths, trampled by war's blindness,
Horses, dogs, that put their faiths in human lovingkindness,

Tamburlane, Napoleon, envious Alexander
Peer in wonder at the wan, tragical commander,
Archduke Francis Ferdinand—when shall his train be ended?—
Of all the lords of Shadow Land most royally attended!

The Little Flag on Main Street (October)
McLANDBURGH WILSON

MADE SAFE FOR DEMOCRACY

"Made safe for democracy" seems mighty fine,
But high-soundin' politics ain't in our line.
'Tain't that made us chuck up our jobs and enlist
For givin' the Kaiser the taste of a fist,
But this is the notion stowed under our lids:
We're makin' it safe for the Missus and kids.

They've taken the men folks and used 'em for slaves,
They've driven the women to worse than their graves,
They've taken the babies and cut off their hands
And murdered the bravest and peacefullest lands,
And this is the notion tucked under our lids:
It's somebody's Missus and somebody's kids.

We ain't any better—it might have been us
And that's why we're doin' our bit in the fuss,
We don't know the rules of the high soundin' game,
Perhaps in the end it all comes to the same,
But this is the notion stowed under our lids:
We're makin' it safe for the Missus and kids.

The Little Flag on Main Street (October)

COMPANY FOR DINNER

Our cousins are coming to dinner,
    The larder is showing a lack,
So pass the kick under the table
    And signal the family, "Hold back!"

You, Mother, decline the potatoes,
    And Father, go light on the meat;
And Sis, have a heart for the sugar,
    And Bub, skip the bread when you eat.

"Food Will Win the War." Color poster. Washington, D.C.: U.S. Food Administration, *1917*. (From original at the Joseph M. Bruccoli Great War Collection, Special Collections Library, University of Virginia Library.)

There—France, have some more, let us beg you;
    John Bull, let us fill up your plate;
And Belgium, another good helping—
    Gee folks, but to have you is great!

New York Call, 19 October
LOLA RIDGE

BREAD

*(Women's demonstration against the high cost of living, N.Y. City Hall,
December, 1916.)*

Shawled women,
Trickling like a sluice out of alleys and side streets;
Swelling, irresistibly growing—
Pouring like an addled river
Through stalled crowds and vehicles cluttered like curses—
And a cry in their lifted throats.

That tatterdemalion cry:
Bread! Bread!
Sung to a rhythm of frenzied fists
And a flut[t]er of rags
And a clatter of feet on the flags;
Bread! Bread!
In ugly and raucous notes
Out of scrawny throats
Falling like pellets of lead.

They heard at their councils:
Bread!
Is it sounding again
Out of the prosperous years?
That bedlam screech,
With its menace of deadly reach—
That tocsin of terror and tears?

No, it was muffled in earth . . .
It is safe with the rotting bones . . .
It was choked with a fatted lie . . .
It died in a song of fire.

Bread! Bread!
This the reply—
Piercing, and harsh, and high—
Sung to a rhythm of upturned faces,
White as under a flame,
And a flashing of slender wrists
And a swaying of unset hips . . .
That desperate, hag-worn cry—
Strange on the dewy lips.

But they heard, with their thumbs on the rye,
That cry like a blazing town—
That tatterdemalion cry:
Bread! Bread!

They shifted their thumbs on the wheat,
At that cry like a bloodied gown,
Flaunting their flags above.

Four Lights, 20 October
MARY ALDEN HOPKINS

THE PICKET

Men tell us women
Not to ask for suffrage now
Lest we hinder the pursuit of war.
Well, for my part,
I would rather have a vote than a war any day.

New York Call, 21 October
BERNICE EVANS

THE SAYINGS OF PATSY

As Recorded by Bernice Evans
  SAYS PATSY:
We're beginning
To hear
That the
American soldiers
Get too much
Money.
They say
Our soldiers
Have so much more
Than the soldiers
Of the Allies
That it is causing
Envy
And discontent
And lack of
Harmony
Among the
Allied soldiers.
When I read
Things like that
I feel
Quite confused.
You see,
I always thought
That if anybody
Talked about
Equal incomes,
And envy,
And discontent,
It was
A sure sign
That person
Was opposed to
Religion

And marriage,
And was
Pro-German,
And a traitor,
And a slacker,
And a copperhead,
And other
Awful things.
But maybe not!
Anyway,
It seems to me
They're establishing
A "dangerous precedent"
When they begin
To talk about
Equalizing incomes
To prevent
Envy,
And discontent,
And lack of harmony
In the armies
In France,
Because
There might be
Some pestiferous folks
Who would want
To apply
The same principle
To civil life
In America.
You know
How some people
Are.
And if
You start
Folks' minds
To working
In that direction
Now
You might not
Be able to
Stop them

When the war
Is over,
Just like
Turning off
A faucet.
But, anyway,
When you consider
That a soldier
Has to carry
Seventy pounds
Of arms
And equipment
It certainly is
Cruel
To make him
Carry around
All that money,
Too.

Chicago Evening Post, 29 October
CARL SANDBURG

THE FOUR BROTHERS

[To the Editor:—The inclosed poem, "The Four Brothers," will appear in Poetry for November. Believing that this poem voices the heart and mind of America at war, we release it to a special list of papers for publication in whole or in part on Oct. 29, due credit being given to Poetry. The author's check in payment for the poem will be given to the fund for American poets' ambulances in Italy. Poetry believes that publication of this poem is a service of loyalty to the democracies at war.—Poetry.]

NOTES FOR WAR SONGS
Make war songs out of these;
Make chants that repeat and weave.
Make rhythms up to the ragtime chatter of the machine guns;
Make slow-booming psalms up to the boom of the big guns.
Make a marching song of swinging arms and swinging legs,
Going along,

Going along,
On the roads from San Antonio to Athens, from Seattle to Bagdad—
The boys and men in winding lines of khaki, the circling squares of bayonet
    points.

Cowpunchers, cornhuskers, shopmen, ready in khaki;
Ballplayers, lumberjacks, ironworkers, ready in khaki;
A million, ten million, singing, "I am ready."
This the sun looks on between two seaboards,
In the land of Lincoln, in the land of Grant and Lee.

I heard one say, "I am ready to be killed."
I heard another say, "I am ready to be killed."
O sunburned clear-eyed boys!
I stand on sidewalks and you go by with drums and guns and bugles,
You—and the flag!
And my heart tightens, a fist of something feels my throat
When you go by,
You on the kaiser hunt, you and your faces saying, "I am ready to be killed."

They are hunting death,
Death for the one-armed mastoid kaiser.
They are after a Hohenzollern head:
There is no man-hunt of men remembered like this.

The four big brothers are out to kill.
France, Russia, Britain, America—
The four republics are sworn brothers to kill the kaiser.

Yes, this is the great man-hunt;
And the sun has never seen till now
Such a line of toothed and tusked man-killers,
In the blue of the upper sky,
In the green of the undersea,
In the red of winter dawns.
Eating to kill,
Sleeping to kill,
Asked by their mothers to kill,
Wished by four-fifths of the world to kill—
To cut the kaiser's throat,
To hack the kaiser's head,
To hang the kaiser on a high-horizon gibbet.

And is it nothing else than this?
Three times ten million men thirsting the blood
Of a half-cracked, one-armed child of the German kings?
Three times ten million men asking the blood
Of a child born with his head wrong-shaped,
The blood of rotted kings in his veins?
If this were all, O God,
I would go to the far timbers
And look on the gray wolves
Tearing the throats of moose:
I would ask a wilder drunk of blood.

Look! It is four brothers in joined hands together.
The people of bleeding France,
The people of bleeding Russia,
The people of Britain, the people of America—
These are the four brothers, these are the four republics.

At first I said it in anger as one who clinches his fists in wrath to fling his
     knuckles into the face of some one taunting;
Now I say it calmly as one who has thought it over and over again at night,
     among the mountains, by the sea-combers in storm.
I say now, by God, only fighters today will save the world, nothing but
     fighters will keep alive the names of those who left red prints of bleeding
     feet at Valley Forge in Christmas snow.
On the cross of Jesus, the sword of Napoleon, the skull of Shakespeare, the
     pen of Tom Jefferson, the ashes of Abraham Lincoln, or any sign of the
     red and running life poured out by the mothers of the world,
By the God of morning-glories climbing blue the doors of quiet homes, by
     the God of tall hollyhocks laughing glad to children in peaceful valleys,
     by the God of new mothers wishing peace to sit at windows nursing
     babies,
I swear only reckless men, ready to throw away their lives by hunger,
     deprivation, desperate clinging to a single purpose imperturbable and
     undaunted, men with the primitive guts of rebellion,
Only fighters gaunt with the red band of labor's sorrow on their brows and
     labor's terrible pride in their blood, men with souls asking danger—only
     these will save and keep the four big brothers.
Good-night is the word, good-night to the kings, to the czars,
Good-night to the kaiser.
The breakdown and the fadeaway begins.
The shadow of a great broom, ready to sweep out the trash, is here.

One finger is raised that counts the czar,
The ghost who beckoned men who come no more—
The czar gone to the winds on God's great dustpan,
The czar a pinch of nothing,
The last of the gibbering Romanoffs.

Out and good-night—
The ghosts of the summer palaces
And the ghosts of the winter palaces!
Out and out, good-night to the kings, the czars, the kaisers.

Another finger will speak,
And the kaiser, the ghost who gestures a hundred million sleeping-waking
     ghosts,
The kaiser will go onto God's great dustpan—
The last of the gibbering Hohenzollerns.
Look! God pities this trash, God waits with a broom and a dustpan,
God knows a finger will speak and count them out.

It is written in the stars;
It is spoken on the walls;
It clicks in the fire-white zigzag of the Atlantic wireless;
It mutters in the bastions of thousand-mile continents;
It sings in a whistle on the midnight winds from Walla Walla to
     Mesopotamia:
Out and good-night.

The millions slow in khaki,
The millions learning "Turkey in the Straw" and "John Brown's Body,"
The millions remembering windrows of dead at Gettysburg, Chickamauga
     and Spotsylvania Court House,
The millions dreaming of the morning-star of Appomattox,
The millions easy and calm with guns and steel, planes and prows:
There is a hammering, drumming hell to come.
The killing gangs are on the way.

God takes one year for a job.
God takes ten years or a million.
God knows when a doom is written.
God knows this job will be done and the words spoken:
Out and good-night.
The red tubes will run,
And the great price be paid,
And the homes empty,

And the wives wishing,
And the mothers wishing.
There is only one way now, only the way of the red tubes and the great price.

Well . . .
Maybe the morning star is a five-cent yellow balloon,
And the evening stars the joke of a God gone crazy.
Maybe the mothers of the world,
And the life that pours from their torsal folds—
Maybe it's all a lie sworn by liars,
And a God with a cackling laughter says:
"I, the Almighty God,
I have made all this,
I have made it for kaisers, czars and kings."

Three times ten million men say: No.
Three times ten million men say:
God is a God of the People.
And the God who made the world
And fixed the morning sun,
And flung the evening stars,
And shaped the baby hands of life,
This is the God of the Four Brothers;
This is the God of bleeding France and bleeding Russia;
This is the God of the people of Britain and America.

The graves from the Irish Sea to the Caucasus peaks are ten times a million.
The stubs and stumps of arms and legs, the eyesockets empty, the cripples,
ten times a million.
The crimson thumb-print of this anathema is on the door panels of a
hundred million homes.
Cows gone, mothers on sick-beds, children crying a-hunger and no milk
comes in the noon time or at night.
The death-yells of it all, the torn throats of men in ditches calling for water,
the shadows and the hacking lungs in dugouts, the steel paws that clutch
and squeeze a scarlet drain day by day—the storm of it is hell.
But look, child! The storm is blowing for a clean air.

Look! The four brothers march
And hurl their big shoulders
And swear the job shall be done.

Out of the wild finger-writing north and south, east and west, over the
blood-crossed, blood-dusty ball of earth,
Out of it all a God who knows is sweeping clean,
Out of it all a God who sees and pierces thru, is breaking and cleaning out an
old thousand years, is making ready for a new thousand years.
The four brothers shall be five and more.

Under the chimneys of the winter-time the children of the world shall sing
new songs.
Among the rocking restless cradles the mothers of the world shall sing new
sleepy-time songs.

Crisis, November
JAMES WELDON JOHNSON

TO AMERICA

How would you have us, as we are
Or sinking 'neath the load we bear?
Our eyes fixed forward on a star
Or gazing empty at despair?

Rising or falling? Men or things?
With dragging pace or footsteps fleet?
Strong willing sinews in your wings?
Or tightening chains about your feet?

Suffragist, 10 November
WOMAN'S SUFFRAGE PRISONERS AT OCCOQUAN WORK HOUSE

[WE WORRIED WOODY-WOOD]

"[A]n enlivening ballad to the dogged tune of 'Captain Kidd'"
We worried Woody-wood,
As we stood, as we stood.
We worried Woody-wood,
As we stood.

We worried Woddy-wood,
And we worried him right good,
We worried him right good, as we stood.

We asked him for the vote,
As we stood, as we stood.
We asked him for the vote,
As we stood.
We asked him for the vote,
But he'd rather write a note,
He'd rather write a note—so we stood.

We'll not get out on bail,
Go to jail, go to jail—
We'll not get out on bail,
Go to jail.
We'll not get out on bail,
We prefer to go to jail,
We prefer to go to jail—we're not frail.

We asked them for a brush,
For our teeth, for our teeth.
We asked them for a brush,
For our teeth.
We asked them for a brush,
They said, "There ain't no rush,"
They said, "There ain't no rush—darn your teeth."

We asked them for some air,
As we choked, as we choked.
We asked them for some air,
As we choked.
We asked them for some air,
And they threw us in a lair,
They threw us in a lair—so we choked.

We asked them for our nightie,
As we froze, as we froze.
We asked them for our nightie, as we froze.
We asked them for a nightie,
And they looked—hightie-tightie—
They looked hightie-tightie—so we froze.

Now, ladies, take the hint,
As ye stand, as ye stand.
Now, ladies, take the hint,
As ye stand.
Now, ladies, take the hint,
Don't quote the President,
Don't quote the President, as ye stand.

New York Call, 20 November
ZELDA

TO THE PATRIOTIC LADY
ACROSS THE WAY

She wore a Liberty loan button
And above it a silken American flag,
And her knitting needles clicked
Through some soldier's sweater.
A youth came on the subway
And sat beside her—
A comely youth, neat, intelligent,
Yes, even respectable;
But his skin was black
And his lips were thick
And his nose was broad and flat.
She gathered her knitting needles together
In unseemly panic,
And as she fled, with disdainful nose, tip-tilted,
To the lower end of the car
I noticed that she wore a Liberty loan button
And a silken American flag—
And I do believe she thinks she's helping
To make the world safe for democracy.

Outlook, 21 November
AMELIA JOSEPHINE BURR

FATHER O'SHEA

Father O'Shea was his regiment's pride.
Sturdy, fine sons of the emerald sod,
Like heroes they fought and like children they died
With their Padre beside them to help them to God.
Four times court-martialed for risking his life
In No Man's Land, seeking his lost where they lay.
"They are my sons as the Church is my wife,
And I never will fail them," said Father O'Shea.

They were called for their turn in the terrible drive,
And the Padre went up with his boys to the town
Where host upon host passed their last night alive—
Ah, the few that came back where the many went down!
He had looked in those simple young hearts to the deep,
He had shriven their souls for the perilous way.
"It's clean wheat for heaven the Berthas will reap
In the battle to-morrow," said Father O'Shea.

But the blood will run hot when it soon may be cold,
And life's lure is stronger with death just ahead.
There were women with eyes that were shallow and bold
In the quarter inclosed, where a narrow gate led
To the chambers a man need not visit by stealth,
That stood open shameless to all who could pay.
The authorities gave them a clean bill of health,
But they never could get one from Father O'Shea.

That night, every Irishman bound for that gate
Stopped at salute—there was no room to pass
The figure that sat there as steady as fate
With a quizzical glitter of spectacle glass.
He shut for a marker his thumb in the book.
"Is it me that ye want, son?" he glanced up to say.
They all turned abashed from the probe of that look,
And back to his reading went Father O'Shea.

The shadows of sleeplessness circled his eyes
When at morning he heartened his lads for the test,

But through a worse danger he'd guarded his prize,
And in the tired body his heart was at rest.
If I had a son where the red rivers roll,
With every breath of my lips I would pray,
"God save him, God keep him in body and soul—
And send him a Padre like Father O'Shea!"

New York Call, 30 December
BERNICE EVANS

THE SAYINGS OF PATSY

As Recorded by Bernice Evans
  SAYS PATSY:
Sometimes,
These days,
I really don't know
Just where
My place is.
That certainly is
Confusing.
You see,
I'd always been
Solemnly assured
That it was
"In the home,"
But recently,
It's been pointed out
That, unquestionably,
My place is
Half way up
A step ladder
Cleaning windows,
So that
One more man
Can go to fight.
It really seems
That my place
Has been mislaid—

Not to say
Permanently lost.
And I begin
To suspect
That it is
Wherever
It's most convenient
For some folks
To place me.
We're getting
A lot of praise,
Just now,
For our "patriotism"
In taking
Men's jobs.
There's a
Horrible Grin,
Up on Oyster Bay,
Sometimes known as
The Battle Him
Of the Republic,
Who, in times past,
Never deigned
To notice us
At all,
But who writes
A whole column
About us now.
Indeed,
Praise
Is about all
We do get,
Considering that
Women are paid
Just about half
The regular wages
For their work,
Patriotism included.
But,
Be sure of this—
Women aren't going
To stay fooled

Very long.
It's a case of
"Timeo Danaos et dona ferentes,"
Which, being interpreted,
Readeth,
When interested folks
Wax eloquent
In their praises
Of your patriotism,
And nobility,
And self sacrifice,
And other virtues,
Carefully count
The contents
Of your pay envelope.
But, really,
They ought to be
Grateful to us,
Because
I honestly don't see
Whom they would do
Without us.

PART 6
1918

Today.
A Man Burned Alive.
Not in Prussia—
Here in America.
And a Lady Applauds.

Excuse the omission of any reference to "Prussian brutality" from this column for just one day.

We Americans in the proud and civilized State of Tennessee have just burned a Negro to death. Details of this interesting performance should take our minds off Prussian cruelty for a while.

The Negro was not accused of "the usual crime," an attack on woman, supposed to explain any brutality. He had shot two men and wounded a third.

When they [got] him they tied him to hot irons to make him confess something—which is going some distance back in history of justice.

Then they piled up wood around him and burned him up.

And note this refining touch of civilization: a lady made a speech requesting the burning of the Negro and other ladies seconded the motion.

—Arthur Brisbane, *Chicago Examiner,* 18 February

Germany has once more said that force, and force alone, shall decide whether Justice and peace shall reign in the affairs of men, whether Right as America conceives it or Dominion as she conceives it shall determine the destinies of mankind. There is, therefore, but one response possible from us: Force, Force to the utmost, Force without stint or limit, the righteous and triumphant Force which shall make Right the law of the world, and cast every selfish dominion down in the dust. The world must be made safe for democracy.

—Woodrow Wilson, "President Wilson Condemns German Peace
Treaties with Russia and Rumania—And Accepts the German
Challenge of Force (An Address at Baltimore, April 6, 1918)"

In January 1918 Woodrow Wilson finally discovered the democratic logic behind votes for women, as he publicly called for Congress to pass the suffrage amendment. Whether Wilson was moved more by the war work of the National American Woman Suffrage Association or by the picketing and protests of the National Woman's party, both groups' arguments made their impression on his September 1918 address to Congress. Besides emphasizing women's contributions to the war effort—contributions organized and encouraged by the association and used as its central pro-suffrage argument behind the scenes—Wilson explained that suffrage needed to be treated as essential wartime legislation because "the plain, struggling, workaday folk" of Europe were "looking to the great, powerful, famous democracy of the west to lead them to the new day for which they have long awaited; and they think, in their logical simplicity, that democracy means that women shall play their part in affairs alongside men and upon an equal footing with them" (1:530). Wilson's condescending tone aside, this was precisely the argument made the previous year by the party's White House picketers.

But the success of the woman's suffrage campaign was not an unequivocal triumph of democratic principle and persuasion. Carrie Chapman Catt, president of the association, appealed to the prejudices of lawmakers as well as to their sense of justice as she testified before a congressional committee: "Every slacker has a vote. Every newly made citizen will have a vote. Every pro-German who can not be trusted with any kind of war service will have a vote. Every peace-at-any-price man, every conscientious objector, and even the alien enemy will have a vote. . . . It is a risk, a danger to a country like ours to send 1,000,000 men out of the country who are loyal and not replace those men by the loyal votes of the women they have left at home" (qtd. in Schaffer 91–92). The great victory of the National Woman's party was founded on public outrage that genteel society women should be held in a debtor's prison, subjected to undignified conditions, and mistreated by lower-class female guards who did not properly temper their 100 percent Americanism with class deference. At the very same time, many IWW members imprisoned in Leavenworth suffered similar beatings and deprivations. Unlike the suffrage prisoners, the Wobblies were held for months without any charges being brought against them, and their abusive treatment, to the extent it was noticed by anyone, was considered appropriate. The government was congratulated for arresting IWW national and regional leaders as a preventive measure, *before* they could commit any of the crimes they certainly would have as slackers, aliens, and secret German sympathizers. Thus, the War for Democra-

"Colored Man Is No Slacker." Color Poster. *1918*. (From original
at the George C. Marshall Research Library, Lexington, Va.)

cy generated strange juxtapositions. Genuine democratic reform, al-
beit forged through political pressure and compromise, took place
alongside some of the most blatant infringements of civil rights in U.S.
history. Acts of courage and self-sacrifice, by both those who support-
ed and those who opposed the war, coexisted with the selfish greed of
war profiteers and the shaming of young men into enlisting. In 1918,

outright brutality and illegality could pass as patriotic service; what criticism existed of the war effort emerged almost exclusively from *within* it, slyly and subversively in texts that otherwise professed loyalty to the national mobilization.

The criminal conviction of the national IWW leadership, brought to trial in Chicago in the summer of 1918, was a foregone conclusion. On 30 August, having deliberated for about an hour, the jury convicted ninety-six IWW leaders on over one hundred charges each, ranging from individual acts of war sabotage to participation in a general conspiracy to disrupt war mobilization. The conspiracy theory was crucial, for a number of the defendants never had evidence presented against them individually and prosecutors never produced credible evidence that the IWW engaged in the destructive sabotage with which its members were charged (Dubofsky 163). But the Espionage Act had, after all, focused on treasonous speech rather than action. Accordingly, federal prosecutors simply quoted correspondence seized in the September 1917 searches of IWW headquarters, read *Solidarity* editorials and songs from the "Little Red Song Book," and displayed cartoons from IWW newspapers and stickerettes—small gum-backed publicity stickers sold to union members. Neither the presiding judge, Kenesaw Mountain Landis, nor the jury seemed bothered that many of these materials had been written or published prior to the U.S. declaration of war, some of it even before August 1914 (Peterson and Fite 238). With these documents, the IWW members were convicted of impeding the U.S. war effort before any such effort had existed. Judge Landis's pronouncement at the sentencing hearing was chilling: "In times of peace, you have a legal right to oppose, by free speech, preparations for war. But when war is declared, that right ceases" (qtd. in Peterson and Fite 240). Public commentary was less likely to focus on the ruling's implications for free speech than on the political opportunity it provided for suppressing the IWW and other radical groups. The *Kansas City Journal* claimed that the IWW represented the "hellish character of the Bolsheviki of America" and that 1918 was the time "to wipe out the I.W.W., the Non-Partizan League, the radical Socialists, and all other un-American and anti-American organizations on this continent" (qtd. in "Branding" 14).

In light of these sentiments, it may be surprising to find any dissenting poetry published in 1918. In "The Captain Said," Covington Hall (writing under his pen name Covington Ami) uses a Bolshevik ship's captain as a vehicle to ridicule capitalists who claim to be "true democrats." It was one of several confrontational poems and articles published in the IWW's western organs *Industrial Worker* and *Lumberjack*

Bulletin, the latter a single-page publication run on odd weeks to compensate for the loss of staff and income during the sedition trials. Additional installments of "The Sayings of Patsy" ran in the *New York Call.* The last, appearing on 17 March, has much the same bravado as the segments from the previous fall, though the poem's satire peters out into serious wishful thinking by the final lines:

> Anyway,
> We don't need
> To be worried,
> Because
> "The forces of reaction"
> Really are not so forceful
> As they would like
> To seem.

Since the *Call* was permitted to continue publishing throughout the year, there might have seemed some truth to Patsy's remarks, yet radical critics actually were being overwhelmed by the collective forces of patriotic enthusiasm: editorial collaboration at the "capitalist" newspapers, war posters and Vigilantes' poems provided gratis to the national mobilization, the Four Minute Men giving patriotic speeches during movie intermissions, liberty bond campaigns, food conservation programs, and on and on.

The systematic harnessing of poetic craft to the war machine was relished by both professional and amateur American poets. Published in 1917 just prior to the U.S. declaration of war, John Curtis Underwood's *War Flames* had hymned the powers of modern industrial machinery and Taylorite organization, steel, fire, and high explosives—albeit selectively, only when such powers were wielded by Allied forces. Underwood's group of poems published in June 1918 in *Poetry* magazine, including "At Bethlehem," just as vigorously applied the same poetic and rhetorical techniques to the American military-industrial complex. Meanwhile, in March *Poetry* magazine premiered the work of soldier-poet. Baker Brownell, who perhaps outdoes Underwood in substituting the "certainty" of inanimate steel for the troubling, human task of ethical choice: "the soldier loved his steel, / . . . Its fearlessness of fact, its bitterness of line, / Its certainty and decision."

Writers who had always thought of themselves—and would always subsequently think of themselves—as connoisseurs of high culture wrote doggerel verse supporting the war effort. Alice Corbin Henderson, associate editor at *Poetry,* wrote a poem entitled "The Planting of the Green" that celebrated the mobilization of American agriculture

by the Food Administration. Private citizens felt obliged to publish, at
their own expense, the one book of poetry they would ever write in
their lives. Poets who had earlier expressed reservations about—or
outright protest of—intervention now proclaimed America's "crusade"
in Europe. Edith Matilda Thomas, who had once written in praise of
the women's peace parade and enjoined Russia's soldiers to resist
mobilization, wrote many heartily patriotic poems, including some for
the Vigilantes, and one for the *New York Times* entitled "'Verses'—for
an Unknown Soldier" that compared the art of poetry with the patri-
otic knitting of countless women across the country. Next to food con-
servation, knitting socks, sweaters, and other woolen garments for the
soldiers "over there" was probably the national service most engaged
in by American women, and in 1918 the *New York Sun* initiated a poet-
ry contest with the express purpose of stimulating both this patriotic
knitting and the composition of poems about it. From 12 May until 10
November, the Sunday edition of the *Sun* published first, second, and
third prizewinners and ten honorable mentions selected by the edito-
rial staff, and these, "a few of which we did not hesitate to acclaim as
genuine poems!" (Dounce viii) were published in 1919 as a book-length
collection entitled (what else?) *Sock Songs.*

Many patriotic poems from the year are verse of the lightest variety,
perhaps surprising given that by the fall American soldiers were fully
engaged on the Western Front and suffering higher casualty rates than
their more seasoned Allies and that on the home front Americans were
suffering their own staggering losses from the influenza epidemic. Yet
the levity of the verse surrounded disparate content: expressions of
Yankee good humor and high spirits; ridicule of persistent war oppo-
nents like Wisconsin senator Robert M. La Follette; but also wry, if not
quite protesting, commentary on the disjunctions between patriotic
rhetoric and praxis. Like the most famous of the English soldier-poets,
some versifiers of the American Expeditionary Force described the
disparity between the facts of military life and the enthusiasm of civil-
ian friends and relatives for it. Sidney G. Doolittle, an ambulance driver,
spares not even the patriotic knitters, who "send me . . . strange things
called sweaters, / And are always knitting miles of mufflers." Poets on
the home front, even if their witticism avoided the positively subver-
sive, likewise found plenty to satirize. "O, You Hoover!" published
anonymously in the *Detroit Labor News,* says nothing that the postmas-
ter would trouble himself over. But from its opening lines poking fun
at the Food Administration—"My Tuesdays are meatless, / My Wednes-
days are wheatless; / I am getting more eatless each day"—to the emp-

ty and just-too-emphatic final line—"My! how I do hate the Kaiser!"—
the poem undermines the pomp and certainty of patriotic rhetoric.

While black Americans were generally supportive of intervention,
they could find as much cause for criticism in their country's war pol-
icy as any other group, and their poems contain some of the sharpest
critiques of any published in 1918. Black Americans were drafted just
as whites—a policy fought for by leaders in the black community—but
once in the armed services they were treated very differently. Black
enlisted men were placed in segregated army units; they were officered
mostly, and in the upper ranks entirely, by whites; and they were ex-
cluded from the marines, the Coast Guard, and the Army Aviation
Corps. The 10,000 African Americans in the navy were assigned exclu-
sively to mess duty and coal-shoveling, and blacks in the army were
assigned disproportionately to various services of supply, almost ex-
clusively providing the stevedore labor in French ports, for example
(Wynn 178). In spite of a considerable military record proving other-
wise, black soldiers were thought unreliable in combat, so while two
out of three white soldiers who reached France saw action at the front,
only one in five of their black counterparts did (Kennedy 162). In
American industry, black labor migrating from the South provided the
ready source of cheap labor that had dried up since 1914, when Euro-
pean immigration was greatly curtailed. Whereas in the forty years since
the end of Reconstruction these migrants had numbered around
67,000, in the six years following the outbreak of the Great War the
number leaped to somewhere between 300,000 and 500,000 (Wynn
180–81). But if job opportunities in the urban North were better than
in the South, racial tension was no less sharp; lynching was replaced
by antiblack rioting. The worst incident occurred in East St. Louis in
the summer of 1917, when the Aluminum Ore Company used black
replacement workers to break a strike by the American Federation of
Labor and white workers retaliated by attacking black neighborhoods.
Over four days of rioting in July, 39 blacks and 8 whites were killed, over
6,000 people, mostly blacks, were left homeless, and $400,000 worth
of property was burned or looted (D. Lewis 536–37).

As if to prove that dilemmas for black Americans could get still more
complicated, on 23 August 1917 black soldiers of the regular army sta-
tioned in racially hostile Houston went on a rampage after a member
of their unit was wrongfully arrested. They descended upon the police
station where he had been held, killing sixteen whites and wounding
eleven in the space of two hours. Nineteen attackers were subsequent-
ly executed by hanging, and another sixty-seven were court-martialed

and sent to prison for terms varying from a few years to life. Thirteen with death sentences were executed in December without being allowed to appeal (D. Lewis 542–43). Among black Americans, sympathy for these black soldiers wrestled with alarm at the possibility of white reprisals; rage at the discrimination that had driven the soldiers to violence contended with respect for nonviolence and law, however imperfectly administered. Though the NAACP's W. E. B. Du Bois made no effort to exculpate the black soldiers' actions, he did compare the two incidents to show racial inequality under the law: while many more blacks were killed in East St. Louis than were whites either there or in Houston, as many blacks as whites received sentences of up to fifteen years for the northern rioting, whereas in Houston all the blacks accused were convicted, forty-one receiving life sentences in addition to the nineteen executed ("Houston"). A poem published in the February 1918 issue of *Crisis*, "These" by Lucian Watkins, went farther, commemorating the executed as black heroes. "Lord, these are Thine who pay their price / For what a freeman's soul is worth," Watkins wrote in this short, nine-line poem elaborately illustrated with a scene echoing Augustus Saint-Gaudens's bronze relief of Colonel Shaw and his black soldier-martyrs of the Civil War—but minus the paternalistic figure of Shaw on his horse (reproduced in my *Partisans and Poets* 209).

Yet if black Americans sympathized with the Houston mutineers, most leaders and the communities they represented came to support the war, and Du Bois and the NAACP clearly contributed to this trend. The crucial factor was almost certainly the overwhelming number of black Americans in uniform. African American troops of the regular army were among the first to go into action in France; four separate regiments were assigned to fight with the French, and some units were in combat already in May and June 1918 helping to stem the final German offensive. The work of their 400,000 men in uniform was a natural source of pride, and their families and communities could hardly be anything but supportive. Already before the intervention, blacks had seized upon their soldiers as models of initiative and action; in 1916 Major Charles Young, then the highest-ranking black officer in the army, had won the NAACP's Spingarn Award for distinguished achievement (Du Bois, "Young"). Interest in the military profession and in the fate of the U.S. Army—coupled with the hope that black military service would pave the way for greater political and social freedom at home—do much to explain Du Bois's infamous "Close Ranks" editorial of July 1918 in which he declared, "Let us, while this war lasts, forget our special grievances and close our ranks shoulder to shoulder with our white fellow citizens and the allied nations that are fighting for democracy. We make no ordinary sacrifice, but we make it gladly and willingly with our eyes lifted up to the hills."

But although acquiescence to the powerful forces of national mobilization was the de facto position of the black community generally and of Du Bois specifically, Du Bois was not suggesting either that black "grievances" be set aside permanently or that black civil rights could be achieved without further political and social struggle. A poem such as Allen Tucker's "The 367th Infantry" that sees equality for black Americans as an accomplished reality did not represent Du Bois's position; even that the *Crisis* reprinted the poem from the *New York Times* does not indicate Du Bois's endorsement but rather his tendency to reprint or report on virtually anything in the mainstream press that touched on black America, however flawed its politics. Although in wartime black activists and intellectuals could not press demands for civil rights as the suffrage activists did, they were far from being passively accepting and uncritical of the war. Of this, poems published by black authors in 1918 leave little doubt. Besides his tribute to the Houston mutineers, Lucian Watkins's "The Negro Soldiers of America: What We Are Fighting For" pledges fealty to Woodrow Wilson's war for democracy only, and perfunctorily, in its first stanza, then goes on for seven more to denounce a recent Tennessee lynching and to proclaim the centrality, for black soldiers, of the war for civil rights. Furthermore, black poets were among the first to step forward after the armistice to call attention to the unfinished work of building true democracy at home. Published in December in William Stanley Braithwaite's anthology *Victory!* Fenton Johnson's "The New Day" adapts the form of a gospel acclamation to celebrate the end of the war, but also asserts plainly that black Americans were fighting in Europe to restore political liberties that they themselves did not enjoy in their own country: "We were not free, our tawny hands were tied; / But Belgium's plight and Serbia's woes we shared / Each rise of sun or setting of the moon." Published in the *Liberator* the same month, Mary Burrill's memorial "To a Black Soldier Fallen in the War" plays on its theme with only the subtlest, yet unmistakable, irony: "'Why should *he* thus perish? / Why, for freedom, die?'" The question galled many African Americans, who, like critics on the political Left, could not in 1918 apply the term *freedom* to the United States without uncertainty, equivocation, or downright ridicule.

Newspaper clipping
McLandburgh Wilson

POETIC JUSTICE

If any man is found
  With treason on his tongue,
What justice shall we mete?
  How shall his doom be rung?

To make him kiss the flag
  Atonement will not suit;
From such polluted lips
  Quite useless to salute.

On war stamps make him spend
  All riches he has gained,
And have him lick them fast
  Until his tongue is sprained.

Detroit Labor News, 1 February
Anonymous

O, YOU HOOVER!

My Tuesdays are meatless,
My Wednesdays are wheatless;

I am getting more eatless each day.
My home it is heatless,
My bed it is sheetless;
   They're all sent to the Y.M.C.A.
The barrooms are treatless,
My coffee is sweetless;
   Each day I grow poorer and wiser;
My stockings are feetless,
My trousers are seatless;
   My! how I do hate the Kaiser!

Poetry, March
BAKER BROWNELL

FREEBOURNE'S RIFLE

"It's an old gun," the major said,
"But clean—give him excellent;"
And pushed the oil-scrubbed gun
Back on private Freebourne's chest.
"An old gun! Hell, yes!" said Freebourne,
When he tried to turn it in
To the Q. M. for a new one;
"I put two hours a day on it."
But Freebourne loved its steel;
He never took the other.
Two hours on steel, man's metal,
Till the inner twirl of bore
Carried the light in gleaming gutters
Round, coiled round on itself,
To lurch pointed bullets true
A thousand yards. Two hours
Testing the severe materiality of steel:
Steel thought, steel calculation,
Severe, absolute in hardness,
Loyal to existence—
It could transcend sense sogginess and flesh.

Two hours the soldier loved his steel,
Its truth, its edge,
Its fearlessness of fact, its bitterness of line,
Its certainty and decision.

Richmond Planet, 2 March
LUCIAN B. WATKINS

THE NEGRO SOLDIERS OF AMERICA: WHAT WE ARE FIGHTING FOR

We fight—and for DEMOCRACY
  Lord, we are glad of this sweet chance
To brave whatever hells there be
  Beside the bleeding heart of France!

We fight—for all who suffer pain,
  We give our souls in sympathy;
We fight that Liberty may reign
  From Berlin unto Tennessee.

To Tennessee—where last we saw
  Infernal brands of death applied
To men—our men, within the law,
  But "lawless" as they moaned and died.

In Tennessee—where vain, it seems,
  Have been the gifts of passing years,
Where vain have been the eternal dreams
  And toil of Lincoln, sad with tears;

In Tennessee—where Life's best part
  Rich "pearls are cast before the swine,"
CHRIST'S GOLDEN RULE that rules the heart
  And keeps man nearer The Divine.

In Tennessee—where Wrong is Might
  With Hate and Horror on the throne,
Where GOD'S DEMOCRACY of LIGHT
  AND LOVE, it seems, has never shone.

In Tennessee—and all her kin
  Of sister criminals, year by year,
Who've lost the consciousness of sin,
  The tenderness that is a tear.

We fight—and for DEMOCRACY
  We'll dare Atlantic's tragic foam,
Go "over the top"—Lord, let us see
  PEACE AND ITS HAPPINESS AT HOME!

Rimes in Olive Drab [ca. March]
JOHN PIERRE ROCHE

"YOU WERE SO WHITE, SO SOFT"

I knew your gentle touch
  Through all those many years—
Unheeding then, but now
  How memory endears
That golden span of time
  And makes me wish anew
That, since you could not come,
  I might have stayed with you.

We said good-bye, and yet
  I went without a thought
Of what my going meant,
  Or how you held me taut;
And yet the thought of you
  Each night repose defeats—
Oh, would I knew again
  The luxury of sheets!

Lumberjack Bulletin, 9 March
COVINGTON AMI

THE CAPTAIN SAID

A stout ship to Seattle came;
Her flag was red, her crew the same,
And Shilka was the good ship's name.

A rumor roamed that in her hold
Were oodle tons of purest gold,
And awesome plots, and fearsome plans,
And secret codes of Rebel Clans.

The Plutes and Pollies fumed for fair,
And Mimic Men mussed up the air;
They called a pow-wow, then a troop,
And swarmed down on the red-flagged sloop.

They raked the good ship fore and aft,
From bowsprit to propeller shaft;
They searched the cook, they searched the crew,
The bosun, mate and captain, too.

They seized their papers, pens and books,
And likewise grabbed their grappling hooks;
They chased a clue, they smelt a rat,
And swore they saw a sabby cat.

They heard his silent footsteps fall,
His grey ghost scratch and cat-a-waul;
Their Christian charity awoke,
And, conscience stricken, thus they spoke:

"O comrades of the Shilka, hear!
Some ass has blunderbussed, we fear;
Regretting that we showed our cards,
The chamber begs your pardon, pards."

And then they asked them for to ride,
The Rebels with the Sons of Pride;
They fed them up in sumptuous style,
And, talked of dollars all the while.

They cursed the Czars; the Kaisers damned;
They threw the bull, they flimmed and flammed;
They spake of soul and sourmash,
But evermore came back to CASH.

It was "some" outing for the Rebs,
"Some" entertainment for the plebs;
But when they heard the Dicks and Fats
All swear themselves "true democrats,"
The captain loosed a loud guffaw,
A Bolsheviki big haw-haw,
And, sailing, said: "Like hell you are!"

Vigilantes Press Release, 18 April
WALLACE IRWIN

ODE TO TONSILITIS

Since Senatorial Rules decree once more—
    Even while Prussia threatens us with slaying—
That one wild donkey still may hold the floor
    And block an entire nation with his braying;

Yea, since the chin is mightier than the sword,
    The lung and larynx deadlier than reason
And Robert spurns the Flag beneath the Ford
    In one continuous honk of windy treason;

Ah! then come forth, thou dread but welcome one,
    Nymph of the swollen throat, fair Tonsilitis!
Go gulping to the Sage of Madison,
    Woo him with wreaths of asthma and bronchitis!

Snuggle beside his Senatorial seat,
    Lure him with kisses sneezy, damp and reckless
Until the cold which now afflicts his feet
    Climbs to the place where Mabel wore the necklace.

Then must that rare trombone grow fogged and cease,
    That wealth of words lie fallow in his wallet;

There'll be no more Atrocities of Peace
   Committed then by Robert M. La Follette.

Then will the eagle o'er the rostrum shriek
   While patriots clasp hands in satisfaction,
"The gentleman from Wisconsin cannot speak—
   Rejoice, ye nations! Now we'll get some action!"

Poetry, May
WALLACE STEVENS
From Lettres d'un Soldat

V

> *J'ai la ferme espérance; mais surtout j'ai confiance en la justice*
> *éternelle, quelque surprise qu'elle cause à l'humaine idée que nous*
> *en avons.*
>
>   *(26 novembre)*

THE SURPRISES OF THE SUPERHUMAN

The palais de justice of chambermaids
Tops the horizon with its colonnades.

If it were lost in Uebermenschlichkeit,
Perhaps our wretched state would soon come right.

For somehow the brave dicta of its kings
Make more awry our faulty human things.

VI

> *Bien chère mère aimée, . . . Pour ce qui est de ton coeur, j'ai telle-*
> *ment confiance en ton courage, qu'à l'heure actuelle cette certitude*
> *est mon grand réconfort. Je sais que ma mère a atteint à cette lib-*
> *erté d'âme qui permet de contempler le spectacle universel.*
>
>   *(7 décembre)*

There is another mother whom I love,
O chère maman, another, who, in turn,
Is mother to the two of us, and more,

In whose hard service both of us endure
Our petty portion in the sacrifice.
Not France! France also serves the invincible eye,
That, from her helmet terrible and bright,
Commands the armies; the relentless arm,
Devising proud, majestic issuance.
Wait now; have no rememberings of hope,
Poor penury. There will be voluble hymns
Come swelling, when, regardless of my end,
The mightier mother raises up her cry:
And little will or wish, that day, for tears.

VII

La seule sanction pour moi est ma conscience. Il faut nous confier à une justice impersonelle, indépendante de tout facteur humain; et à une destinée utile et harmonieuse malgré toute horreur de forme.

(15 janvier)

NEGATION

Hi! The creator too is blind,
Struggling toward his harmonious whole,
Rejecting intermediate parts—
Horrors and falsities and wrongs;
Incapable master of all force,
Too vague idealist, overwhelmed
By an afflatus that persists.
For this, then, we endure brief lives,
The evanescent symmetries
From that meticulous potter's thumb.

VIII

Hier soir, rentrant dans ma grange, ivresse, rixes, cris, chants, et hurlements. Voilà la vie!

(4 février)

John Smith and his son, John Smith,
    And his son's son John, and-a-one
    And-a-two and-a-three
And-a-rum-tum-tum, and-a

Lean John, and his son, lean John,
   And his lean son's John, and-a-one
   And-a-two and-a-three
And-a-drum-rum-rum, and-a
Rich John, and his son, rich John,
   And his rich son's John, and-a-one
   And-a-two and-a-three
And-a-pom-pom-pom, and-a
Wise John, and his son, wise John,
   And his wise son's John, and-a-one
   And-a-two and-a-three
And-a-fee and-a-fee and-a-fee
   And-a-fee-fo-fum—
Voilà la vie, la vie, la vie,
   And-a-rummy-tummy-tum
   And-a-rummy-tummy-tum.

IX

   La mort du soldat est près des choses naturelles.

                                   (5 mars)

Life contracts and death is expected,
As in a season of autumn.
The soldier falls.

He does not become a three-days' personage,
Imposing his separation,
Calling for pomp.

Death is absolute and without memorial,
As in a season of autumn,
When the wind stops.

When the wind stops and, over the heavens,
The clouds go, nevertheless,
In their direction.

New York Times, 6 May
BERTON BRALEY

CONSEQUENCES

He "wanted to go," but his wife said "No!"
　And she wept at the very thought,
So he stayed at home while across the foam
　The war of the worlds was fought!
He was held and bound to the daily round
　By the toils of a clinging love
That would make the goal of an eagle's soul
　The cote of a cooing dove.

He "wanted to go," but his wife cried "No!"
　And she held him there with her,
While the news that came from the war's great game
　Set his brain and his heart awhirr;
He was "mad" to sail on the soldier's trail,
　To venture and risk and dare,
To face the brunt at the very front
　Of the fighting over there.

He "wanted to go," but his wife wailed "No!"
　Unequal to sacrifice.
Though the chains might chafe she would hold him safe—
　And she paid a heavy price!
For his love turned hate for his selfish mate,
　As the strongest passion can,
So she lost her "romance"—and he his chance
　To live or to die a Man!

Vigilantes Press Release, [May]
VACHEL LINDSAY

THE JAZZ BIRD

The Jazz Bird sings a barnyard song,
  A cock-a-doodle bray,
A jingle-bells, a boiler works,
  A he-man's roundelay.

The eagle said: "Son Jazz Bird,
  I send you out to fight."
And the Jazz Bird spread his sunflower wings,
  And roared with all his might.

And they woke to it in Oregon,
  In Florida and Maine,
And the land was dark with airships
  In the darting Jazz Bird's train.

Crossing the roaring ocean
  His bell-mouth shook the sky,
And the Yankees in the trenches
  Gave back the hue and cry.

And Europe had not heard the like,
  And Germany went down.
The Jazz Bird with the headlight eyes
  Tore off the Kaiser's crown.

At midnight on a haunted road
  A star bends low and sees
The Kaiser and his row of sons
  Marching at their ease.

Their necks are broken by the hemp,
  They goose-step in a line,
Their stripped bones strutting in the wind
  Swinging as a sign

That Jazz Birds come on sunflower wings
  When loathsome tyrants rise . . .
The Jazz Bird guards the gallows,
  He lights it with his eyes.

Poetry, June
JOHN CURTIS UNDERWOOD

AT BETHLEHEM

Twenty-six thousand men are building at Bethlehem
Armor plates and palisades and props of steel for the peace of Christ,
That comes momently, by breathing spells, in a world forever at war:
Twenty-six thousand men sweating blindly to build a world forever
    beginning to fall;
Twenty-six thousand men are making tools for breaking, scrapping, scraping
    and fixing foundations anew.

For life ever fuses and glows,
Like the heart of a rose in the fire that eats up red billets of steel like raw
    fagots of wood.
And a war is as good as a rose in the eyes of the Watcher of Space;
A war is as brief as a rose in its growth and its death in the fire of the Forger
    of Stars.
And the fire ever burns out the dross in the depths of the stone and the soul.
All the fires that ape or man ever kindled on earth were lit and fused to keep
    these crucibles boiling.

And now they roll a loaded crucible that flames white-hot along the level rails
    and swinging truck-ways overhead.
And the moulds are made ready and prepared.
And they look like trenches of shadow, before the raw red tide of war pours
    into them.
And one half-naked foreman of his gang is a general of today's grim shaping
    of life.

A general who knows his job and holds it hard-fisted,
Holds it and sways it like a tool he beats and welds and batters with.
For the war is a job and a tool, that must be beaten out and battled with to
    the bitter end of the stint; and finally finished.

Ten huge trip-hammers rising and falling in cadenced choruses affirm it.
Twenty-six rolling-mills, that print a gospel new and red in steel still raw, are
    ready to publish it.
Twenty-six thousand men, twenty-six million men, in smoke and fumes and
    mud and grime, assert and by their blood and breath maintain it.

Poetry, June

THE RED COFFINS

After the revolution in Petrograd,
They made a great common grave in a vaster parade ground outside the city.
And they brought the red coffins of those who fell fighting for freedom
To honor and bury them.

They piled them tier by tier while the crowd in silence watched them.
And as the pile rose and spread, to many it seemed
Like the red blood of Russia welling from a mortal wound.
And some saw red fagots of freedom rising and kindling a fire that would
  warm all the world.
But no man there could tell the truth of it.

Vigilantes Press Release, 3 June
ALICE CORBIN

THE PLANTING OF THE GREEN

Oh, Woody dear, and did ye hear
The noise that's going round?
We are rising by ten thousands
And we're ploughin' of the ground!
We are droppin' in the corn and beans,
We are plantin' wheat for all,
We are mobilizin' turnips, too,
An' answerin' the call!

Your Auntie Sam is makin' jam
For all the boys to eat,
And when she gets her dander up,
You know she can't be beat!
She's bossin' all the folks about,
The farm's no home at all!
It's just a mobilizin' camp
For answerin' the call!

So, Woody dear, ye need not fear.
The country's coming strong;
You can hear the factories' whistles,
You can hear the dummy's gong,
You can hear the crops a-sproutin',
You can hear the seedlings say,
"We're pushing up for freedom, too—
We'll do our bit today!"

Your Uncle Sam says, "Here I am!"
We're marching everywhere;
We are planting beets an' bayonets,
Oh, we've hayseeds in our hair!
But we're marching to the music
Of a lasting peace for all—
With our reapers and our muskets
We are answering the call!

New York Sun, 9 June
HELEN TOPPING MILLER

[SOCK SONG]

Will Cosette or Adelaide or Jeanne with eyes of blue,
Pick up the stitch I drop by chance, and mend the toes of you?
Threading a loyal smile for France the dainty stitches through.

Or will those downcast maiden eyes see, through a golden haze,
Some gallant lad, some khaki lad, with brave audacious ways?
Hear the little lilting pipes that play, above the Marsellaise?

Methinks it were the wisest thing to knit you strong and true,
Lest Cosette or Adelaide or Jeanne with eyes of blue,
Should drop another stitch, perchance, and spoil the toes of you!

New York Times, 12 June
ALLEN TUCKER

THE 367TH INFANTRY

Down the street, between the waiting crowds, they come—
The Buffaloes,
The Black Regiment!
The band ahead,
Thumping, crashing,
Booming, smashing,
"Onward, Christian soldiers," fills the air.
Black are the lines—
All splendid black,
Beneath the sharp bayonets,
Under the high waving flags;
A long way they have marched,
Down the long years they have come,
Through suffering and despair,
From Africa to Manhattan,
From slavery to freedom,
Men—citizens—at last!
No masters, no protectors!
Owning themselves,
Saving themselves,
Marching, marching,
Rank on rank,
Black—all black!
Africa here—
Embattled!
Free!
Now ready to fight for us,
Now ready to fight with us,
Ready to fight for themselves—
Ready to fight,
Ready to die,
For Freedom!

Poetry, August
AJAN SYRIAN

THE PRAYER RUG OF ISLAM

Men there are who live among flowers
And the colors of the rose are known to them in the seed—
Even as the hands of a woman in the dark
Make of the shadows a garden,
Filling the night of her husband with fragrance.
Men there are who know the stars:
To them, the night sky is a velvet woof
Crossed with the tint of jewels and April waters.
It is a carpet infinitely patterned,
Whereon the Poet-God lies, half dreaming—
Amid the perfect and the boundless
Yearning for the wistfulness of things imperfect,
And so making the Song that is Humanity.

Even so am I to the roseate carpets of the Orient.

The Magic of Khorassan weavers is known to me:
The dyers of Khiva and Damascus,
And the Arabian dreamers in purple,
The resonant color-singers of old Turkestan,
Have come to me out of the dim shadows
Of the carpet-bales,
Under the flickering gas-jets,
In the back room of a little shop on upper Broadway.
For—how long ago!—in the time of peace
I was a rug vendor.

Nineteen Hundred and Sixteen, *Anno Domini*:
And Spring bursting with young green in the parks,
And bird-wings rhythmically weaving
Into the New Earth's carpet
Little mottoes of freedom!
Gajor wept and said, "You will never return."
And my friends in the Syrian café on Tenth Avenue
Laid their hands heavily upon me.
But I saw only the hands of the ancient color-singers beckoning;

Heavier were their ghostly fingers tapping at my soul.
Oh! never were the lips of her I love
More desirous and more dear
Than when she alone whispered:
"If thou diest, I die; yet go!"

Makhir Subatu!
Nineteen Hundred and Sixteen, the Year of Our Lord,
And Spring; and the Rose of Sharon blooming
By crimson-clotted brooks:
And gold-tongued lilies
That once, with my youth, answered the nightingale,
Now dumb beneath the moon,
Their white throats choked with blood!
Among the trampled green of olive-groves
Are strewn the stained girdles of young women,
Or wrapped about small—pitifully small—black mounds of death.

Sky-blue, sea-blue, girdles of young women
That once sacredly bound the Hope of a Race,
Waiting the loosening hands of Love;
And little tunics of slain children
Woven through the woof, like the snow-flower pattern,
Under triumphant spring-green banners
Blowing from the four corners of the hills.
And the fringes that hold the Sacred Carpet up to Heaven—
The countless thick-packed white fringes—
These are the bones of men who loved their Christ.
For this is the great Prayer-rug of Islam.

I have seen the Turk weaving his Sacred Carpet,
I have knelt on the Prayer-rug of Islam!
I am apostate, dear Christ!
Christian and poet no longer, lover no more,
How shall I lay hands on my beloved's blue girdle?
My heart is a place of swords!

Songs of the Trenches (September)
BYRON BEARDSLEY

THE NATIONAL GAME

The "Huns" had not been challenged nor scheduled to appear,
But the game began four years ago on the German-Belge frontier;
The Allied team was crippled, but had no time to stall,
For the voice of domination had plainly cried, "Play ball!"

In the early innings of the game the Germans took the lead,
Their forty years of practice had developed lots of speed;
The Allies' southpaw, Belgium, was pitching clever ball,
But his comrades and his captains considered him too small.

So rather than to lose the game by taking such a chance,
They shifted him to second and substituted "France";
The Germans thought the time was ripe to carry out their mission,
And figured they could win the game through "France's" poor condition.

A "Boche" came up and toed the plate and tripled over Arras;
He decided he could stretch the hit and slide right into Paris;
But the ball was neatly handled, by fielders that were clever—
In the famous battle of the Marne he was tagged by General Joffre.

The "lucky seventh" rolled around—the Allies came to bat;
Old Kaiser Bill was pitching, and his arm was sore at that.
Canada singled o'er Vimy Ridge (he willingly paid the price);
Then Edith Cavel[l] walked up to the plate and came through with a
    sacrifice.

Italy slammed an offensive, which rang with a sounding thud;
His spikes got tangled in German intrigue and he tripped and fell in the
    mud.
The next ball pitched was a beauty—knee-high and close to the shanks,
And a clever drive for a double was made by the Britisher "tanks."

The splendid Allied rally had filled the "Huns" with doubt.
With two men on and no one down the "Russian Bear" struck out;
So Hindenburg, who's catching, has called for the Kaiser's "spitter,"
And swinging his bats on the side-line is "Sammy," the club's pinch hitter.

His eye is keen, his spikes are sharp—he's filled with the courage of youth;

Democracy gleams in his clear gray eyes—his bat bears the trade-mark of
   Truth.

Now this is as far as the game has advanced, so of course we can tell you no
   more;

But soon every fan in this troubled old world will know the completed box
   score.

Sergeant Byron Beardsley, Q.M.C.,

War Risk Insurance Department

Songs of the Trenches (September)
SIDNEY G. DOOLITTLE

ENTHUSIASTS

I hate Enthusiasts:
They fret me.

There are the Bachelor Aunts;
The ones who make the patent-medicine business pay,
And who go around expecting to die with every step.
They send me abdominal bands and psalm-books,
And what to do for lumbago;
When I'm worrying if the next shell has my name on it.
They are always trying to impress upon me
That the Kaiser is a dreadful man
And that this war is a terrible thing—
As if I thought it was
A blooming picnic!
Will some kind soul enlighten them?

And there are the Sweet Things,
The little original "bit-doers."
They write me letters about dances and teas and things,
While I sit in the mud and read them.
Their ideas of how to show their spirit are funny,
But perhaps it's punishment for my sins.
They send me chewing-gum and strange things called sweaters,
And are always knitting miles of mufflers.
They often wish they could come over here

And get right into it.
I wish they could, too—
Then I wouldn't have to answer their letters.

Then there are the Fire-Eaters
Who go around crying for raw meat and blood,
And who belong to the Odd Fellows.
They want me to hang the Kaiser in every letter,
But don't tell me how to go about it.
They like to tell me how I'm helping
Make the world safe for Democrats,
As if that would spur me on.
And, Lord! how they'd like to get into the army!
They'd show the Boche what's what!
Well, I won't stand in their way—
They can have my place any day.

And then there are the Family Friends,
The ones who used to hold me in their laps,
But suppose I've forgotten them.
Now I'll have to forget all over again.
They have always just seen my folks,
And think Mother is bearing up well
But Father is looking older,
They complain about the restrictions in America—
"Why, I can hardly get enough meat for Rover!"
They wish they could do something for me,
Just for old times' sake.
They can—just one thing:
Stop writing me!

I hate Enthusiasts:
They fret me.

                                        Sidney G. Doolittle

S.S.U. 621, Convois Automobiles.

Joseph Pennell Del. "That Liberty Shall Not Perish from the Earth."
Color Poster. Washington, D.C.: U.S. Treasury Department, 1918.
(From original at the Joseph M. Bruccoli Great War Collection,
Special Collections Library, University of Virginia Library.)

The Drums in Our Street (September)
MARY CAROLYN DAVIES

FIRE OF THE SUN

Passionate children of the sun—
You are one and I am one.
A piece of his fire burns still in you;
And in me, too.

Lower your lids and veil your eyes.
Let us pretend that we are wise,
That we are very wise, and that you
Can smother that fire, and that I can, too.

Let us forget that we are young,
And have wanting in us. Let us go
Walking cautiously and slow
All these folk among.

(Fire of the sun, smother, smoulder!)
Let us pretend that we are older;
And that we are calm, and do not know.
(Fire of the sun, burn low!)

Let us laugh and let us sing,
That will be a pleasant thing.

Let us look at life, and weigh,
And scrutinize it well, and say,
"We think we will not buy today."

     ଶ ଶ ଶ

But war, war, war!—
Let us flame now before
It quenches us. Let us flame high
Ere it is on us; you and I!

New York Sun, 1 September
EDWARD TEN BROECK PERINE

MY AUNT'S LITTLE NOTE

With Loving Memories of Peter I. and Jeanette Ford Ten Broeck

It happened in April, '61; she pinned within the toe
   A note that read: "I hope they fit—and
Perhaps you'll let me know."
   Soon a soldier boy wrote thankfully, and
Then they both wrote more,
   While she kept that Yank in woollen socks,
Until the end of the war.

Four years passed by before they met (now
   You'll guess the rest, no doubt);
Gun and needles were laid aside, and the
   Wedding bells rang out.
'Twas long ago, but the tale is true, with a
   Moral for those who knit:
Pin a little note in the toe, my dears,
   For perhaps your socks may fit!

New York Times, 8 September
EDITH MATILDA THOMAS

"VERSES"—FOR AN
UNKNOWN SOLDIER

> (Said the Old Professor: "The etymology is probably false: but as
> I watch those rhythmical fingers traveling back and forth, I find
> myself associating the two words—plain English, *stitch,* and
> *stich*—Greek for *verse.*)

These verses I have made for you
Had not the Muse's strict review,
Yet prize them none the less for this—
The measure does not run amiss.

Ere ever they took rhythmic form,
Within my heart the thought was warm;
And, as I turned them, without flaw,
Your face before me oft I saw!

That face, my boy, I never knew;
Yet Fancy all its features drew:
And Fancy saw your hand uplift,
And your eyes scan my simple gift.

So happily the work was done!
For, though you were another's son,
I always thought of you as mine,
While I, long hours, knit line to line.

My boy—and yet, another's son,
What mattered? On the verses run:
And, ere my labor reached its goal,
You were the comrade of my soul!

For me you never knew you fought;
And I—a spark from you I caught,
That fired my thoughts with derring-do—
I dreamed I was a fighter, too!

Now, soberly, I have come back;
Not mine to drive on battle's track.
What are these verses I can give
To one who shall an epic live!

But here's my work—in stanzas twain.
Oh, may it not seem quite in vain,
When your eyes scan, your hands uplift,
This pair of socks—my heart-warm gift!

Scribner's, November
EDITH WHARTON

"ON ACTIVE SERVICE"

American Expeditionary Force

(R.S., August 12th, 1918)
He is dead that was alive.
How shall friendship understand?
Lavish heart and tireless hand
Bidden not to give or strive,
Eager brain and questing eye
Like a broken lens laid by.

He, with so much left to do,
Such a gallant race to run,
What concern had he with you,
Silent Keeper of things done?

Tell us not that, wise and young,
Elsewhere he lives out his plan.
Our speech was sweetest to his tongue,
And his great gift was to be man.

Long and long shall we remember,
In our breasts his grave be made.
It shall never be December
Where so warm a heart is laid,
But in our saddest selves a sweet voice sing,
Recalling him, and Spring.

August, 1918

Newspaper clipping, [ca. November–December]
EDGAR A. GUEST

AT THE PEACE TABLE

Who shall sit at the table, then, when the terms of peace are made—
The wisest men of the troubled lands in their silver and gold brocade?
Yes, they shall gather in solemn state to speak for each living race,
But who shall speak for the unseen dead that shall come to the council place?

Though you see them not and you hear them not, they shall sit at the table, too;
They shall throng the room where the peace is made and know what it is you
    do;
The innocent dead from the sea shall rise to stand at the wise man's side,
And over his shoulder a boy shall look—a boy that they crucified.

You may guard the doors of that council hall with barriers strong and stout,
But the dea[d] unbidden shall enter there, and never you'll shut them out.
And the man that died in the open boat, and the babes that suffered worse,
Shall sit at the table when peace is made by the side of a martyred nurse.

You may see them not, but they'll all be there; when they speak you may fail
    to hear;
You may think that you're making your pacts alone, but their spirits will
    hover near;
And whatever the terms of the peace you make with the tyrant whose hands
    are red,
You must please not only the living here, but must satisfy your dead.

Victory! [December]
MARY CAROLYN DAVIES

FIFTH AVENUE AND GRAND
STREET

I sat beside her, rolling bandages.
I peeped. "Fifth Avenue," her clothes were saying.
It's "Grand Street," I know well, my shirtwaist says,
And shoes, and hat, but then, she didn't hear,

Or she pretended not, for we were laying
Our coats aside, and as we were so near,
She saw my pin like hers. And when girls are
Wearing a pin these days that has a star,
They smile out at each other. We did that,
And then she did n't seem to see my hat.

I sat beside her, handling gauze and lint,
And thought of Jim. She thought of someone too;
Under the smile there was a little glint
In her eyelashes, that was how I knew.
I was n't crying—but I have n't any
Pride in it; we've a better chance than they
To take blows standing, for we've had so many.
We two sat, fingers busy, all that day.

I'd spoken first, if I'd known what to say.
But she did soon, and after, told of him,
The man she wore the star for, and the way
He'd gone at once. I bragged a bit of Jim;
Who would n't who had ever come to know
Him? When the girls all rose to go,
She stood there, shyly, with her gloves half on,
Said, "Come to see me, won't you?" and was gone.

I meant to call, too, I'd have liked it then
For we'd a lot in common, with our men
Across. But now that peace is here again
And our boys safe, I can't help wondering—Well,
Will she forget, and crawl back in her shell
And if I call, say "Show this person out"?
Or still be friendly as she was? I doubt
If Grand will sit beside Fifth Avenue
Again, and be politely spoken to.

We're sisters while the danger lasts, it's true;
But rich and poor's equality must cease
(For women especially), of course, in peace.

Victory! [December]

FENTON JOHNSON

THE NEW DAY

From a vision red with war I awoke and saw the Prince of Peace hovering
over No Man's Land.
Loud the whistles blew and the thunder of cannon was drowned by the
happy shouting of the people.
From the Sinai that faces Armageddon I heard this chant from the throats
of white-robed angels:

Blow your trumpets, little children!
From the East and from the West,
From the cities in the valley,
From God's dwelling on the mountain,
Blow your blast that Peace might know
She is Queen of God's great army.
With the crying blood of millions
We have written deep her name
In the Book of all the Ages;
With the lilies in the valley,
With the roses by the Mersey,
With the golden flower of Jersey
We have crowned her smooth young temples.
Where her footsteps cease to falter
Golden grain will greet the morning,
Where her chariot descends
Shall be broken down the altars
Of the gods of dark disturbance.
Nevermore shall men know suffering,
Nevermore shall women wailing
Shake to grief the God of Heaven.
From the East and from the West,
From the cities in the valley,
From God's dwelling on the mountain,
Little children, blow your trumpets!

From Ethiopia, groaning 'neath her heavy burdens, I heard the music of
the old slave songs.
I heard the wail of warriors, dusk brown, who grimly fought the fight of
others in the trenches of Mars.

I heard the plea of blood stained men of dusk and the crimson in my veins
    leapt furiously.

Forget not, O my brothers, how we fought
In No Man's Land that peace might come again!
Forget not, O my brothers, how we gave
Red blood to save the freedom of the world!
We were not free, our tawny hands were tied;
But Belgium's plight and Serbia's woes we shared
Each rise of sun or setting of the moon.
So when the bugle blast had called us forth
We went not like the surly brute of yore
But, as the Spartan, proud to give the world
The freedom that we never knew nor shared.
These chains, O brothers mine, have weighed us down
As Samson in the temple of the gods;
Unloosen them and let us breathe the air
That makes the goldenrod the flower of Christ.
For we have been with thee in No Man's Land,
Through lake of fire and down to Hell itself;
And now we ask of thee our liberty,
Our freedom in the land of Stars and Stripes.

I am glad that the Prince of Peace is hovering over No Man's Land.

Liberator, December
MARY BURRILL

TO A BLACK SOLDIER FALLEN
IN THE WAR

O Earth, lie light upon him
Deep pillowed on thy breast;
O Winds, blow soft above him
And gently lull to rest.

O questioning Heart, be silent,
Allay the bitter cry—
"Why should *he* thus perish?
Why, for freedom, die?"

PART 7

REPERCUSSIONS

While the big coal and railroad strikes were on this summer we had considerable trouble to hold some of the I.W.W. prisoners in check. . . . When they were first brought to this penitentiary they got up riots in the dining room, refused to work and made much trouble for a former warden and a deputy warden.

Chaplin is more cunning than the average I.W.W. prisoner and he tries in sneaking ways to make trouble for the prison officials, and he is meddlesome and I have had to stop him several times in attempting to send out letters about other prisoners' affairs. . . . Chaplin poses as a painter and poet and is a loafer.

—Leavenworth Penitentiary warden, letter to Assistant Attorney
    General Mabel Walker Willebrandt, September 30, 1922

By the time of the armistice, most poems ever written about the Great War already had been. In 1919 came many single-author collections, but a good number of these were in press prior to November 1918. The anthologies published after 1918 consisted almost exclusively of poems that had first appeared during the war. The corpus of war poetry and of wartime experience embodied therein was treated as something like a holy object, beyond which further literary art seemed not so much superfluity as profanity. The critic John Erskine had written in December 1914, "When we have become hardened to this war or have got further away from its horrors, we may begin to make literary use of them, but at present, it seems, the poets and their readers think it a kind of sacrilege to convert any of this stupendous misery to the purposes of art" (4–5). Writing in July 1917, *Poetry* editor Harriet Monroe goes further, to suggest that the immediate, horror-stricken responses that Erskine found most ethically valid were also likely to be the most aesthetically powerful: "Some critics try to comfort us with the assurance that the best war poem will be written after the war. But history is not convincing on this point. . . . The poet who waits to mature his thought may prove as impotent as the laggard in battle. He should take a gambler's chance of immortality today—tomorrow may be too late" ("Will" 204). Monroe might not have been shocked that Pound's "Hugh Selwyn Mauberley" and T. S. Eliot's *The Waste Land,* both written after the war, would eventually become the best-known Great War poems by Americans. Eliot and Pound, after all, were among her regular contributors. But Monroe and Erskine would presumably have been surprised to learn that these and a handful of other postwar poems would be the *only* ones to secure a place in the literary canon.

I would nevertheless contend that Monroe's and Erskine's assumptions about the importance of the immediate, wartime context are essentially right. The postwar poetry of Eliot and Pound is, of course, not altogether removed from the war's horrors. Both men lived in Europe through much or all of the war. In 1915 Pound had written the text for a book commemorating the young sculptor Henri Gaudier-Brzeska, killed that year in service with France's army. Eliot's 1917 book, *Prufrock and Other Observations,* was dedicated to Jean Verdenal, the French poet and army officer killed in action the previous year, and *The Waste Land,* published in 1922, may be read, Sandra M. Gilbert and Susan Gubar

Armistice Day *1918*, San Francisco. Photograph. (From original at the
San Francisco History Center, San Francisco Public Library.)

argue, "as a dirge for Verdenal" just as satisfactorily as a "generalized meditation on civilization and its discontents" or a specific one on the poet's unhappy marriage (311). Yet the multiple facets of the poem, so prized by modern readers, unmistakably stamp *The Waste Land* as a postwar poem, for "civilization and its discontents" and Eliot's unhappy marriage not only reinforce the elegy for Verdenal but also become, in effect, metonymic substitutions for the war experience: the big picture—the larger cultural vision—and the little one—the personal reference—become the main narratives. Similarly, Pound makes of "Mauberley" an occasion for both denouncing the wartime conduct of England's politicians and military strategists—the old men of Siegfried Sassoon's and Wilfred Owen's verse—and proclaiming agendas more strictly personal and more broadly cultural: it is Pound's renunciation of England as his expatriate home and the first clear enunciation of his peculiar view of "usury" that was to lead him in subsequent years to support Mussolini and flaunt his anti-Semitism publicly. Pound's "Mauberley" and Eliot's *Waste Land* are thus valedictions: farewells not only to the naively optimistic world that preceded the war but also to the world war itself.

By rearticulating the poetic and historical resources of the Great War according to the need of a later historical moment, Eliot's *The Waste Land* and Pound's "Mauberley" do precisely what any postwar war poem must do. Indeed, this rearticulation is just the kind of work that must be done by any postwar *reader* of Great War poetry. Other poets and poems treated the Great War less obliquely, however. Americans who had been most persecuted during the war also suffered most afterward, whether under the suppression of political nonconformity in the Red Scare of 1919–20 or under the more benign neglect of the Republican administrations of the 1920s. Accordingly, the most critically and socially engaged postwar poetry emerged from the ranks of African Americans, Socialists, and conscientious objectors.

W. E. B. Du Bois, reporting from France on the conduct and treatment of African Americans in the armed forces, abruptly recanted his former position that black Americans held common cause with whites in fighting the war. Du Bois's "Documents of the War" revealed to *Crisis* readers that American Expeditionary Force headquarters had advised the French military command that between blacks and whites "relations of business or service only are possible" and that, in the United States, "the black is constantly being censured for his want of intelligence and discretion, his lack of civic and professional conscience and his tendency toward undue familiarity" (17). A letter by Colonel Allen J. Greer, chief of staff of the African American 92d Division, reported on the conduct of the division as follows: "There have been numerous accidental shootings, several murders, and also several cases of patrols or sentinels shooting at each other. . . . They kept their animals and equipment in good condition. . . . They have in fact been dangerous to no one except themselves and women. . . . Accuracy and ability to describe facts is lacking in all [of the officers] and most of them are just plain liars in addition" (19).

Race relations were no better, if not worse, at home. Race riots consumed 1919: more people, blacks and whites alike, were killed in riots during that year than in riots during the war. The worst violence was in Chicago, where thirty blacks and fifteen whites were killed; but some twenty-five other significant disturbances broke out in communities as various as Washington, D.C.; Elaine, Arkansas; Omaha, Nebraska; Knoxville, Tennessee; Longview, Texas; and Charleston, South Carolina (Wynn 189). Whereas most previous riots had followed the pattern of those in East St. Louis, in which casualties and property damage were suffered almost exclusively in black communities, in 1919 blacks lashed out, as had the black soldiers of the 24th Infantry in Houston, destroying white-owned property and doing bodily harm to whites. It was as if blacks took quite literally Du Bois's first editorial advice upon disembarking:

> We are returning from war! *The Crisis* and tens of thousands of blackmen were drafted into this great struggle. . . .
> But by the God of heaven, we are cowards and jackasses if now that the war is over, we do not marshal every ounce of our brain and brawn to fight a sterner, longer, more unbending battle against the forces of hell in our own land.
> We return.
> We return from fighting.
> We return fighting. ("Returning")

It is this spirit of militancy, nurtured in the environment of wartime mobilization, sharpened in the experiences of combat success and state-sponsored prejudice, and acted out in riots that finds expression in Claude McKay's "If We Should Die" and "The Little Peoples."

Unrest was also on the rise elsewhere. Organized labor, hopeful of extending wartime gains but confronted by bosses no longer constrained by the War Industries Board, went out on a series of bitterly fought strikes that fanned public fears of a Bolshevik-style revolution in America and, largely as a consequence, brought ruinous reversals to labor. In 1919, virtually all steelworkers and coal miners went on strike. So did the Boston city police. In June, July, and August alone, the country saw over one thousand strikes (Levin 31). The repressive, red-baiting pattern for putting down these disputes was set early, however, during the Seattle general strike of January and February. When some 25,000 workers in nonessential industries walked out in support of roughly 35,000 ship and dock workers already on strike, Seattle mayor Ole Hanson called in the national guard and launched a publicity barrage, denouncing the strike in newspapers across the country as Bolshevist and un-American (Murray 59, 61, 63). The strike committee—made up of local labor representatives who neither drew funds nor any particular inspiration from abroad and whose goals had been limited to better hours and wages—gave up the strike with no gains (Murray 64). The triumphant Hanson resigned his job and toured the country, lecturing on the national peril posed by Bolshevik labor radicals and earning the equivalent of his annual mayoral salary five times over in a little more than half a year (Levin 31). Red hysteria was fueled when, just in advance of May Day, 1919, thirty-six mail bombs were discovered posted to prominent public officials and business leaders. Only one actually reached its destination and went off, but a general radical plot to destroy the government and undermine business seemed indicated by the addressees: Attorney General A. Mitchell Palmer, Chief Justice of the Supreme Court Oliver Wendell Holmes, federal judge Kenesaw Mountain Landis (who had heard the IWW sedition trial in Chicago), Postmaster General Albert Burleson, J. P. Morgan, and John D. Rockefeller (Levin 32). Gains for labor were virtually impossible in this political atmosphere; the steelworkers, the miners, the Boston police, and almost all other striking workers met with no more success than the Seattle workers had.

Just two years before, Americans of many political stripes had welcomed the March revolution in Russia. Now, those who admired its November successor, the Bolshevik Revolution, were branded as un-American and threatened with deportation. The Wobblies who took over from the jailed union leaders of 1917 were locked in a desperate, vicious cycle: demonized in the United States, IWW poets such as John E. Nordquist and Covington Hall looked to Bolshevik Russia as to a Messianic hope; but their affection for the Bolsheviks, publicly expressed in print, made the IWW's declining popularity and failure all the more certain. The IWW leaders of 1919 and 1920 were, in fact, all too ready to believe the hysteria of mainstream newspapers and the bombast of their own newspaper headlines; instead of resuming active organizing among American workers, they waited for the irresistible, inevitable Revolution to arrive from abroad. Revolutionary enthusiasm and misguided, hysterical patriotism made a volatile combination. On

Armistice Day, 1919, American Legionnaires on parade in Centralia, Washington, assaulted the local IWW union hall and were met by gunfire. Four legionnaires were killed and those in the union hall were arrested. One Wobbly, Wesley Everest, happened also to be a U.S. soldier recently home from Europe and was—coincidentally?—the most implacable in the clash. Aided by a suspicious power failure, a vigilante mob stormed the town jail, hauled Wesley out, beat him, castrated him, hanged him from a railroad trestle, and riddled his corpse with rifle bullets. Such inhumanity, reminiscent of the treatment of Frank Little in 1917 and more blatant than the injustices against Joe Hill in 1915, were largely ignored. While in IWW newspapers Everest became the latest in a series of labor martyrs, conservatives treated his murder as well-deserved retribution; progressives saw it as too controversial for the kind of spirited defense they had offered in Hill's case.

Chillingly, the law did not simply fail to protect radicals but was used to drive them out of the country. The nationwide Red Scare of 1919–20 is most commonly associated with Attorney General A. Mitchell Palmer; the arrests and deportations of radicals during that period are known collectively as the Palmer Raids. But the Immigration Bureau, the FBI, the Labor Department, and the Justice Department were all involved in the deportation of radicals and came into conflict only to the extent that each wanted primary control over the procedure (Preston 220–23). The English poet Charles Ashleigh was among the ejected IWW members. In the most spectacular deportation, immigrants belonging to the Union of Russian Workers and anarchists including Emma Goldman and Alexander Berkman were rounded up in November 1919. Of the 249 swiftly packed off to Russia on a troop transport, many were presented with no evidence against them but their association with the union (Murray 207). This coup was followed by a massive, nationwide sweep on 2 January 1920, when over four thousand people suspected of radical political views were arrested (217). While from this group only about one in eight were actually deported (251), and by 1920 the government agencies' wide-ranging powers of search and seizure were reined in, the raids dramatically undermined radical political groups. The Socialist Party of America renounced all ties with the international soviet and grew quiescent. The IWW likewise distanced itself from the soviet, though it could never be effectively revived anyway. The Communist party's membership of some 70,000 in 1919 dropped to an insignificant 16,000 or fewer by the mid-1920s (276).

With the severest repression of left-wing politics having been meted out in the final two years of the Wilson administration, the Republican administrations of the twenties inherited a repressive regime under which dissent was customarily interpreted as disloyalty and leftist politics automatically considered un-American. By his term, Warren Harding could afford to put a more benign face on postwar reaction, as he commuted the long sentences of most political prisoners in 1921, including nearly all of the IWW leaders and the most famous Socialist, perennial presidential candidate Eugene V. Debs. The challenge for wartime dissenters thus became maintaining some vital cultural memory of what all the fuss had been about. In poetry, they had to face a formidable assortment of patriotic anthologies that reprinted a great many nationalist poems alongside a few pacifist classics but with little of the wartime context crucial to understanding the difference. *Armistice Day,* from Dodd, Mead's Our American Holidays series, presents a virtually seamless progression of verse written prior to, during, and after the war, from Katharine Lee Bates's "America the Beautiful" to W. N. Ewer's "Five Souls" to Dana Burnet's "Peace at Morning," as if the antiwar, and antinationalist, stance of Ewer's poem were not in any way at odds with Burnet's patriotic celebration of Armistice Day (Sanford and Schauffler). After all, the nationalisms critiqued by Ewer were *European,* not American, right? And its adoption by the Woman's Peace party and the additional stanzas written by others about American nationalism went unmentioned. Burton Stevenson used the same tack when he included Vachel Lindsay's "Abraham Lincoln Walks at Midnight" in his anthologies *Poems of American History* (1922) and *American History in Verse for Boys and Girls* (1932). Stevenson's themes of national unity and military heroism diverted readers's attention from potentially embarrassing applications either of Lindsay's socialist-leaning ideals—"The league of sober folk, the Workers' Earth"—or of his general condemnation of militarism—"The sins of all the war-lords." In the latter collection Stevenson explains that "America has no reason to be ashamed of any of her wars, and every reason to be proud of two of them," these being the American actions in the Spanish-American War, "motivated by a fine ardor for human liberty," and in the Great War, "undertaken in complete disregard of selfish gain" (v). Just for good measure he glosses Lindsay's poem thus: "For many years the nations of Europe, urged on by age-old hatreds, had been arming against each other, but it was Germany which finally delivered the attack, and to most Americans it seemed clear that the struggle was one of despotism, as typified by Germany and Austria, against democracy, as typified by France and England" (397).

Postwar dissenting poetry had continually to confront this kind of historical forgetfulness. Misremembrance was inculcated on a national scale and was greatly aided by the general political anesthetic of pros-

perity administered more or less successfully by three Republican administrations. The political criticism of Brent Dow Allinson's "Mr.
Bryan Enters Arlington" remains sharp, as the poem berates former
secretary of state William Jennings Bryan for not leading the peace
movement after his much publicized 1915 resignation on pacifist principle. The poem's bitterness toward Bryan's repudiation of pacifism
underscores the depth of Allinson's commitment to pacifism—strong
enough for him to go voluntarily to jail as a conscientious objector. But
Allinson was speaking to a diminished and disheartened pacifist audience by the midtwenties, when Bryan died: with the war over and the
United States opting out of the League of Nations, only the staunchest
core of antiwar activists saw the practical use of organizing for the next
war. Similarly, Sarah Norcliffe Cleghorn's *Ballad of Gene Debs* reflects
clearly the need to cultivate political integrity in the face of public cynicism and apathy. Cleghorn's ballad records Debs's actions, words, and
even his clothing in great historical particularity as if to ensure that the
myth of his person could not be entirely reframed by national demonology. At the same time, however, the poem is a valediction to Debs and
his gradualist socialism; like Allinson's attack on Bryan, the ballad refers to a then-deceased political leader with no well-established constituency to carry on his legacy.

If remembering Gene Debs helped some radicals keep faith in a
politics of egalitarian activism until a more propitious time, a greater
number of Americans added historical amnesia to the delusions of the
war years. Thus could George Sylvester Viereck, expelled from the
National Poetry Society during the war because of his pro-German
propagandizing in *Fatherland: Fair Play for Germany and Austria-Hungary*, reasonably enough conclude in 1930,

> Now, with unfolding eyes, I see
> The paradox of every fight,
> That both are wrong and both are right,
> The friend is foe, the foe is friend,
> And nothing matters in the end.
>
> (Cane, Farrar, and Nicholl 287)

Viereck's posturing about the vicissitudes of time and fortune, which
amounts to surrendering ethical determinations in favor of submission
to (seemingly) irresistible historical forces, was not far from the general view of disengaged Americans in the twenties. But such a stance is
hardly without political ramifications, as Viereck's case illustrates. For
armed with this philosophy and assured of the apathy of most Americans, Viereck could readily enough sign on as Nazi Germany's chief

publicist in the United States. Informed by a philosophy similarly indifferent to political principle and oriented to pragmatism and expediency, U.S. political leaders and the general populace barely heeded the Nazis until forced to, just as they concerned themselves with the ills of the American political economy only when compelled to by the Great Depression and a revitalized American Left.

New Solidarity, 9 February 1919
John E. Nordquist

THE UNEMPLOYED SOLDIER

(Air: "John Brown's Body")

Now the great world war is over and the fighting is all done,
All the soldiers are returning from the conquest of the Hun;
We are anxious for the old job—we've laid down the bloody gun.
    Now there is no job for us.

(Chorus)
Soldier boys we'll join the union!
Soldier boys we'll join the union!
Soldier boys we'll join the union!
Industrial Workers of the World.

When we went away to battle to maintain democracy,
We were cheered in camp, on train; we were cheered across the sea;
And they called us noble heroes—just as noble as could be.
    Now there is no job for us.

(Chorus)

When we left the busy workshop; left the mine and farm and mill,
Then our bosses grandly told us they would keep our jobs until
We returned across the ocean after spanking Bloody Bill—
    Now there is no job for us.

(Chorus)

Now we soldiers who are jobless shall we meekly starve and die,
While the bosses who have lied to us, enjoy their steaks and pie?
We who fought the war for freedom now must ask with many a sigh,
  Why there is no job for us.

(Chorus)

Why not do just like the workers far across the ocean do?
Take the ruling of the nation from the tyrant greedy few;
For just One Big Mighty Union—soldiers, workers, sailors, too,
  Then there will be jobs for us.

(Chorus)

Commemorative booklet, 14 February 1919
WALLACE IRWIN

THOUGHTS INSPIRED BY A
WAR-TIME BILLBOARD

I stand by a fence on a peaceable street
  And gaze on the posters in colors of flame,
Historical documents, sheet upon sheet,
  Of our share in the war ere the armistice came.

And I think about Art as a Lady-at-Arms;
  She's a studio character most people say,
With a feminine trick of displaying her charms
  In a manner to puzzle the ignorant lay.

But now as I study that row upon row
  Of wind-blown engravings I feel satisfaction
Deep down in my star-spangled heart, for I know
  How Art put on khaki and went into action.

There are posters for drives—now triumphantly o'er—
  I look with a smile reminiscently fond
As mobilized Fishers and Christys implore
  In a feminine voice, "Win the War—Buy a Bond!"

There's a Jonas Lie shipbuilder, fit for a frame;
  Wallie Morg's "Feed a Fighter" lurks deep in his trench;

There's Blashfield's Columbia setting her name
  In classical draperies trimmed by the French.

Charles Livingston Bull in marine composition
  Exhorts us to Hooverize (portrait of bass),
Jack Sheridan tells us that Food's Ammunition—
  We've all tackled war biscuits under that class.

See the winged Polish warrior that Benda has wrought!
  Is he private or captain? I cannot tell which,
For printed below is the patriotic thought
  Which Poles pronounce "Aladami Ojcow Naszych."

There's the Christy Girl wishing that she was a boy,
  There's Leyendecker coaling for Garfield in jeans,
There's the Montie Flagg Guy with the air of fierce joy
  Inviting the public to Tell the Marines.

And the noble Six Thousand—they count up to that—
  Are marshalled before me in battered review.
They have uttered a thought that is All in One Hat
  In infinite shadings of red, white, and blue.

And if brave Uncle Sam—Dana Gibson, please bow—
  Has called for our labors as never before,
Let him stand and salute in acknowledgment now
  Of the fighters that trooped from the studio door.

New Solidarity, 26 April 1919
COVINGTON AMI

I AM REVOLUTION

I am Revolution.
Hunger is my mother—
Hunger of soul and body.
Suppression is my father—
Suppression of soul and body.—
I rise when they think me dead.
I come like a thief in the night.
I strip the old lies naked.

I make the ancient good uncouth.
I force society to face reality.
With the winds of life I lash the stagnant seas of love to action.

I am the Race-Soul waking.
I Speak, and there is light.
I lift my hand, and Croesus falls, thrones topple, and the old Gods die.
I am the Masses making dreams come true.
I am the higher hope, the wider world.
The spirit and substance—
The Destroyer and Renewer of all that was, is, and is to be—
The child of war and the death of war—
The peace that the Prophets have visioned—
The Idea winning its place in the sun—
The Omega and Alpha of all Evolution.

Liberator, July 1919
CLAUDE McKAY

THE LITTLE PEOPLES

The little peoples of the troubled earth,
The little nations that are weak and white;—
For them the glory of another birth,
For them the lifting of the veil of night.
The big men of the world in concert met,
Have sent forth in their power a new decree:
Upon the old harsh wrongs the sun must set,
Henceforth the little peoples must be free!

But we, the blacks, less than the trampled dust,
Who walk the new ways with the old dim eyes,—
We to the ancient gods of greed and lust
Must still be offered up as sacrifice:
Oh, we who deign to live but will not dare,
The white world's burden must forever bear!

Liberator, July 1919

IF WE MUST DIE

If we must die—let it not be like hogs
Hunted and penned in an inglorious spot,
While round us bark the mad and hungry dogs,
Making their mock at our accursed lot.
If we must die—oh, let us nobly die,
So that our precious blood may not be shed
In vain; then even the monsters we defy
Shall be constrained to honor us though dead!

Oh, Kinsmen! We must meet the common foe;
Though far outnumbered, let us still be brave,
And for their thousand blows deal one death-blow!
What though before us lies the open grave?
Like men we'll face the murderous, cowardly pack,
Pressed to the wall, dying, but—fighting back!

There and Here (1919)
ALLEN TUCKER

"LES FLEURS DU MAL"

From the battlefield,
From the ground uptorn, overturned,
Blasted, ruined, defiled,
Grow flowers;
Strange flowers,
Flowers hitherto unseen,
Flowers never known before,
Flowers dreadful, unearthly.

In the deep shell holes,
Among the unexploded bombs,
Twisting about the broken wire,
From beneath the half-buried corpses,
Creep flowers;

Flowers of horror,
Some noxious, spotted grey,
With dripping, loathsome lips;
Some a cruel, dusty red,
With bloated, purple veins;
Some thin, slimy black
Rank with the odour of the lost;
Ghastly flowers,
Flowers of hell,
Fit only for nosegays of the damned,
Flowers that frighten one to see.
But beyond,
For Beauty never dies,
Bloom masses of blue,
Blue incredible, unbelievable,
Sweet, unutterably sweet,
Star shaped,
With the piercing blueness
That grows only from the heart of love.

Captain Billy's Whiz Bang [1921]
J. EUGENE CHRISMAN

POPPIES

Poppies?
Not for me, buddy!
Buds o' Hell I'd call 'em.
Plain red hell—they—
They remind me—

And folks plant 'em around
Gardens—huh!
Says one old dame to me,
"Don't they bring back," says she
"The poppied fields of Flanders?"
"Poppied fields of—" Ain't that a heluva—
But who wants 'em brung back—huh?
Say, buddy,

If she'd seen poppies
Like I've seen 'em—millions—acres—
Scattered through the wheat-fields,
Red—and gettin' redder—mostly poppies—
Yeah—mostly!

Slim—my buddy—old scout
Slept under the same handkerchief,
Me 'n' Slim—clean through from the word go!
I'm liable to forgit—ain't I—
Day we kicked off west o' Château-Thierry
Down the valley—
Poppies—say,
You couldn't rest for poppies.

Then the Jerries cut loose
Machine-gun fire—reg'lar sickle.
Poppy leaves—bits o' red
Flickin' and flutterin' in the wind.
Mowed 'em, buddy—and us—I'll tell the world!
Got old Slim—got him right!
Down in the poppies he goes—kickin'—clawin'!

Don't talk poppies to me—
Skunk-cabbage first—*compree?*
If you'd seen old Slim—
Boy, he died *wallerin'* in poppies!
Poppies—
            Hell!

Periodical clipping, [ca. 1925]
Brent Dow Allinson

MR. BRYAN ENTERS ARLINGTON

"Long John Abraham—lazy black bones!
What are you doing behind those stones?
Tell me the news, lad; ship ahoy! . . .
Why don't you answer, curly black boy?

Can he have gone asleep, or gone beyond
Earshot on the long range? . . . Oh, damn the rain
That's never stopped since April! It comes again
Rat-tatting like machine-guns from our train
In the steel-drenched Argonne. This water-cure
Is a strange absolution. . . . Where's that blond? . . .
How long, how long, Lord Jesus must I endure? . . .
John! John! John Abraham!—You grinning ghoul!—"

"Coming, Lootenant, coming! . . . Now jes' keep cool
And patient-like, 'cause you know I ain't no fool
And I don' need those compliments you're throwin'!"

"Where in the sacred twilight were you going?"

"Now where do you s'pose? Couldn't you hyear that noise
Above the snickering of all de boys?
They was blowin' their horns and a-firin' that volley
Till it sounded like the screech of the damned old trolley
A-grindin' round the curves in Geo'getown. . . . Gee!—
I couldn't stand it longer, and I had to go see!
But I couldn't see much fer the crowd there. . . . Whist!—
Who's that Big Beggar a-gropin' through de mist?"

"Stand by, Black Boy, and tell me all you see,
For they left my eyes in France when they exhumed me!"

"S'help me, Lawd!—as sho' as you're dead,—
They ain't a single halo round his old bald head!"

"What is it, John Abraham; who is it your see?—
Don't keep me guessing, browny. Be quick! tell me!"

"Boy!—it's Mistah Bryan comin', as sho' as I'm hyere,—
With the same big smile that he used to wear
In the good old summer time, on Chautauqua days. . . .
Sit up, Lootenant, quick!—It's the grand old man;
All de boys are crowdin' 'round fer to hyear what he says. . . .
Now bless me, Lawd! Look how he rais' his hand!—
An' he done forgotten his ol' palm-leaf fan!"

   Mr. Bryan approaches and speaks:

"Serene in honorable death, O, thou Unknown
But unforgotten Soldier who hast trod

The path of glory to a patriot throne!—
You gave your life for Freedom and to God,
As I gave Him my own, once, long ago,
And giving all, gained priceless blessings so!"

"You are much mistaken, Colonel Bryan, I did not!"

"Who is there, speaking? . . . What was that he said?"

"I said: You are mistaken; I did not!
I gave my life, but to the girl I wed. . . .
You and the elders took that life away
And gored and trampled it under the War,—
Their God-confounded thrice accursed war! . . .
They sent me into Hell; and on the way
They cheered me with your Christian metaphor.
They did this, Mr. Bryan,—and even you
Propitiated patriotic gods,
Although in honesty you once resigned
Your office when you felt yourself at odds
With the proud perfidy that stooped to do
The Hell-evoking mischief of the blind!—
But where were you upon youth's fateful day?
Where was your Christ? And what had you to say?"

"I did my duty, Soldier, and I prayed;
And so, I trust, did you. . . . Can man do more?"

"Strange that your duty your own God betrayed
And mocked the Price of Peace whom you adore! . . .
Why, in the name of God, did you not speak
With the old fire for us and for the weak
Who could or dared not? Why did you not cry
With your own Christ a clear denial of war?
You did your 'duty' well. . . . You let us die
More maddened than the Gadarenian swine!
They damned us all,—and you who might have saved
Young hearts from doom—by silence you enslaved
The sons of prostrate Freedom's noble line! . . .
You and the Church—you had a chance to speak,
To 'thunder in the Index' and be heard—
From Gath to Babylon; but you were weak,
Paltering, dumb, official—Oh, sacrosanct

267

In Florida! . . . And you will not be thanked
For what you did for God in Tennessee!"

"Is it a man that's saying this to me?"—

["]Whose lying exhortations charged our dreams
Of young adventure with cremating hate,—
When I remember the heartrending fate
Of the ten million torn from Joy and Beauty
Of whom I am the symbol,—then it seems
It were far better were boys left unborn,
Or born, ungifted with the power of speech,—
Or speaking, only your own words to cry
Down Time's long corridor to all, to each:
   'Beware! You shall not press a crown of thorn
   Upon the brow of Youth, or crucify
   Upon a cross of gold or war mankind!' . . .
This is the word that, blind, I speak to the blind:
This is the prayer that, dumb, I pray for my kind!—
'The rest is silence'—both for me and you,
Until the star-dust and the quivering dew
Hungry for Joy and Love shall merge anew,
Molding a lovelier Form for God to wed,—
And thence a fairer world for Youth to tread. . . .
But there is no amnesty, now, for the dead."

July 1928
SARAH N. CLEGHORN

BALLAD OF GENE DEBS

A tall, thin, elderly man
   Was pouring a great speech
Into a crowd that leaned to hear
   As far as they could reach:

To see Gene, to hear him,
   That well-beloved Gene:
To feel the good warmth of his voice,
   And all that his talk would mean.

For the words he used another might use,
    And it would not be the same,
Without the thousand layers of love
    Men wrapped around his name.

They saw Gene, they heard him
    Say in a gallant tone,
"Yes! I would stand against the war
    If I stood all alone.

They do not come by chance, these wars;
    They are not accidental:
When profits need a market place
    Your blood must pay the rental.

Because you make so many goods,
    And you can buy so few,
Foreign markets for what you make
    Must be won with a gun by you.

But, comrades, men are worth too much,—
    A man is much too good,
To be but a wheel in a factory,
    Or to be the cannon's food.

Comrades, the time will come,
    In this and every nation,
When we humanize humanity
    And civilize civilization.

Where is Rose Pastor Stokes?
    Do you all know where?
Do you know that she is locked in jail
    As well as Kate O'Hare?

If Rose Stokes, if Kate O'Hare,
    Those champions of the poor,—
If prison is the place for them,
    Why are we outside the door?

This town of Canton has a house
    Intended for disgrace;
And three good comrades, yours and mine,
    Are locked into that place.

Wagenknecht, Ruthenberg
   And Baker, all were strung
By handcuffs in that workhouse,
   And fainted as they hung.

If stringing up was good for them,
   Let me be cuffed and tied!
Let lovers of their fellow men
   Be punished side by side."

The pencilling stenographers
   Took down the words alone;
They could not indicate the look
   Nor memorize the tone.

"Jefferson—Garrison,—
   They too were the rich man's dread:
And men will speak well too of us
   When we are also dead.

But comrades, be that as it may,
   Let's turn our hands and eyes
To the mighty work we labor in
   Till the toiling classes rise."

The hurrying stenographers
   Left out the living love,
The loyal human fellowship
   His words were fashioned of.

"Arrest him!" the order
   Came out to Terre Haute
"Arrest him for the dangerous words
   His traitor fingers wrote."

Calm were his long, thin fingers:
   Calm were his deep-set eyes.
To think of twenty years in jail
   His pulse did not rise.

The Judge looked at Gene Debs.
   The Judge smiled—and frowned.
The crowds filled the courtroom
   And all the streets around.

"Gentlemen of the jury",
   The Government began,
"This man Debs opposed the war;
   Deny it if he can.

He knifed our soldiers in the back
   And down he tried to drag
The good name of his country
   And the honor of his flag.

And for his fellow traitors
   Who safe in prison lie
He used the words of comradeship
   And praised them to the sky.

This war, and wars to come,
   He undertook to say
Were made because of business
   For the profits they would pay.

Business, business,
   He hates with frantic hate:
He seeks to cripple industry
   And overthrow the state."

Gene Debs in his own defense
   Arose to take the stand,
Smiled at the prosecution's men
   And shook them by the hand.

"The witnesses speak true," he said,
   "The court is fair to me;
But one among the charges
   Is false as false can be.

In all my speech from end to end
   No man or woman heard
One word to hurt our soldiers
   Or one pro-German word.

When all your warrior statesmen
   Were loud in the Kaiser's praise,
We Socialists, the same as now,
   Disdained his words and ways.

My blood is French Alsatian;
   I learned the sweet French tongue
From my father's and my mother's lips
   In the years when I was young.

And I to hurt our soldiers!
   By deed or word not I!
I did not drag them from their homes
   And march them off to die!

The man who thinks this war is right,
   He should not sit at ease
And argue in a courtroom here;
   He should be overseas.

But true it is I hate the war;
   I loathe its very name.
To knife the bowels of living men!
   It sickens me with shame.

Most true it is I honor
   My captive comrades dear:
I know their good and glorious deeds:
   I'll keep their records clear.

Well would it serve me
   In friendless hands to die
If I did not praise and honor them
   Who now in prison lie.

True and most true it is
   I take the workers' part,
And keep their weary lives of want
   Forever in my heart.

What man can keep his manhood
   And still be well content
To house the man that built his house
   In leaking tenement?

Or see the skill that wove his shirt,
   And the strength that mined his coal
Shiver in line on a winter night
   For a coffee and a roll?

No! While they stand and shiver,
   And I, like you, behold,
There's little savor in my food;
   My body and soul are cold!

—Freely to say, your honor,
   What a man thinks is true,
That constitution guarantees
   In simple words and few.

This for their fundamental law
   The fathers firmly planned,
And wrote it down in language
   A child could understand.

This liberty, your honor,
   They risked and struggled for,
Is it to be a scrap of paper
   For the bloody sake of war?"

Gene Debs sat down again:
   His potent voice was still.
Upon his slender body now
   The powers would do their will.

At peace were his long thin fingers,
   At peace were his deep-set eyes:
To think of twenty years in jail
   Made all his calmness rise.

"We must hand it to the old man;
   I take off my hat to Gene,"
The prosecuting lawyer said;
   "The old man came through clean."

Back into the courtroom
   The jurymen were led,
"We find Gene Debs is guilty,"
   The foreman said.

Three days from that day
   The court convened again.
The sentence might have been sixty years;
   The court pronounced it ten.

Southward the train sped
　That bore him to his cell.
He looked around the countryside
　And said he loved it well.

"All through this pleasant country
　Again and again",
He said, "I've met in council
　With the union railroad men."

Smiling, in silence,
　His thoughts began to dwell on
Another man who came this way
　To be punished as a felon.

"John Brown", he said, "was taken
　To his hanging by this way,
I own a button from the coat
　He wore that day."

That evening, at Moundsville,
　He went the bars behind,
Entering into captivity
　With a free and tranquil mind.

"Goodbye, my friends." said Gene Debs:
　"Dave Karsner, don't forget
The love that will be yours until
　The last sunset.

New friends are here, black friends and white,
　Who'll let me share their life;
And I can write one letter a week
　To my dear wife."

One of his new friends said to Gene,
　"Your cell would open wide
If you would forget your red ideas
　And talk on the government's side."

The blood came into Gene's thin cheek;
　"Before I will sell my soul,
These flies may carry me grain by grain
　Through that keyhole!"

They moved Gene Debs from Moundsville
   Where the warden was friendly and kind,
And the grim walls of Atlanta
   They locked him in behind.

While he was in Atlanta
   Came round election year,
And the Socialists made him their candidate
   With a loud rousing cheer.

But when he had been three years in jail
   The government let him go.
And which of his fellowcountrymen
   Would not have had it so.?

Yet as he left Atlanta
   A mourning sound began.
It was lonely in jail without Gene Debs
   For many a lonely man.

Gene Debs went east and west,
   And spoke to the world outside.
A hundred thousand lovers heard
   Gene Debs before he died.

I wish I had a word or two
   That Gene Debs wrote.
I wish I had a piece of cloth
   From his old coat.

🌿 NOTES

Each item in this collection is glossed with an author biography with a focus on World War I, a limited list of reprintings, and explanatory notes for individual lines or words. The obscurity of some authors has occasionally reduced the amount of biographical information available to a bare minimum—sometimes to only what can be deduced from the publishing context and guessed from the poem. The list of reprintings cannot be comprehensive, of necessity: the huge number and variety of sites of publication during the Great War have naturally prevented anything like a complete record. The importance of the public reception of these poems makes it imperative, however, at least to *represent* their various sites of publication and to pass on what information I have gathered for the benefit of future researchers. The textual notes attempt to gloss only those references that might demand specialized knowledge, such as of literary biography or of World War I history.

PRESENTIMENTS

Katharine Lee Bates

Though most famous for her one great hit as a lyricist, "America the Beautiful," Bates (1859–1929) was an influential literature professor at Wellesley College from 1885 to 1925. She edited many standard textbooks for classroom use, ranging from *Old English Ballads* to *American Literature,* the latter a widely adopted text and one of the first to promote American literature as a college subject. Her twenty-five books also include collections of her own poetry, children's literature, and travel writing. During the war Bates was one of the more indefatigable of the patriotic, pro-interventionist poets, publishing in the *New York Times, Outlook, Leslie's, Bellman, Contemporary Verse,* and many anthologies. She was also an active participant in the Vigilantes syndicate. The best-known arrangement of "America the Beautiful" was completed by Samuel Ward in 1902, but the lyric was enormously popular in its own right from the time of its initial publication in 1895. The Bates archive at Wellesley College lists over eighty different musical arrangements by various hands, both preceding and following the one by Ward that has come down to us today.

America the Beautiful

1895. Site of publication unidentified.
St. Nicholas 43 (Nov. 1915): 72.
World Outlook 2 (Feb. 1916): 16–17.
Anthologized in U.S. Committee 46; Sanford and Schauffler 4–5.

William Lloyd Garrison Jr.

Like his father, the famous abolitionist activist, William Lloyd Garrison Jr. (1838–1909) was a notable public reformer, supporting free trade, the single tax, woman's suffrage, anti-imperialism, and open immigration.

[The Anglo-Saxon Christians, with Gatling gun and sword]

1899. Site of publication unidentified.
Solidarity 4 Dec. 1915: 2.

"And merrily the hunt goes on throughout the Philippines": Although the war with Spain lasted only a few months in 1898, American troops waged a series of major campaigns between 1899 and 1902 to put down Filipino guerrillas fighting for their national independence. Police actions against such fighters had to be carried out periodically for as long as the United States maintained control of the Philippines—until the Japanese occupation of World War II.

"What though the Boers are Christians": The Boer War, between Great Britain and the Dutch-descended Afrikaners of South Africa, lasted from 1899 to 1902.

"The mahdis and the sirdars along the great Soudan": While consolidating its control over Egypt in the 1880s, Britain relinquished Egyptian claims to the Sudan but sent the mercurial general Charles Gordon to superintend the evacuation of government officials, a decision that made a martyr of Gordon when he chose to stay in Khartoum and was killed in 1885 by an encircling army commanded by Mohammed Ahmed, hailed as "the Mahdi" or "the messiah." It was Gordon's death as well as a more expansionist government policy that sent Anglo-Egyptian forces back into the Sudan, where in 1898 they subjugated the independent, anticolonial government of the Mahdi's successor. The commanding general of the operation, Herbert Kitchener, became a national hero.

Wallace Irwin

Wallace Irwin (1875–1959) made a living by writing light verse. His first two books, *Rubaiyat of Omar Khayyam, Jr.* and *Love Sonnets of a Hoodlum* (Petrarchan sonnets in working-class dialect), were published in 1902, and his career continued over the next forty years with some twenty additional books, mostly satirical poetry culled from his poems first appearing in magazines or in newspapers through syndication. A staff writer for *Collier's* in 1908–9, he contributed to the Vigilantes and also served with the Committee on Public Information during the war. I discovered "A Few Words from Wilhelm" as a clipping in the Swarthmore College Peace Collection that identifies *Collier's* as the publisher and 8 July 1905 as the date of publication. No issue of *Collier's* for 1905 was dated 8 July, however, and the poem appears in neither the nearby issues nor issues thus dated from other years. Given the unlikelihood of a collector of newspaper clippings mistaking the year of publication, 1905 seems credible, and the style of the format and fonts in the clipping does match the *Collier's* issues of this period.

A Few Words from Wilhelm

Collier's [1905?].

"Choost Europe, Asia, Africa": Kaiser Wilhelm did not keep to himself about
his wishes for a German empire to rival the colonial holdings of other Euro-
pean powers.

"Die Wacht am Rhein": "The Watch" (as in guard) "on the Rhine," a patriotic
song popular in Germany.

"Each hour I shange mein uniform": The kaiser's fondness for extravagant
military uniforms was a subject of ridicule in the press, satirized here also
in E. W. Kemble's accompanying illustrations: cartoons of the emperor in
four ridiculous declamatory poses and four different costumes.

"Ven Gott iss in der Trust!": Reference to the popular German expression *"Gott
mit Uns,"* "God [is] with us."

"Und all iss right vas Iss!": Sardonic allusion to Hegelian social philosophy, in
which the seeds of future progress are already contained in the present order,
and for which the Prussian constitutional monarchy was supposed to repre-
sent the highest form of government yet to be revealed.

Paul Laurence Dunbar

Born in Ohio in 1872, his mother a former slave, Paul Laurence Dunbar is best known
for his local color poetry and his use of black dialect, but he was equally a practitioner
of formal verse of high diction. He authored six collections of poetry, most famously
his *Lyrics of Lowly Life* (1896). Dunbar died young, in 1906, but in his relatively short
life he gained nationwide recognition for his talent, arguably the first African Ameri-
can poet to do so.

Black Samson of Brandywine

Life and Works of Paul Laurence Dunbar. Ed. Lida Keck Wiggins. Naperville, Ill.:
J. L. Nichols, [1907]. 186–87.

Crisis 14 (June 1917): 255.

"Straight through the human harvest": The stanza beginning with this line is
omitted in Du Bois's reprinting of the poem.

Joe Hill

Born in 1879 in Sweden, Joel Hagglund adopted the name Joe Hill after immigrating
to the United States in 1902. From 1902 to 1908, Hill labored as a porter, longshoreman,
and harvest hand, among other jobs, in places including Philadelphia, Pittsburgh,
Cleveland, Chicago, the Dakotas, Spokane, and Portland. In 1910, while working on the
docks in San Pedro, California, Hill joined a local of the IWW. The next year he wrote
his first song for the IWW, "Casey Jones—the Union Scab," in support of strikers on
the Southern Pacific railroad, and in 1911 he made his first of many contributions to
the union's famous "Little Red Song Book," or *Songs of the Workers on the Road, in
the Jungles, and in the Shops.* He was one of the most published of all Wobbly song-
writers and was catapulted to international notoriety and martyrdom when in 1915 he

was convicted of murder and executed. Hill's funeral procession in Chicago drew an estimated thirty thousand mourners. "Should I Ever Be a Soldier" appeared in nearly all nine editions of "The Little Red Song Book" published between 1913 and September 1917, the month the IWW leadership was arrested. It did not return to the song book until 1925, eight editions later, but has appeared in virtually all subsequent editions.

Should I Ever Be a Soldier

Songs of the Workers on the Road, in the Jungles, and in the Shops. 5th ed. [1913]. 5.
Anthologized in *Songs of the Workers* 6th ed., [1913]; 7th ed., June 1914; 8th ed.,
 Dec. 1914; 9th ed., Mar. 1916; 10th ed., Feb. 1917; 11th ed., [1917]; 13th ed., Sept.
 1917; 21st ed., 1925.

Katherine Devereux Blake

Of Katherine Devereux Blake I have discovered little beyond what may be inferred from this one-stanza poem. Although Elizabeth Devereux Blake—a sibling or mother, I would conjecture—is named by Charlotte Perkins Gilman as the president of the New York State Suffrage Association in 1895 (Gilman), of Katherine I can find nothing. Nevertheless, the publication of "O say can you see" in 1929 on a postcard-sized broadside together with another pacifist stanza written by Blake after the war and the inclusion of that broadside by archivists in the Swarthmore College Peace Collection strongly suggest Blake's long-term association with the peace movement. The item includes a footnote explaining that Blake's 1914 verse was endorsed by the "President of the Board of Education" of New York City for use in all city schools and that "It was sung in schools in places all over the United States until we entered the war." A date of composition prior to the outbreak of war in Europe cannot be established for certain, but the widespread practice of parody and the active prewar peace movement certainly make it possible. Indeed, it is included with the prewar poems to underscore this possibility and because a verse written after August 1914 would be likely to include (like all poems from fall 1914 included here) some unmistakable reference to the present war.

[O say can you see, you who glory in war]

1914. Site of publication unidentified.
Broadside. 1929. Peace Poems subject file, box 1, folder B. Swarthmore College
 Peace Collection, Swarthmore, Pa.

AUGUST TO DECEMBER 1914

George Sylvester Viereck

George Sylvester Viereck was born in Munich, Germany, in 1884, but before his second birthday he immigrated with his family to the United States. That country remained his home until his death in 1962, although his parents returned to Germany in 1911. Yet Viereck became the foremost U.S. apologist for imperial Germany during the war. His father was allegedly the child of the famous actress Edwina Viereck and Wilhelm I; George Viereck was only too happy to pass on the rumor. Already the editor and publisher of a German-language magazine assumed from his father, Viereck moved rapidly in August 1914 to bring forth an English-language journal supporting Germany's war cause. *Fatherland: Fair Play for Germany and Austria-Hungary* was published first on 10 August, a week after Germany invaded Belgium, and continued its weekly publication undeterred until the end of January 1917. Under other titles, primarily *Viereck's: The American Weekly,* essentially the same journal was published through the war's end. In August 1915 the *New York World* alleged that Viereck's magazine was subsidized by the German government. A Justice Department investigation in 1918 failed to produce enough evidence to bring Viereck to trial as a foreign agent. But his dogged advocacy of Germany and attacks against its enemies, especially Britain and Russia, earned him contempt among other American intellectuals and publishers; in 1918 he was expelled from the Author's League and the Poetry Society of America, of which he had been a cofounder. In the 1930s and 1940s he supported Nazi Germany, and from March 1942 to March 1943 and again from July 1943 to May 1947 he was imprisoned on charges of disloyalty and subversion.

The German American to His Adopted Country

> *Fatherland: Fair Play for Germany and Austria-Hungary* 17 Aug. 1914: 10.
> *Songs of Armageddon and Other Poems.* New York: Mitchell Kennerley, 1916. 9–10.

Edith M. Thomas

By the time of World War I, Edith M. Thomas had had a long and distinguished career as a poet. She had served as a reader for *Harper's* magazine and published poetry in *Scribner's,* the *Atlantic, Harper's, The Nation,* and the *Century,* among other places. Born in Chatham, Ohio, in 1854, Thomas was a resident of New York City during the war and died in 1925. The war summoned Thomas, like other poets, to write much more politically engaged poetry than she had theretofore. Her poetry also mirrored closely the changing attitudes toward the war typical of WASP intellectuals. Initially she denounced the war and supported pacifist agitation, writing, besides "The Woman's Cry," a poem entitled "We Mourn for Peace" that described the women's peace parade held in New York City on 29 August 1914. But several pieces in her collection *The White Messenger,* published in the fall of 1915, and most of her thirty-nine poems that appeared in the *New York Times* were sympathetic to the Allies and critical of the Central Powers. In June 1917 she contributed poetry to the Vigilantes' *Fifes and Drums.*

The Woman's Cry

> *New York Evening Post?* [Aug.]
> *Literary Digest* 29 Aug. 1914: 357.
> *The White Messenger and Other Poems.* Boston: Badger, 1915. 56–57.
> Anthologized in Wheeler 161–62.

Carl Sandburg

Carl Sandburg (1869–1967) was one of several poets whom *Poetry* is credited with having "discovered"; he published his first poems in the magazine in March 1914. But by that time Sandburg had already been discovered by the American Left; he had worked as an organizer in the Wisconsin Social Democratic party and regularly contributed his investigative journalism to the *International Socialist Review*. Both "Ready to Kill" and "Buttons" reveal Sandburg's early contempt for the war—typical of American poets from across the ideological spectrum, though in Sandburg's case informed by a socialist analysis. Sandburg joined in the patriotic enthusiasm in 1917, as did most intellectuals whether liberal or conservative. Significantly, *Poetry* published not only "Ready to Kill" in 1914 but also "The Four Brothers" in 1917, the latter poem revealing the degree to which a socialist perspective on the war could be twisted to suit the needs of mobilization. "The Four Brothers" also marked Sandburg's debut as a popular poet; *Chicago Poems* (1916) had been a critical success, but "The Four Brothers" was reprinted in newspapers throughout the country.

Ready to Kill

> *Poetry* 4 (Sept. 1914): 238–39.
> *Chicago Poems*. New York: Holt, 1916. 60.
> *International Socialist Review* 16 (June 1916): 710.
> *Industrial Worker* 25 Sept. 1920: 3.

> "This is a bronze memorial to a famous general": The statue Sandburg describes is of Ulysses S. Grant and stands to this day in Chicago's Grant Park.

Sara Beaumont Kennedy

Born in Somerville, Tennessee, Sara Beaumont Kennedy made her living as a journalist on various Memphis newspapers. She also published four volumes of fiction (in 1901, 1902, 1908, and 1911) and two of poetry, *One Wish* (1915) and *Poems* (1919). She died in Memphis in 1921. "The Call to the Colors" is the product, then, of a poet both very much at home with the milieu of the daily newspaper poem and ambitious to produce durable volumes of literary work. The editors of the *Literary Digest,* bringing the poem to national attention, remarked that it was "a peculiarly American poem." It certainly was prescient of what was becoming a central concern in U.S. war policy: the "problem" of America's ethnic diversity and the corresponding fear that, as the *Digest* suggested, "this great war shows that the various metals [of the American melting pot] are not as yet absolutely fused."

The Call to the Colors

> *Memphis Commercial Appeal* 6 Sept. 1914: 6.
> *Literary Digest* 28 Nov. 1914: 1082–83.
> Reprinted in Wheeler 89–90.

Vachel Lindsay

Prior to the war Lindsay traveled the lecture circuit for the Anti-Saloon League, and in the summer of 1912 he went, on foot and by rail, from Illinois to New Mexico on a mission to proclaim the "Gospel of Beauty," during which he exchanged copies of his poems for food and shelter. After his publications in *Poetry* magazine attracted attention in 1914, he became famous in England and the United States for his public recitals, wherein he typically invited his audiences to join him in reciting the refrains of his poems. Lindsay was born in Springfield, Illinois, in 1879, and revered Springfield's most celebrated resident, Abraham Lincoln. Influences on Lindsay's work include Edgar Allan Poe, Sidney Lanier, Walt Whitman, gospel songs, Salvation Army bands, revival meetings, and jazz. Lindsay committed suicide by poison in 1931.

Abraham Lincoln Walks at Midnight

> *Independent* 79 (21 Sept. 1914): 408.
> *Survey* 33 (6 Mar. 1915): 636.
> *The Congo and Other Poems.* New York: Macmillan, 1915. 145–47.
> *Independent* 97 (15 Feb. 1919): 205.
> *Collected Poems.* New York: Macmillan, 1927. 53–54.
> Anthologized in Erskine 7; Cunliffe 159; Clarke (1917) 6–7; U.S. Committee 68; Eaton 144–45; Rittenhouse 157–58; Stevenson (1922) 661–62; Stevenson (1932) 197–98.

> "It breaks his heart that kings must murder still": For three of the five major combatants entering the war in 1914, a king held final authority over whether the nation was to fight: Nicholas II in Russia, Wilhelm II in Germany, and Franz Joseph I in Austria-Hungary.

Percy MacKaye

Percy MacKaye (1875–1956) enjoyed a long career as a poet and playwright, composing over thirty dramas that were performed and published between 1903 and 1949. In addition to his plays intended for the professional theater, MacKaye wrote masques and public dramatic programs including the 1914 production *St. Louis,* which demanded seventy-five hundred performers. During the war his writing regularly addressed the conflict: *The Present Hour: A Book of Poems* (1914), *Poems and Plays* (1916), and *Roll Call: A Masque of the Red Cross* (1918) all contain work explicitly concerned with the war. The sonnets "Doubt" and "Destiny" reprinted here were the first and last in a cycle of six sonnets, the other four being "The Great Refusal," "Louvain," "Kultur," and "Rheims." MacKay's use of "lurking Hun" in "Doubt" suggests what is made more explicit in the other four sonnets: his tendency to assign primary blame for the war and its atrocities on Germany.

From Carnage: A Meditation on the European War: I. Doubt, VI. Destiny

> *Boston Transcript* 26 Sept. 1914: sec. 3: 16.
> Anthologized in Erskine 22; Holman 142–45; Wheeler 100–101.

Mary White Ovington

Born in New York City in 1865, Mary White Ovington was a leader in social work, serving as the head of the Greenpoint Settlement from 1895 to 1903 and then as a member of the Greenwich House Committee on Social Investigations in 1904–5. She helped found the NAACP in 1909, published a ground-breaking study of sociological conditions among New York City blacks, *Half a Man,* in 1911, and served as a board member of the NAACP and as chair after the war. During the war she was a member of the Woman's Peace party and contributed to its bimonthly, *Four Lights.* Poetry was an avocational interest, as it was for many Americans of the period, but she brought to it her passion and perspective as a champion of people of color.

War

> Crisis 8 (Oct. 1914): 297.

> "Thy most lovely island in the western ocean": The eastern half of New Guinea and its surrounding islands made up a Germany colony, Kaiser Wilhelm Land.

Ernst Lissauer

A German Jew who was an enthusiastic patriot, Ernst Lissauer lived to regret both his "Hassgesang gegen England" and his unquestioned loyalty to Germany, as he died in 1937 when the pro-Nazi Anschluss was imminent. Although he authored twenty-one books between 1907 and 1930, including novels, dramas, poems, and essays, he was remembered almost exclusively for his jingoist poem dashed off in August 1914. Soon after its publication in the *Berlin Jugend,* the "Hassgesang" made a sensation, with Kaiser Wilhelm according military honors to its author and Prince Rupprecht making copies for his entire army. It was first published in English translation in the *New York Times,* where it caused a sensation of another sort. The translation by Barbara Henderson was published on 15 October 1914 along with a lengthy letter by her husband, Archibald, a University of North Carolina math professor who had studied in Germany with Albert Einstein. Archibald's letter charged the *Times* and other newspapers of favoritism toward the Allies, requested the newspaper's publication of "the best German poems evoked by the war" as a corrective measure, and suggested, to begin with, a poem he called "a symbol of the spirit which has welded together into a marvelous union the entire German people of seventy millions and made of them a fighting unit of almost incredible force and cohesiveness." What the Hendersons, would-be apologists for Germany, did not foresee was the tremendous backlash that would greet the poem's U.S. publication. For a week afterward, the *Times* editorial page ran rejoinders, and the "Hymn of Hate," the short-hand title for "A Chant of Hate against England," came almost immediately to signify for many Americans the irrational malignity of imperial Germany.

A Chant of Hate against England

> *New York Times* 15 Oct. 1914: 12.
> *Outlook* 112 (28 Oct. 1914): 439.
> *Saturday Evening Post* 17 Apr. 1915: 22.
> Anthologized in Erskine 38–39; Grumbine 42–43.

> "Cut off by waves that are thicker than blood": Allusion to the Germanic heritage of England, which supposedly increased the offensiveness of Great Britain's entry into the war as a member of the Triple Entente.
> "Spoke three words only: 'To the Day!'": This was indeed a common expression among expansionist Germans, referring to the day when war with the Triple Entente came, presumably offering an opportunity for Germany to beat back foes who intended to strangle its national aspirations by encirclement and containment.

McLandburgh Wilson [Florence McLandburgh]

McLandburgh Wilson was the pen name of Florence McLandburgh, born in 1850 in Ohio, later a resident of Chicago, and a frequent poetry contributor to both the *New York Times* and *New York Times Magazine*. Whereas "Motherhood's Chant," McLandburgh's reply to Lissauer's "Hassgesang," indicates McLandburgh's early attraction to the women's peace movement, her later poems chart responses much more typical of the WASP intelligentsia: wholehearted support for war involvement and caustic ridicule for dissenters. Her war poetry in these later modes appeared in periodicals including *Ainslie's, Bookman, Current Opinion,* the *Living Age, Munsey's,* and the *Survey*. A sampling of this poetry is collected in her *Little Flag on Main Steet*.

Motherhood's Chant
> *New York Times* 21 Oct. 1914: 10.
> Anthologized in Erskine 42.

Charles Ashleigh

One chronicler of the IWW calls Ashleigh "an English hobo-intellectual and poet" (Tyler 77). Sentenced to ten years, Ashleigh was among the IWW activists convicted of sedition and sent to Leavenworth 1918. His prison record offers the following information: age at time of incarceration, twenty-nine; mother's address, West Hempstead, London; time of U.S. residency, six years; occupation, "News-paper man"; place of arrest, San Francisco. Ashleigh was a contributor to the *International Socialist Review* in 1914, reporting on migratory labor and on Chicago labor affairs. Ashleigh's semi-autobiographical novel, *Rambling Kid,* suggests that he lived and worked in South Dakota, Minnesota, and North Dakota before moving on to the West Coast—becoming an IWW member at some point along the way. The ending of the novel is fictionalized: instead of being arrested, Ashleigh's alter ego, Joe, sneaks out of the country and goes to Russia as a special IWW representative. In reality, Ashleigh was deported to England upon the commutation of his sentence on 26 December 1921—though his warden does report that he later traveled to Russia. In reply to an inquiry about Ashleigh's poetry, the warden further opines, "Ashleigh is an I.W.W. agitator and trouble-maker and I think the United States is well rid of him." For Ashleigh's prison record, consult Inmate Case File 13115, U.S. Penitentiary, Leavenworth (KS), Bureau of Prisons, Record Group 129, National Archives and Records Administration—Central Plains Region (Kansas City, Mo.).

The Anti-Militarist
> *Solidarity* 31 Oct. 1914: 1.

Louise Driscoll

Born in Poughkeepsie, Louise Driscoll (1875–1957) lived most of her life in Catskill, New York, where she worked as a public librarian. She published volumes of poetry in 1922 and 1924, but arguably the high point of her poetic career came in November 1914, when her poem "The Metal Checks" won the *Poetry* magazine prize for the best war or peace poem submitted, beating out contributions by Richard Aldington, Amy Lowell, Carl

Sandburg, and Wallace Stevens. Considered in terms of this coup, she published there-after a fairly modest number of war poems—thirteen—though three of those, like "The Metal Checks," were anthologized in at least one collection.

The Metal Checks

> *Poetry* 5 (Nov. 1914): 49–54.
> Anthologized in Cunliffe 78–83; Monroe and Henderson 80–84.

Maxwell Bodenheim

A poet, dramatist, essayist, and novelist, Maxwell Bodenheim (1893–1954) was born in Mississippi but lived in or near New York City for most of his adult life. He would publish eight collections of poetry between 1920 and 1946, but in 1914 he was a nearly unknown young poet when included in *Poetry*'s special war poetry issue and thus is one of several poets (including Vachel Lindsay and Carl Sandburg) whom the maga-zine may take some credit for discovering. Bodenheim was soon to be a regular in sev-eral of the most famous little magazines of the 1910s, including *Others, Little Review,* and *Seven Arts,* as well as *Poetry.*

The Camp Follower

> *Poetry* 5 (Nov. 1914): 65.
> Anthologized in Cunliffe 29.

> "She spoke of a woman she had known in Odessa": Mention of Odessa, a Black Sea port in far southern Ukraine, appears to place the poem's conversation somewhere in imperial Russia, which, as we see also in Thomas's "The Woman's Cry," was a safely distant (and presumably corrupt) locale for ex-pressing strident antiwar attitudes.

Wallace Stevens

Wallace Stevens's war poems were both pivotal and problematic in his development as a poet. In the fall of 1914 Stevens (1879–1955) wrote a series of short poems—eleven altogether—which he submitted to *Poetry* magazine's war poetry competition. They arrived too late to be properly considered for the one-hundred-dollar prize, but Mon-roe did nevertheless make space for four of them, grouped together as "Phases." "Phases" was only the second publication of Stevens's poetry since his undergraduate days at Harvard (1897–1900) and his first publication of poems that break from the genteel manner of his earliest writing. "Phases" marks the beginning of Stevens's mature, elliptical idiom, as it juxtaposes seemingly contrary points of view regarding the war: section 2 indicating there is no glory in modern warfare, section 4 suggesting that death in battle is the *only* possible (and not insignificant) triumph for exploited working-class people. Stevens, however, later spurned these poems; they reappeared only in his *Opus Posthumous.* The pattern set by "Phases" was closely repeated with Stevens's second group of war poems to appear in the magazine, "Lettres d'un Sol-dat." See also the notes to that poem on 325–27.

Phases

> *Poetry* 5 (Nov. 1914): 70–71.
> *Opus Posthumous.* Ed. Samuel French Morse. New York: Knopf, 1957. 3–5.

> The following epigraph from Pascal is included in the manuscript: *"La justice sans la force est contredite, parce qu'il y a toujours de mechants: la force sans la justice est accusee."* [Justice without force is contradictory, because there are always those who are wicked: force without justice is reprehensible. Translation by Scott Fish.]

Karle Wilson Baker

Born in 1878 in Little Rock, Arkansas, Karle Wilson Baker was educated at the University of Chicago, Columbia, and the University of California. Although by no means as famous today as some of the company she kept in the *Poetry* war issue, Baker published fiction, essays, and poetry in journals such as *Harper's, Scribner's,* the *Atlantic Monthly, Century,* and *Yale Review.* Her nine books included three of poetry, published in 1919, 1922, and 1931. A professor at Stephen F. Austin Teacher's College, Texas, from 1925 to 1934, Baker died in 1960 in Nacogdoches, Texas.

Unser Gott

> *Poetry* 5 (Nov. 1914): 75–77.
> Anthologized in Cunliffe 11–14.

> *"Ein Feste Burg Ist Unser Gott!":* "A Mighty Fortress Is Our God," highly popular hymn written by Martin Luther in 1529.
> "With Zeppelins": Airships used by the German army for observation and bombing both military and civilian areas. Zeppelins attacked targets in France and Belgium in the fall of 1914; beginning on Christmas Day 1914, they began to attack sites in England.
> "And much concerned to keep Alsace-Lorraine": This region at the border between Germany and France, actually two separate provinces, had long been disputed by the two countries. Germany annexed Alsace-Lorraine after success in the Franco-Prussian War of 1870. But many residents retained their loyalty to France, and the recovery of the provinces was the central objective of the French battle plan of August 1914.

Morrie [Ryskind]

Born in 1895, Morrie Ryskind was an undergraduate at Columbia when the war began and an active leader in the small but vocal group of students opposed to U.S. involvement. Indeed, on account of his dissent—which included criticism of the hawkish Columbia president Nicholas Murray Butler—Ryskind was expelled in the spring of 1918, his senior year. He gained a measure of revenge, however, when *Of Thee I Sing,* a musical satire of patriotism Ryskind cowrote with George S. Kaufman that was scored by George Gershwin, was awarded the Pulitzer Prize in 1932—an accomplishment made all the more satisfying since the awards committee was headquartered at Columbia. Ryskind, who died in 1985, wrote in his lifetime two collections of poetry, six Broadway plays, and numerous Hollywood scripts, including some for the Marx Brothers. In the fall of 1914 Ryskind was already honing his satirical gift, casting aspersions on the poetic rhetoric of English mobilization in this poem subsequently entitled "Who Dies if England Live?"—a quote from Rudyard Kipling's "For All We Have and Are."

[Ten thousand Tommy Atkinses went forth into the fray]

> *Columbia Jester* 15.2 (Nov. 1914): 10.
> Anthologized in Erskine 25 as "Who Dies if England Live?"

> "Tommy Atkinses": Generic name for British soldiers popularized by Rudyard Kipling and used widely in both military and civilian life.

Civis Americanus [Henry van Dyke]

"A Scrap of Paper" was originally published by "Civis Americanus" because Henry van Dyke (1852–1933) was the U.S. ambassador to the Netherlands between 1913 and 1916, and it would have been unseemly for a representative of neutral America to neutral Holland to publish such partisan sentiments. Van Dyke's name would have counted for something, as he was a widely read author of moralistic, aphoristic poetry, a Presbyterian minister, and a professor of literature at Princeton University. When he returned to the United States he campaigned vigorously for U.S. intervention and in 1917–18 served as a navy chaplain. "A Scrap of Paper" joined a general outcry throughout Great Britain and the Commonwealth—and among Anglophile Americans—at Germany's violation of Belgian neutrality. On 3 August, presented with an ultimatum that Great Britain would declare war if Germany invaded Belgium, German chancellor Theobald von Bethmann-Hollweg reportedly remarked, "Will you go to war just for a scrap of paper?" The "scrap of paper" was the treaty, signed by England, France, Austria, Russia, and Prussia in 1839, that guaranteed Belgian independence and neutrality. The reporter of the remark was Sir Edward Goschen, the British ambassador; it was subsequently included in the British government's *Blue Book* justifying its war participation and thereupon reported widely by the English-speaking press throughout the world.

A Scrap of Paper

> *Outlook* 112 (4 Nov. 1914): 560.
> *The Red Flower.* New York: Scribner's, 1918. 7.
> Anthologized in Broadhurst and Rhodes 51.

Charles W. Wood

Charles W. Wood's "National Anthem" was widely known among American radicals and was cited in the mainstream press to demonstrate the un-Americanism of the Left. Wood's commentary "Am I a Patriot?"—accompanying the publication of his "National Anthem" in the *Masses* of 1916—offers a little help on this author's background. Wood identifies his birthplace as Ogdensburg, in upstate New York. The prominence and tenor of the article in the *Masses,* along with other articles contributed to the journal, identify Wood as an established radical spokesman; the arguments set forth in "Am

I a Patriot?" reveal Wood to be a thoroughgoing Marxist and internationalist. "Patriotism," Wood writes, "is evidence of a small or undeveloped mind. It is especially a disease of childhood and is most virulent in such underdeveloped persons as . . . Theodore Roosevelt." "Nationalism," he continues, "made the world war possible." The only "isms" about which he feels any enthusiasm whatsoever are internationalism and materialism: "The idealist gives his life for geography and 'colors.' The materialist saves his for concrete, tangible things like wives and children. The realities of life—the things we want and know we want—are material. The lies, the frauds, the things that turn us from our real purposes and make us the slaves of other people's ambition, these are uniformly handed to us in the guise of ideals." Writing with equal vehemence and eloquence in the less well known "King of the Magical Pump," Wood calls these ideals, or Marxist "false consciousness," simply "flapdoodle."

King of the Magical Pump

Masses Dec. 1914: 3.

1915

Alfred Bryan

The lyricist Alfred Bryan (1871–1958) had his greatest popular success with "I Didn't Raise My Boy to Be a Soldier," released in January 1915 with music by his frequent collaborator Al Piantadosi (1884–1955). Within weeks it was the most popular song in the country and was one of the best-selling songs—if not the best—of 1915. Bryan was not a committed pacifist but instead responded to what his listening, singing, and piano-playing audience wanted. Indeed, the song came to signify, for proponents and opponents of pacifism alike, a nearly undisputed American consensus. The *Literary Digest* reported that British observers were astonished "how America can be so sunk in pacifist conviction as to elevate such a ditty . . . into a song of nation-wide popularity." When popular attitudes toward the war shifted in 1917, however, Bryan followed. For example, his lyrics published in 1917 included "Lorraine, My Beautiful Alsace Lorraine" and "Joan of Arc, They Are Calling You."

I Didn't Raise My Boy to Be a Soldier

New York: Leo Feist, Jan. 1915.

As "Our 'Ignoble, Rancid' Popular Song." *Literary Digest* 21 Aug. 1915: 350–51. Excerpt.

Olive Tilford Dargan

Born in 1869 in Kentucky, Olive Tilford Dargan attended George Peabody College for Teachers in Nashville and Radcliffe College. Moving with her husband to New York City after graduation, Dargan published four collections of drama and three of poetry between 1904 and 1922. After her husband's early death in 1915 (she survived him by fifty-three years), she returned to Kentucky and focused on fiction; seven novels and collections of stories appeared between 1925 and 1962. In the 1930s, writing under the pseudonym Fielding Burke, she wrote her best-known work, proletarian fiction entitled *Call Home the Heart* (1932) and *A Stone Came Rolling* (1935) that represented the poor and exploited of Appalachia.

From This War

Scribner's 57 (Jan. 1915): 89–91.
As "Beyond War." Pamphlet for the Woman's Peace party. Riverside, Conn.:
    Hillacre Bookhouse, 1915.
Anthologized in Braithwaite (1915) 101–6; Wheeler 40–45.

"This War": The poem was retitled "Beyond War" for the Woman's Peace party
    pamphlet and retained this title in later reprintings.

Louis Untermeyer

Born in 1885, Louis Untermeyer is today most widely known as an anthologist, beginning with *Modern American Poetry* (1919) and proceeding through nine other volumes, the last appearing in 1961. But from 1911 onward he was also a regularly publishing poet and a correspondent with a variety of leftist and progressive journals. Even while working in a family jewelry manufactory by day, at night Untermeyer was an assistant editor on the staff of the *Masses* from 1912 until the journal was banned from the mails in 1917. In 1917 Untermeyer also was a frequent contributor and an advisory board member to James Oppenheim's little magazine *Seven Arts.* In the summer and fall of 1918 he was one of the codefendants in two separate federal trials of the *Masses* staff on charges of sedition, both of which resulted in acquittal. Beginning in February 1918, Untermeyer joined with virtually the same staff—albeit with slightly greater care to avoid the censor—in publishing the *Liberator.*

To a War Poet

Masses Jan. 1915: 3.
Current Opinion 58 (Feb. 1915): 122.

"You sang the battle": It is tempting to identify Untermeyer's "war poet" with a
    particular British poet—Rudyard Kipling, for example. But since the poem's
    physical description of a corpulent man does not fit Kipling, it may suggest a
    physical and moral type more than a particular person. Assuming a British
    author—the patriotic war poet most on display to U.S. readers in 1914—we
    may choose, according to Catherine Reilly's tally, among the 1,276 British
    civilian males who published war poetry between 1914 and 1918, as compared
    to 532 women and 417 military personnel (*English Poetry* xix).

Carl Sandburg

For Sandburg's biography see 281–82.

Buttons

Masses Feb. 1915: 10.
Current Opinion 58 (Mar. 1915): 201.
Chicago Poems. New York: Holt, 1916. 92.

Angela Morgan

Angela Morgan (d. 1957) was the author of twenty-four books, nine of poetry. *The Hour Has Struck (A War Poem) and Other Poems,* her first poetry collection, helped establish her as a war poet in 1914. She was also quick to associate herself with the women's peace movement, joining the Woman's Peace party at its inception and serving as a delegate to the international women's peace conference at The Hague in March 1915. Later she traveled as a journalist throughout Germany and reported on the hardships of German women. An orator as well as a poet and journalist, Morgan spoke on the chautauqua circuit prior to the war, and in November 1915 performed her poetry, including "Battle Cry of the Mothers," at a mass peace meeting held in Detroit—a meeting that led, indirectly, to Henry Ford's active support for pacifism and, in turn, to the debacle of the Ford Peace Ship delegation. She participated after the war in other, less radical, public gatherings, reading a poem at the dedication of the Tomb of the Unknowns in Arlington National Cemetery and another at the dedication of Will Rogers's mausoleum.

Battle Cry of the Mothers

Independent 81 (1 Feb. 1915): 167.

Utterance and Other Poems. New York: Baker and Taylor, 1916. 43–46.

New York Evening Sun. N.d. Angela Morgan file. Swarthmore College Peace Collection, Swarthmore, Pa.

Pamphlet published by the Church Peace Union. N.d. Angela Morgan file. Swarthmore College Peace Collection, Swarthmore, Pa.

W[illiam]. N[orman]. Ewer

Born in 1885 in London, William Norman Ewer graduated from Trinity College of Cambridge University; he was a foreign correspondent with the *London Daily Herald* after the war. During the war he was active as a civilian dissident; "Five Souls" was initially published on 3 October 1914 in the *Nation* (London), one of the few British periodicals critical of the nation's war effort. The poem enjoyed its greatest popularity in the United States, however, where it was introduced in a musical arrangement by Frances Frothingham drawn from the Allegretto of Beethoven's Seventh Symphony. Published in this musical version for the Woman's Peace party and sung across the nation by the Fuller Sisters, an English quartet, "Five Souls" became a standard not only in the women's peace movement (sung at meetings twenty years after the armistice) but also as a lyric poem in many war poetry anthologies. When the United States began to contemplate, and then in fact initiated, intervention, several authors wrote additional stanzas describing a sixth, U.S. soldier. One of these stanzas is included in part 5 (see 166). A third extant version of the poem, credited to Rev. H. W. Pinkham, was part of the program for the presentation of the 1921 World Peace Prize to Rosika Schwimmer.

Five Souls

Musical Arrangement by Frances Frothingham. Clayton F. Summy [Mar. 1915].

As "Five Dead Men." *Literary Digest* 27 Mar. 1915: 703.

Advocate of Peace 78.7 (July 1916): 211.

International Socialist Review 17 (Apr. 1917): 588.

"Presentation of the World Peace Prize to Rosika Schwimmer," 4 Dec. 1921. Peace Poems subject file, misc. box 2. Swarthmore College Peace Collection, Swarthmore, Pa.

Broadside. N.d. Peace Poems subject file, box 1, folder E-G. Swarthmore College Peace Collection, Swarthmore, Pa.

Anthologized in Holman 112–13; Wheeler 46–47.

On the format: The verse format and the punctuation follow the lyric as published with music for the Woman's Peace party. Most versions of the lines as a printed poem are quite different: The stanzas are typically headed "FIRST SOUL," "SECOND SOUL," etc.; the choruses are in italic; and the rhyme pattern is reinforced by standard indention of lines 2, 3, 5, and 6.

Charles Hanson Towne

Though born in Louisville, Kentucky, Charles Hanson Towne (1877–1949) lived most of his adult life in New York City. He was the author of twenty-seven books, including six of poetry, the editor of three more, and the lyricist for eight song cycles with various composers. A published magazine poet by the age of seventeen, Towne later worked as a writer and editor for the *Designer, Smart Set, McClure's, Harper's Bazaar,* and the *New York American.* From 1915 to 1920, Towne was the managing editor at *McClure's.* Early in his tenure, even before the *Lusitania* was sunk, he commissioned Cleveland Moffett to write a series for the magazine about "what would happen if the Teutonic powers invaded the United States" (Towne, *So Far* 178). Towne published similar incendiaries against U.S. neutrality by Porter Emerson Browne and Hermann Hagedorn and joined with these writers, plus Julian Street, in founding the Vigilantes in November 1916.

To My Country

Everybody's Magazine 32 (Apr. 1915): 484.

Literary Digest 24 Apr. 1915: 961.

Today and Tomorrow. New York: Doran, 1916. 22.

Anthologized in Braithwaite (1915) 183; Cunliffe 265; Wheeler 166–67.

Frank L. Stanton

From 1890 until his death in 1927, Stanton (b. 1857) produced a daily column on the editorial page of the *Atlanta Constitution,* "Just from Georgia," which included extracts from other Georgia newspapers, news from a fictional rural town, "Billville," and, most famously, his own homey lines of poetry, often dialect verses imitating southern working people. Stanton's poetry typically idealized the rural and unreconstructed South, and his appropriation of black dialect poetry is likewise problematic. But he also criticized lynchings, and his poem "Missionary and Hottentot" places condemnation of white "civilization," as evidenced in the European combatants of World War I, into the mouth of a black African resisting Christian conversion. Stanton was appointed poet laureate of Georgia in 1925.

Missionary and Hottentot

> *Atlanta Constitution* 2 May 1915: pictorial sec.: 1.
> *Portland Oregonian* 9 May 1915: magazine sec.: 1.

> "We are our brother's keepers"—Alludes to Cain's excuse to God in Genesis,
> after murdering his brother Abel but denying knowledge of his whereabouts:
> "Am I my brother's keeper?" Although the line reverses Cain's denial of re-
> sponsibility, the mere association of missionaries with Cain is hardly flattering.

Joyce Kilmer

Although in later years Kilmer's 1913 poem "Trees" has made him among the most rid-
iculed as well as the most quoted of American poets, its publication in *Poetry* helped
give him a national reputation and considerable influence as a critic. Already on the staff
of the *New York Times Magazine* and the *New York Times Book Review* in 1913, he subse-
quently became poetry editor for the *Literary Digest* and *Current Literature.* Aged thirty-
one in 1917, Kilmer volunteered for military service and qualified for officer's training
camp but, eager to see combat more quickly, subsequently volunteered in the New York
National Guard. He rose to the rank of sergeant but was killed in action on 30 July 1918;
he received the Croix de Guerre posthumously for his war service. "The White Ships
and the Red" was written on assignment for the *New York Times Magazine* immediate-
ly after the sinking of the *Lusitania* and was reprinted numerous times throughout the
United States and Europe. The poem originally appeared on the front cover of the mag-
azine with an illustration. See my *Partisans and Poets* (8) for a reproduction.

The White Ships and the Red

> *New York Times Magazine* 16 May 1915: cover and illus.
> *Literary Digest* 28 May 1915: 1287.
> *New York Times Magazine* 7 May 1916: 10.
> Anthologized in *The Haunted Hour: An Anthology.* Ed. Margaret Widdemer.
> New York: Harcourt, Brace, and Howe, 1920. 70–73; Cunliffe 151–54; Broad-
> hurst and Rhodes 24–25 (excerpt); Powell and Curry 283–85; Stevenson
> (1922) 663–64; Stevenson (1932) 400–403.

Gerald G. Lively

No dictionary of literary biography that I have consulted offers information on Ger-
ald G. Lively. We can, however, say something about his composition of this particu-
lar poem, for in imitating (or is it parodying?) Bryan's lyric "I Didn't Raise My Boy to
Be a Soldier," Lively joined a host of poets and songwriters who used the sentiments
and form of the original to join the debate on American pacifism, neutrality, and in-
tervention. At least nineteen musical sequels were published between 1915 and 1918, a
few titles supporting the original song's attitude but most contesting or simply ridi-
culing it: "I Didn't Raise My Dog to be a Sausage" (Apr. 1915), "I Did Not Raise My
Girl to Be a Soldier's Bride" (June 1916), "America, Here's My Boy" (Feb. 1917), "I Didn't
Raise My Boy to Be a Slacker" (July 1917), and "I Didn't Raise My Boy to Be a Soldier,
But!" (Aug. 1918). Printed poems, as opposed to lyrics set to music, made similar mis-

chief with the original: verses like Lively's, which basically agrees with the pacifist philosophy of Bryan's lyric, formed a distinct minority; the scornful verse that follows, the anonymous "M. O. R. C.," was more typical.

'Twas You Who Raised Your Boy to Be a Soldier

San Francisco Bulletin 5 June 1915: 20.

Anonymous

M. O. R. C.

Detroit Saturday Night. Date of publication unidentified.
Western Medicine. N.d. (Rpt. from Detroit Saturday Night, n.d.) Peace Poems
subject file, box 3, misc. folder 2. Swarthmore College Peace Collection,
Swarthmore Pa.

"M. O. R. C.": Not only the author but also the title of this poem is mysterious. The acronym suggests, perhaps, "Mothers Of Rank Cowards." Given the straightforwardness of the poem generally, the "they" of the opening lines almost certainly connects to a noun in the cryptic title, and "Mothers" of some sort would be the likely choice.

George Sylvester Viereck

For Viereck's biography see 280–81.

The Neutral

Fatherland: Fair Play for Germany and Austria-Hungary 7 July 1915: 6.
Songs of Armageddon and Other Poems. New York: Mitchell Kennerley, 1916. 11.

"Thou who canst stop this slaughter if thou wilt": This line, coupled with the later phrase "Upon thy White House" and the use of "we" to refer to the nation generally, suggests that the poem is addressed directly to Woodrow Wilson.
"Lo, how with death we freight the unwilling sea!": Overall, the poem denounces U.S. policies that proclaim neutrality yet allow extensive arms trade with the Triple Entente. This line suggests, in addition, the argument that the U.S. manufacturers who shipped contraband on the Lusitania, not the German sub that sank it, are primarily responsible for those killed.
"Upon thy White House falls a streak of red": In Songs of Armageddon, revised to "Upon these harbors falls a streak of red."

Amy Lowell

Born in 1874 in Brookline, Massachusetts, Amy Lowell joined one of the most venerable, prosperous, and influential families in New England. A great-great-uncle on her father's side was the namesake of Lowell, Massachusetts; a forebear on her mother's side was the namesake of Lawrence; both families increased their fortunes by developing, financing, and managing textile mills in these towns. The poet James Russell

Lowell was a cousin. Amy Lowell was near the center of the formation and publicizing of the "New Poetry": she was the leading exponent of Imagism, sticking with the movement long after Ezra Pound had abandoned it (and rechristened it "Amygism"). The war years marked the height of Lowell's production and influence as a poet-critic. Four of her seven poetry collections published in her lifetime appeared between 1914 and 1919. Between 1915 and 1918 she also edited or coedited five anthologies, including the three annual editions of *Some Imagist Poets* (1915–17), and published critical studies of French Symbolist poetry and of contemporary American poetry. While her chief occupation during this period—and, truly, throughout her life—was her work as a poet and poetic proselytizer, Lowell was certainly willing to make felt her support for the Triple Entente and, later, of the U.S. war effort. In December 1914 she joined in a poetry reading to benefit the Belgian relief; in the summer of 1917 she volunteered to select volumes for poetry reading libraries in army training camps; and in the fall she refused to finance the struggling *Seven Arts* because its editor, James Oppenheim, defended Randolph Bourne's antiwar commentary in the journal. Lowell was an enthusiastic and dedicated ornamental gardener, a point with some bearing on both the setting of "Patterns" and the central image of "Orange of Midsummer" (see 157).

Patterns

> *Little Review* 2.5 (Aug. 1915): 6–8.
> *Literary Digest* 4 Dec. 1915: 1300.
> Anthologized in Braithwaite (1915) 22–25; *Some Imagist Poets* 77–81; Cunliffe
>   161–65; Monroe and Henderson 182–86; Rittenhouse 105–9.

Percy MacKaye

For MacKaye's biography see 283.

The Return of August

> *Independent* 9 Aug. 1915: 185.
> *Literary Digest* 28 Aug. 1915: 411–12.
> Anthologized in Braithwaite (1915) 137–40.

Dana Burnet

Born in 1888 in Cincinnati, Ohio, Dana Burnet graduated from Cornell University Law School in 1911 and soon became a special columnist at the *New York Evening Sun*. His later poems were to give enthusiastic support to the war effort (see, for example, "Marching Song" in Powell and Curry). "The Return," however, is typical of mainstream poetry published in the first year of the war: Cautious about taking too strong a position, the poet provides a vague setting and action more fantastic than realistic, even while unequivocally and bleakly presenting war's consequences.

The Return

> *Poems.* New York: Harper and Brothers, 1915.
> Anthologized in Cunliffe 41–43.

"Marched the columns of the Emperor . . .": This reference to "the Emperor,"
especially when combined with "The gray tide" in the second stanza identi-
fying the soldiers' uniform color, appears to suggest a German context.

"'*Margot, Margot!*'": French name, indicating that the poem may, after all, be
imagining a scene not altogether tied to the specific sides of the current
conflict.

Lincoln Colcord

Born off Cape Horn, Africa, Lincoln Colcord (1883–1947) spent most of his childhood
on voyages primarily to China with his father, a merchant seaman. He otherwise grew
up in Searsport, Maine. The author of four books published between 1912 and 1922,
Colcord was also a correspondent on the Washington Bureau of the *Philadelphia Public
Ledger* in 1917–18 and an associate editor of *The Nation* in 1919–20. Braithwaite's *An-
thology of Magazine Verse for 1915* identified Colcord as one of the four most impor-
tant emerging poets of the year, which put him in company with another poet not
known today, John Niehardt, and two very well known indeed, Edgar Lee Masters and
Robert Frost. Braithwaite calls *Vision of War* "the greatest poem this war or any war in
modern times has inspired" and Colcord "the authentic Whitman in substance and
form, in the passionate idealization of a world democracy" (227–28). Of the peculiar
stance of the poem at large, which veers from celebration of military heroism to
condemnation of the Triple Entente's righteous attitudes, Braithwaite writes, "We have
in this poem a great vision of sick humanity. . . . [The poet] will not soothe the pains
of these symptoms with the drugs of idealisms, but prepares the patient for the knife
of war" (228).

From *Vision of War,* XIV and XV

Vision of War. New York: Macmillan, Sept. 1915. 81–89.
While section I is reprinted in Cunliffe 58–69, neither XIV, XV, nor any other
canto has been heretofore reprinted.

XIV

"*Our country calls! Our country, and our King!*": Military recruiting slogan used
extensively in Britain, though it would also apply readily enough to the Bel-
gian mobilization led by King Albert.

XV

"I suppose that, by keeping Turkey alive beyond her day, for your designs . . .":
Although formally allied with Russia, Britain prior to August 1914 had pur-
sued an international policy that shored up the power of the Turkish Otto-
man Empire so as to restrict Russian influence in the Middle East.

"dead Christians in Turkey . . . So many massacred in Turkey": The Turkish
campaign to suppress its Armenian minority population, Christians within a
Muslim empire, preceded the war: Armenian civilians were massacred in
1894, 1896, and 1909. But the brutality reached new levels in the spring of
1915, when hundreds of Armenian villages were emptied, their residents ei-
ther summarily executed or deported to the desert, where many starved to

death. Figures vary, but at least half a million Armenians were killed or died of starvation during the war.

"China's opium trade": In the nineteenth century, opium was Britain's primary import from China. During two separate periods, 1839–42 and 1856–60, Britain went to war with China for a freer hand in this trade. The "Opium Wars" resulted in British victories and Chinese concessions, including the ceding of the land that became the colony of Hong Kong. During the latter half of the nineteenth century, the Royal Navy policed the coasts and major waterways of China; coastal cities such as Shanghai had their trade policies set not by China but by Britain and were dominated politically and economically by a resident British elite.

Alan Seeger

Born in New York City in 1888, Alan Seeger attended Harvard University, where he was a coeditor of the *Harvard Monthly* and a contributor of many poems. Between his graduation in 1910 and the war, he lived a bohemian, artistic lifestyle first in New York and then in Paris. Soon after the declarations of war, he joined the French Foreign Legion, though many of his comrades regarded him as aloof and reckless in combat. "Champagne, 1914–15" is one of only a few publications of Seeger's war poems that were not posthumous; "I Have a Rendezvous with Death" first appeared in October 1916, some three months after Seeger had died in the early days of the Somme offensive.

Champagne, 1914–15

North American Review 202 (Oct. 1915): 551–52.
Literary Digest 25 Dec. 1915: 1484.
Anthologized in Braithwaite (1916) 129–32; Clarke (1917) 160–61.

"Champagne": Through virtually the entire war, the battle line on the Western Front bisected the Champagne region; thousands of French, German, and American soldiers were killed or wounded there.

"And round the city whose cathedral towers / The enemies of Beauty dared profane": During September 1914, Rheims, fifty miles from the Belgian border, was initially occupied by the Germans, then abandoned after their defeat on the Marne River and bombarded heavily. The destruction of the city's seven-hundred-year-old cathedral was often cited as proof of "Hun" barbarism.

J[ohn]. F. Kendrick

What we know both of John F. Kendrick's connection with the IWW and of Kendrick's biography generally is sketchy. Joyce Kornbluh, a chief chronicler of the IWW, says only that Kendrick was a newspaper correspondent in Chicago. But the note appearing under "[Onward, Christian soldiers!]" says it "was written especially for Solidarity," so the association between Kendrick and the IWW was evidently close. The connection between the poem and the union was cemented when "Christians at War," the poem's title when it appeared in the "Little Red Song Book," was presented at the 1918 trial of IWW leaders as chief evidence revealing the seditious character of the union.

Like Joe Hill's "Should I Ever Be a Soldier," Kendrick's lyric disappeared from "The Little Red Song Book" for many years after the 1917 round-up of IWW leaders.

> What For?
>
> > *Solidarity* 16 Oct. 1915: 2.
>
> > "praying . . . baying . . . braying . . . war": Kendrick's close, comical adaptation of Edgar Allan Poe's rhyme-rich stanzaic pattern for "The Raven" demands attention.

Robert Underwood Johnson

A well-known genteel poet and editor, Robert Underwood Johnson (1853–1937) worked continuously as an editor of the *Century* from 1873 until 1913 and was editor-in-chief beginning in 1909. His *Poems* was published in 1903 and updated in 1908, 1919, and 1931. Johnson was active in civic affairs: the leading advocate for the formation of Yosemite National Park, a founding member of the American Academy of Arts and Letters, the chief lobbyist for better copyright protections in the United States, and the instigator of a program to provide "American Poets' Ambulances in Italy" during the war. After the war he served as ambassador to Italy. In the tradition of Longfellow, Holmes, and James Russell Lowell, Johnson saw his role as including the function of public poet, and he was often called upon by other editors for poems offering commentary on current affairs. "Edith Cavell" is certainly one such poem, published just twelve days after the English Red Cross nurse Edith Cavell was executed for helping British, French, and Belgian POWs escape to the Netherlands. Like the *Lusitania* sinking, the execution of Cavell seemed, to many Americans, to indicate the humanity of the Allies and the perversity of the Central Powers; portrayals of Cavell such as Johnson's reflected and helped shape these impressions.

> Edith Cavell
>
> > *New York Times* 24 Oct. 1915: sec. 2: 16.
> > *The World War: Utterances Concerning Its Issues and Conduct by Members of the American Academy of Arts and Letters.* New York: American Academy of Arts and Letters, 1919. 23.
>
> > "Whose pure heart harbored neither hate nor blame": The chaplain at the American embassy, who visited with Cavell the evening before her death, reported her saying, "Standing as I do in view of God and eternity: I realize that Patriotism is not enough. I must have no hatred or bitterness toward anyone."

John F. Kendrick

For Kendrick's biography see 297–98.

> [Onward, Christian soldiers!]
>
> > *Solidarity* 4 Dec. 1915: 2.

As "Christians at War." *Songs of the Workers on the Road, in the Jungles, and in the Shops* 9th ed., Mar. 1916; 10th ed., Feb. 1917; 11th ed., [1917]; 13th ed., Sept. 1917; 28th ed., July 1945.

Outlook 119 (17 July 1918): 450.

For initial *Solidarity* publication: Kendrick's poem appeared alongside William Lloyd Garrison Jr.'s parody of 1899 and they were jointly subtitled "Two War Poems . . . 1899 . . . 1915." For Garrison's poem see 42–43.

Grace Isabel Colbron

Born in New York City, Grace Isabel Colbron worked in Germany as a journalist for much of her life. She was a translator of sixteen works, most of them dramas, from German, Italian, Hungarian, Norwegian, and Danish. She was also, apparently, an activist against militarism, as her "Ballad of Bethlehem Steel" casts aspersions on the profits made by U.S. companies selling munitions to European countries—and the further profits to be made if the United States entered the war. Colbron died in 1948 in New Canaan, Connecticut.

The Ballad of Bethlehem Steel; or, The Need for "Preparedness"

Public 18 (Dec. 1915): 1198.

In *Seven Congressmen on Preparedness*. Pamphlet. [1916.] Peace Poems subject file, box 1, folder C. Swarthmore College Peace Collection, Swarthmore, Pa.

"Bethlehem Steel": Of all the major steel companies, Bethlehem Steel was the most opportunistic in making wartime sales. In 1904 the company was nearly bankrupt. Then Charles M. Schwab purchased the steel works, added shipbuilding and munition-making capacities, and aggressively sought contracts in Europe, primarily with the Triple Entente. Schwab rounded up $50 million in orders during a single trip to Europe in the fall of 1914 and had received a total of $246 million from the Allied countries prior to the U.S. declaration of war—nearly twice the amount sold by U.S. Steel, the largest steel producer in the country. Largely on the strength of its munitions and naval production during the war, Bethlehem Steel became the fourth largest steel producer in the country by 1916 and the second largest by 1926.

1916

Harry McClintock

Harry McClintock (1883–1957) first became involved in radical politics around 1908, when he performed in an IWW band organized in Portland, Oregon, to compete with local Salvation Army ensembles. McClintock's "Hymn of Hate," which adapts the sentiments of Lissauer's "Chant of Hate" to the class war, appears to be his lone contribution of poetry to an IWW publication. He was not, it seems, a principal leader of the union—he was not, for example, among those arrested in September 1917. After the war he performed on the radio, between 1925 and 1955 working mostly in San Francisco.

Hymn of Hate

> *Solidarity* 1 Jan. 1916: 2.

> "For Homestead and for Chicago, Coeur D'Alene and Telluride, / For your
> bloody shambles at Ludlow": Allusions to famous labor fights, the first two
> sites suggesting actions preceding the existence of the IWW (the Homestead
> strike and also the Pullman strike and the Haymarket Square Riot, both in
> Chicago), the latter three indicating strikes in which the IWW was a primary
> actor.
> "And The Day shall come . . .": This allusion to (and appropriation of) the
> German military slogan shows McClintock's familiarity with Lissauer's orig-
> inal. See the note to Ernst Lissauer, "A Chant of Hate against England" on
> 284.

Edith Wharton

An indefatigable supporter of the Allies and especially of Belgium and France, Edith
Wharton stayed in Paris for much of the war and on one occasion even visited a quiet
sector of the front. All of her activities between 1914 and 1918 centered on the war,
whether personal involvement in campaigns for the relief of Belgian war refugees, es-
pecially orphaned children, or publications urging closer U.S. support for the Allies.
These two occupations sometimes merged. *The Book of the Homeless,* a high-priced,
deluxe edition edited by Wharton and featuring an international gallery of writers,
artists, and even composers, was published to raise money for the American Hostels
for Refugees and the Children of Flanders Rescue Committee.

The Tryst

> *The Book of the Homeless.* Ed. Wharton. New York: Scribner's, Jan. 1916. 41–42.

Edgar Lee Masters

Born in Kansas but raised in the down state Illinois towns of Petersburg and Lewis-
town, which he was to make infamous in his *Spoon River Anthology,* Edgar Lee Mas-
ters (1868–1950) was a lawyer by profession from 1891 to 1920, practicing with Clarence
Darrow from 1903 to 1911. He continually aspired to a literary career, publishing four-
teen books of poetry and drama before the phenomenal success of *Spoon River* in 1915,
and afterwards publishing forty additional books of poetry, dramatic verse, fiction,
history, criticism, literary biography, and autobiography. Masters made use of the crit-
ical and popular acclaim of *Spoon River* to put two new books into press in 1916. He
also put in a good word for heroic France in "O Glorious France," published in the
first of them, *Songs and Satires,* and reprinted in various anthologies of war poetry.
Later, discouraged by mediocre reviews of the collections following *Spoon River,* Mas-
ters chose a subject linked to the war in hopes of creating another unequivocal suc-
cess. His 350-page-long *Domesday Book* (1920) records the proceedings at the inquest
of a young woman recently returned from military service as a nurse and discovered
dead on an Illinois river bank.

O Glorious France

> *Songs and Satires.* New York: Macmillan, Mar. 1916. 71–73.
> Anthologized in Cunliffe 177–79; Towne (1917) 210–12; Clarke (1917) 35–37;
> Wheeler 104–6.

Mary Carolyn Davies

We know that Mary Carolyn Davies was born in Sprague, Washington (no longer an incorporated town), but otherwise have little personal data. We can deduce from her record of poetry publication, beginning with *The Drums in Our Street* (1918) and continuing through *Youth Riding* (1919), *Marriage Songs* (1923), and *Penny Show* (1927), that Davies was a diligent and respected poet in her time. Her range is aptly indicated by the three selections included here: the biting, unapologetic satire of "To the Women of England"; the romantic but not at all cloudy-headed effusion of "Fire of the Sun"; and the close social observation of "Fifth Avenue and Grand Street." Also worth noting is that Davies's caustic attitude toward women worrying and grieving for their soldiers, on display in "To the Women of England," did shift considerably when her three brothers enlisted in the U.S. Army. One who had joined up early with the Canadian armed forces was wounded seriously while serving with the American Expeditionary Force in France.

To the Women of England

> *Masses* Apr. 1916: 7.

> "They hold a box for pennies in our faces": From the opening months of the war, many war-related relief organizations, almost all dedicated to helping the Allies, solicited donations through charity events, magazine campaigns and advertisements, and, as Davies's line indicates, street corner panhandling. The Commission for the Relief of Belgium and the Red Cross were the most prominent of these organizations, but there were relief funds also for Armenian and Serbian refugees, the American Ambulance Field Service, military horses, and many others.
>
> "Pinned a feather on a boy and killed him": After the opening days of the war when British army recruiting offices were mobbed with volunteers, men of military age not in uniform but evidently fit for service were "recruited" by patriotic women who handed or pinned onto them white feathers signifying cowardice.

Charles W. Wood

For Wood's biography see 288–89. Wood entitled this poem "National Anthem" in his *Masses* article "Am I a Patriot?" accompanying the June 1916 publication of the poem (elsewhere the poem is untitled). Wood says, as well, that he "once wrote" the poem, suggesting a much earlier composition of it and perhaps a prior publication; I have not, however, located any such publication. The poem may well have made the rounds of radical periodicals anonymously, as in 1917 the *Independent Worker* reprints it as "contributed by Salt Lake Local."

National Anthem

> *Masses* June 1916: 8.
> As "A Patriot." *Industrial Worker* 14 Apr. 1917: 4.
> *Chicago Examiner* 2 Aug. 1918.

Ralph H. Chaplin

Born in 1887 in rural Kansas, Ralph H. Chaplin grew up mostly in Chicago after his father's farm went bankrupt and the family moved to the city in search of work. Trained as an artist, Chaplin began working as an illustrator for the *International Socialist Review* while still a teenager and served on the editorial board of the Charles Kerr company, publisher of the review, from 1908 through 1913. Befriended by IWW president Bill Haywood as early as 1907, Chaplin covered the 1912–13 United Mine Workers strikes in West Virginia and, soon after, became a card-carrying Wobbly. By 1916 Chaplin had become the staff artist for *Solidarity*. At this time Chaplin also began to publish his poetry in IWW publications and his song lyrics in "The Little Red Song Book," becoming the most prolific IWW songwriter of the period following Joe Hill's execution. His "Solidarity Forever," set to the tune of "John Brown's Body," is arguably the best-known song in American labor history. In the spring of 1917 Chaplin assumed the position of *Solidarity* general editor, so that he was one of the chief targets of the Justice Department's 1917 sedition investigation and 1918 prosecution of union leaders. Sentenced to twenty years in federal prison, Chaplin bargained individually for clemency in 1922–23. Advised by Roger Baldwin of the American Civil Liberties Union, Chaplin understood his conditional release obtained in 1923 as demanding only that he be law abiding, not that he renounce his radical views. Other Wobblies held in federal pententiaries were released en masse later the same year, and thereafter Chaplin and others who had gained individual releases were looked upon as having betrayed their colleagues. Chaplin subsequently became critical of communist influence in American radical politics and even of the "state socialism" of Roosevelt's New Deal. He died in Tacoma, Washington, in 1961. For an invaluable resource for studying Chaplin's time in prison, see Inmate Case File 13104, U.S. Penitentiary, Leavenworth (KS), Bureau of Prisons, Record Group 129, National Archives and Records Administration—Central Plains Region (Kansas City, Mo.).

Preparedness

> *Solidarity* 24 June 1916: 2.
> *When the Leaves Come Out and Other Rebel Verses.* Cleveland: by the author,
>   Feb. 1917. 12.

Charles T. Dazey

Born in Lima, Illinois, Charles T. Dazey (1855–1938) attended the University of Kentucky and Harvard University, where he was an editor of the *Harvard Advocate* and class poet for 1881. Dazey became a popular dramatist whose greatest commercial success was *In Old Kentucky,* a sensational American Cinderella story set in bluegrass country and featuring Appalachian feuds as well as a climactic horse race. Beginning with an 1892 performance in St. Paul, Minnesota, the play ran continuously, on or off Broadway, for twenty-seven years. Among its main characters is a black servant, Uncle Neb, delineated by broad caricature and a heavy black English dialect and intended, all too predictably, for comic relief. The other characters are equally obvious, one being the stereotypical buck dancer. "At Carrizal" was heavily influenced by Dazey's sentimental view of the Old South and its people. This background explains the primitivist stereotype of a line such as "The strange, wild music of their race" but also makes all the more notable the poem's portrayal of black soldiers' heroism and patriotism.

At Carrizal

New York Times 30 June 1916: 10.

"At Carrizal": Eighty black soldiers and 3 white officers of the Tenth U.S. Cavalry faced some 120 Mexican soldiers loyal to President Carranza. Attacking without proper reconnaissance and acting against orders to avoid confrontation with Mexican government troops, the officers led a charge against a well-prepared defensive position. Two U.S. commanders and 8 soldiers were killed; 9 others were wounded and 22 captured. The Carrizal debacle thus revealed glaring weaknesses in U.S. tactics and command but courage and discipline among the black soldiers.

Lurana Sheldon

The poet Lurana Sheldon has sunk into nearly complete obscurity; what we know of her can only be deduced from her publications. Her war poetry appeared quite frequently on the editorial page of the New York Times: fifteen times in 1918 alone. She also published war poetry in the New York Times Current History Magazine and in Munsey's. In her publications Sheldon consistently and forcefully supports the Allies and intervention; "The Naturalized Alien" describes Woodrow Wilson's campaign theme of "100 percent Americanism" as fundamentally a war preparedness issue.

The Naturalized Alien

New York Times 5 July 1916: 10.

Arturo Giovannitti

In 1884 Arturo Giovannitti was born into a prominent family in Ripabottoni, Campobasso, Italy. Seeking wider religious and political freedom, he immigrated to Canada at age seventeen. Although he studied in seminaries in Canada and in the United States (where he moved in 1903), his calling to political activism soon proved stronger; by 1906 he was active in the Italian Socialist Federation and was appointed editor of Il Proletario in 1911. In 1912 Giovannitti worked as one of the IWW's organizers at the Lawrence, Massachusetts, textile strike and was subsequently arrested and charged with responsibility for the death of a striker killed in antilabor violence. Acquitted of the charges in a highly publicized trial, he emerged from prison a widely acclaimed champion of labor. His 1914 poetry collection, Arrows in the Gale, written for the most part while in prison, brought him to the attention of the literary world. The book was reviewed favorably by both mainstream and left-wing journals, and thereafter he was much sought after as a columnist and poet in the Masses and other radical publications. He continued to be featured in IWW materials even after he quit organizing for the union in 1916, after a falling out with IWW president Bill Haywood. During the war he edited *Il Fuoco* and organized for the International Ladies' Garment Workers' Union. He was also a contributing editor for the *Liberator*. After the war he headed the Italian Chamber of Labor and the Italian Labor Education Bureau and founded the Anti-Fascist Alliance of North America. Throughout his career as a labor activist, Giovannitti continued to publish not only articles on leftist politics but also poetry, drama, and fiction; he published a collection of his poems in Italian, *Quando Canto il Gallo* (When the Cock Crows), in 1957, and at the time of his death in 1959 he was preparing a book of his poems in English, subsequently published as *The Collected Poems of Arturo Giovannitti*.

The Day of War

Masses Aug. 1916: 20.

The Collected Poems of Arturo Giovannitti. Chicago: Clemente, 1962. 31–33.
"Speaks stridulously": "Speaks hotly" in the revised version appearing in *Collected Poems*. Giovannitti revised the poem significantly for this volume. The differences merit closer study; only the most obviously significant alterations are noted below.
"The blast of a trumpet shoots by, its notes ramming like bullets against the white tower": Revised in *Collected Poems* to "The blast of a trumpet shoots by, smiting the white tower like a hail of gold coins."
"'Workers of America, we alone . . .'": In *Collected Poems* the following new line is inserted between this and the next line: "Tramp, tramp, tramp—the soldiers are marching . . ."
"'The great voice of labor . . .'": Another insertion, between this line and the next: "Tramp, tramp, tramp—the soldiers march near by."
"'As sure as this sun . . .'": Third insertion, between this line and the next: "Tramp, tramp, tramp—the soldiers sing as they march!"
"In the whiteness of the noonlight": Revised in *Collected Poems* to read "In the whiteness of the moonlight."

Ida B. Luckie

No definite biographical information is available on Ida B. Luckie. We can reliably surmise, however, that she was African American. W. E. B. Du Bois regularly reprinted white authors in columns of the *Crisis* when they wrote on matters of interest to the black community, but feature articles and poetry such as "Retribution" were reserved, with rare exceptions (such as white NAACP board members like Mary White Ovington), for black authors. The poem indicates effectively the difference that a minority perspective provided on the war. What mainstream white poet would think, for example, of comparing the situation of the United States with that of Turkey, at that moment widely reviled not only for its alliance with Germany and Austria-Hungary but also for persecution of its Armenian Christian minority?

Retribution

> *Crisis* 12 (Aug. 1916): 173.

> "To meet the dread, on-coming Bulgar host": Though longtime rivals, Bulgaria and Turkey came, in fact, to fight on the same side in the Great War, as the Triple Entente declared a state of war existed with Turkey in November 1914 and Bulgaria joined the Central Powers in their campaign against Serbia in October 1915.
>
> "The blood of countless innocents so long / Has cried to God, no longer cries in vain": Reference to many massacres and deportations of Armenians in eastern Turkey, both during the war and over previous decades.

Charlotte Holmes Crawford

Charlotte Holmes Crawford was born into a well-established family from upstate New York; she married into another. Later the coauthor of conservative political tracts such as *Energetics* (1938) and *Reeve's Plan for Economic Democracy* (1944), she did her part for the pro-interventionist lobby by penning *The Night before Birth* in 1915, published by the American Rights League for Upholding the Duty of the Republic in International Relations.

> Vive la France!

> *Scribner's* 60 (Sept. 1916): 306.
> Anthologized in Cunliffe 72–73; Braithwaite (1916) 145–46; Clarke (1917) 31–32; U.S. Committee 102–3; Case 157–58; Eaton 139–40; Broadhurst and Rhodes 31–33.

> "'*Sauterelle*'": grasshopper.
> "'But I'll not say where for fear thou wilt tell'": The line alludes to the military censors' practice of forbidding reference to place names in all correspondence between soldiers and civilians, presumably to prevent information on unit positions from falling into the hands of enemy spies.

Alan Seeger

For Seeger's biography see 297.

> I Have a Rendezvous with Death

> *North American Review* 204 (Oct. 1916): 594.
> Anthologized in Cunliffe 232–33; Holman 172–73; Eaton 99–100; Rittenhouse (1919) 164–65; Broadhurst and Rhodes 178–79; Powell and Curry 356.

John McRae

Born in 1872 in Guelph, Ontario, John McRae was a medical doctor graduated from the University of Toronto in 1898. After serving as an artilleryman with Commonwealth forces during the Boer War, he returned to a medical career in the United States (professor of pathology, University of Vermont) and in Canada (McGill University and Alexandria Hospital, Montreal). In 1914 he received a commission as an officer and surgeon in the medical corps and was serving with the Canadian Expeditionary Force in France by the spring of 1915. It was then, in the first spring of the war, that he wrote "In Flanders Fields," which was to become a close runner-up to Seeger's "I Have a Rendezvous with Death" as the favorite recital piece of American schoolchildren. Although McRae was Canadian and the first publication of "In Flanders Fields" was in the English magazine *Punch*, I reprint it with these poems because of its enduring popularity in the United States and because it represents one of the most famous— and certainly the most incongruous—images of nature to be popularized during the war: the profusion of poppies that in springtime grew on many battlefields. To this day, of course, the poppy remains the emblem of Great War remembrance in English-speaking countries, including the United States. McRae, who had risen from the rank of captain to lieutenant colonel, died of pneumonia in France on 28 January 1918.

In Flanders Fields

Cunliffe 180 (published in Nov.).
In Flanders Fields and Other Poems. New York: G. P. Putnam, 1918.
Also anthologized in U.S. Committee 94; Eaton 101; Broadhurst and Rhodes 36;
    Powell and Curry 360.

John Gould Fletcher

John Gould Fletcher was in the thick of a number of important literary movements in early twentieth-century American letters. Born in Little Rock, Arkansas, to a wealthy and genteel Southern family, Fletcher (1886–1950) attended Harvard University between 1903 and 1907 but left before graduating. Independently wealthy by inheritance, he became an expatriate in 1908, first going to Italy and then to England. An exponent, like Ezra Pound, of the French symbolist poets, Fletcher became associated with American imagism, assisting Amy Lowell with her selection of all three editions of *Some Imagist Poets* (1915–17). Along with Pound, Fletcher was deeply interested in Eastern artistic forms and philosophy. He published regularly in the *Egoist*, the *Dial*, *Poetry*, the *Little Review*, and *Others* during the 1910s and in *Broom* and T. S. Eliot's *Criterion* in the 1920s. During World War I, Fletcher divided his time between Europe and the United States. In June 1916 he had arrived in England just in time to witness the last phase of conscription carried out under the British Military Service Act, described in his poem "The Last Rally."

The Last Rally

Century 93 (Dec. 1916): 297.
Anthologized in Clarke (1919) 146–48.

"The troops set out. Eyes right!": "Eyes right" refers to the practice of soldiers
    on parade turning toward the dignitaries in the reviewing stand as they pass
    by—ironic given that the draftees described in the poem leave home with no
    fanfare and less military pride.

1917

Robert Frost

Robert Frost (1874–1963) was busy making his career as a professional poet when the war intervened in ways both public and deeply personal. Having labored in obscurity for over a decade, Frost traveled with his family to England in 1912 and soon after was able to locate a publisher for his first book, *A Boy's Will* (published in 1913 in England, in 1915 in the United States), and made influential acquaintances of the publisher Harold Monro, the English poets Wilfred Wilson Gibson and T. E. Hulme, and the American expatriate poets F. S. Flint and Ezra Pound. Chief among his concerns when war broke out were how it might damage the publishing trade and, in turn, how it would complicate a return home to neutral America. *North of Boston* appeared in April 1914, *Mountain Interval* in November 1916. With overwhelmingly positive reviews of his first three books, Frost's career was made. By the spring of 1917 he was teaching at Amherst College, summering in Franconia, New Hampshire, and "barding around" (as he termed his guest readings and lectures) at various colleges and universities. Yet when honored as the Phi Beta Kappa poet at Harvard University in June 1916, Frost wrote for the occasion "The Bonfire," offering up a New England conflagration as a rather straightforward metaphor for the European war. Not at all incidentally, prior to returning home in February 1915 (in part of a convoy including the *Lusitania*) Frost had befriended the Welsh critic Edward Thomas—and had encouraged Thomas to begin writing poetry. Thomas, just four years younger than Frost, had enlisted with the British army in the fall of 1915 and was soon writing poetry that put him in the first rank of Britain's soldier-poets (and showed remarkable stylistic resemblances to Frost's works). His *Collected Poems* was in press when he was killed in the April 1917 attack on Vimy Ridge. Frost later wrote a highly personal elegy, "To E.T." Before it he wrote "Not to Keep," seemingly forecasting the death of this departing soldier.

Not to Keep

> *Yale Review* 6 (Jan. 1917): 400.
> *Literary Digest* 7 Apr. 1917: 995.
> *Everybody's Magazine* 38 (Mar. 1918): 124.
> *Literary Digest* 1 June 1918: 46.
> Anthologized in Braithwaite (1917) 163; Clarke (1917) 219; *War Poems from the* Yale Review (1918) 14; *War Poems from the* Yale Review (1919) 14.

Katharine Lee Bates

For Bates's biography see 277.

Soldiers to Pacifists

> *New York Times* 19 Mar. 1917: 10.
> *The Retinue and Other Poems.* New York: Dutton, 1918. 43–44.

Amy Lowell

For Lowell's biography see 294–95.

Orange of Midsummer

> *Seven Arts* 1.6 (Apr. 1917): 601.

> "You called to me across a field of poppies and wheat": Cf. the poppies in John
> McRae's "In Flanders Fields" (143) and Alan Seeger's "Champagne, 1914–15"
> (113); cf. also the images of wheatfields and harvesting in Seeger's poem,
> Edith Wharton's "The Tryst" (130), and Percy MacKaye's "Destiny" (61).

John Curtis Underwood

Born in Rockford, Illinois, in 1874, John Curtis Underwood had his period of greatest
poetic accomplishment during the fifteen years or so surrounding the war, when seven of his eight books appeared: *The Iron Muse* (1910), *Americans* (1912), *Literature and
Insurgency* (1914), *Processionals* (1915), *War Flames* (1917), *Trail's End* (1921), and *Pioneers* (1923). *War Flames,* from which "Essen," "The Lavoir," and "The Machine" are
drawn, is devoted entirely to Whitmanesque war poetry whose venom against the
Central Powers and partisanship toward the Allies closely reflect the national mood
in 1917. *War Flames* was, moreover, regarded highly by critics. Harriet Monroe wrote,
"It has processional feeling, largeness of plan, breadth of sweep; like the moving pictures from the various fronts, it should bring home to our sheltered and peace-stubborn people the bitter meanings of war. The poet has felt them from afar, he presents
his impressions with descriptive power; and his limitations are those of many decorative painters of our time who are camera-tempted to crowd their canvases and systematize their impressions" ("War Poems" 275).

Essen

> *War Flames.* New York: Macmillan, Apr. 1917. 40–42.

> "There they cast their mutilated sanctities that frightfulness and force might
> triumph": "Frightfulness" translates *Schrecklichkeit,* a facet of the total war
> advocated by the nineteenth-century German military strategist Karl von
> Clausewitz, stipulating that enemy civilians, like enemy combatants, must be
> made to suffer in war and to fear their adversaries. "Frightfulness" as a supposedly unique German war policy was a recurrent theme in Allied propaganda.

The Lavoir

> *War Flames.* New York: Macmillan, Apr. 1917. 65–69.

> "Little Angêle was washing the broad brassières trimmed with Bruges": Bruges
> is a city in southwestern Belgium near the English Channel, but here it is
> used to refer to very fine lace made there.
> "The older women went away one by one to men's tasks in the town and the
> prostitute had given her jewels and her motor and herself to the service":
> Whether intentionally or not, Underwood's phrase accurately reflects the
> French army's practice of establishing military brothels, regularly inspected
> and officially approved, for its troops.

The Machine

> *War Flames.* New York: Macmillan, Apr. 1917. 100–103.

A. B. Curtis

No definite biographical information is available on A. B. Curtis. Evidence internal to "A Study in Evolution" points to her being female, British, and a suffrage activist.

A Study in Evolution: From Mr. Asquith and the British Government

> *Four Lights* 21 Apr. 1917: 2.

> "From Mr. Asquith and the British Government": Because H. H. Asquith stepped down as prime minister in December 1916, this reference dates the poem as likely having been composed—and first published, as well—sometime that year, almost certainly in England. Having been pressured by the wartime service of women, by most suffrage activists' backing of the war effort, and by resulting public opinion favorable to suffrage, Asquith declared his support for woman's suffrage in August 1916 after years of opposition. Suffrage legislation bogged down, however, and he left office before it passed.

Berton Braley

Berton Braley was one of the most prolific of all syndicated newspaper poets, publishing some eleven thousand poems in various newspapers and periodicals but never a book of poetry. Born in 1882 in Madison, Wisconsin, Braley (d. 1966) worked as a reporter in Montana before moving in 1909 to New York City, where he first wrote for the *Evening Mail* and then edited *Puck*. For the rest of his journalistic career he was a freelance writer, working as a correspondent from northern Europe in 1915–16 and France, England, and Germany in 1918–19 and constantly dispatching his poems back to the United States for syndicated distribution.

The Traitor

> *New York Call* 1 June 1917: 8.
> *Detroit Labor News* 8 June 1917: 4.
> *New York Call* 14 Oct. 1917: magazine sec., 8.

> "The traitor who holds up a nation for gain": In his first proclamations about the U.S. conduct of the war, Woodrow Wilson took an especially hard line against food speculation, announcing on 16 April 1917 that "there shall be no unwarranted manipulation of the Nation's food supply" and warning "middlemen of every sort," "The country expects you, as it expects all others, to forego unusual profits" (Wilson 1:390–91).

C. Arthur Coan

No biographical information is available on C. Arthur Coan. His poem "The Consequentious Objector" reveals as much about the editors at the *New York Times* as about the author: in particular, that the editors' infatuation with genteel verse (remember that Kilmer was on staff during much of the war) was not inflexible, that a satirist and parodist in the line of Don Marquis and Wallace Irwin could be published as long as the *Times* party line in favor of war involvement and against obstructionism was maintained.

The Consequentious Objector

New York Times 8 June 1917: 10.

"You hear about them Belgians in Louvain?": The medieval library at Louvain was bombarded and destroyed by German guns in the fall of 1914; the destruction was widely publicized as evidence of Germany's disrespect for Western culture.

"An' what if Reems Cathedral does fall?": See the note for Alan Seeger, "Champagne, 1914–15," "And round the city whose cathedral towers / The enemies of Beauty dared profane" on 297.

"Nor all the highfalutin talk / Of 'rights' at Sea": American rights to safe passage were part of Wilson's formulation of the U.S. *causus belli*.

"'N' I hear I only gotta join a League": The Anti-Enlistment League was founded in 1917 by Tracy Mygatt and Fannie Witherspoon. The league was affiliated with the Civil Liberties Bureau, soon to be renamed the American Civil Liberties Union.

An English Schoolgirl

The *Advocate of Peace* identifies the author of this addendum to W. N. Ewer's "Five Souls" as a fourteen-year-old English schoolgirl. I include the stanza with the 1917 poems to represent its reprinting in the *New York Call* in June 1917 together with the following selection, Ellen Winsor's "The American Conscript, 1917," and to facilitate comparison with Coan's similarly entitled poem, just preceding. Juvenile poetry was an important subgenre in many periodicals, as editors made use of romantic notions about children to underscore the political innocence and logical obviousness of their perspective on the war.

The Conscientious Objector

Advocate of Peace 78.7 (July 1916): 211.
New York Call 13 June 1917: 8.
As appendix to "Five Souls." Broadside. N.d. Peace Poems subject file, box 1, folder E-G. Swarthmore College Peace Collection, Swarthmore, Pa.

Ellen Winsor

No biographical information found.

The American Conscript, 1917

New York Call 13 June 1917: 8.

See the note for An English Schoolgirl, "The Conscientious Objector," which immediateley precedes this note. See also W. N. Ewer's biography on 291.

Marion Patton Waldron

Little biographical information is available on Marion Patton Waldron. Born in Oberlin, Ohio, she was a book illustrator as well as a published author of both novels and poetry. Her best-known work, *Dance on the Tortoise,* was published in 1930. "Victory" appears to be the only war poem she published, yet in exploring the agonizing human consequences of less-than-mortal battle wounds the poem compares provocatively with Robert Frost's much better known "Not to Keep."

Victory

> *Century* 93 (July 1917): 459–60.

Edith M. Thomas

For Thomas's biography see 281.

Aquila: (A War Change)

> *New York Times* 25 July 1917: 10.

> "Aquila": A northern constellation, the Eagle.

Florence Guertin Tuttle

Florence Guertin Tuttle (1869–1951) came from an eminently respectable family and, whether in spite of or because of this, remained a steadfast pacifist throughout her life. In "Who's Who among the Editors of Four Lights," which the New York Woman's Peace party published to debunk the federal government's claim that the editors were foreigners and Germanophiles, Tuttle wrote, "My mother was a descendant of Patrick Henry. I have always felt that I inherited my radical views from this one of the world's great rebels. My husband is descended from Mayflower ancestry" (*Four Lights* 28 July 1917: supp.). Prior to the war Tuttle helped edit Margaret Sanger's *Birth Control Review.* In 1916 she served as one of the three vice chairs of the New York Woman's Peace party and remained active in this branch of the national party—the only branch to continue pacifist agitation throughout the war. After the war, believing that U.S. involvement in the League of Nations was crucial for the continuance of peace, Tuttle served as the chair of the Women's Pro-League Council and headed the New York branch of the League of Nations Non-Partisan Council.

IF. A Mother to Her Daughter

> *Four Lights* 28 July 1917: 3.

> "IF. . . . (After Rudyard Kipling.)": "If" was a widely known poem of fatherly advice to a son by Rudyard Kipling first published in 1910. The poem's four stanzas consist of a series of conditional clauses beginning with "if," with the corresponding "then" clause arriving only in the final two lines: "[Then] Yours is the Earth and everything that's in it, / And—which is more—you'll be a Man, my son!"

Sarah Norcliffe Cleghorn

Although Sarah Norcliffe Cleghorn had achieved some popularity as a novelist before the U.S. intervention, publishing *The Turnpike Lady* (1907) and *The Spinster* (1916), her associations with antiwar activism and her pacifist publications during the war made her work virtually unsalable thereafter. Cleghorn belonged to the New York branch of the Woman's Peace party, was an editor of the party organ, *Four Lights,* and attended the Washington, D.C., demonstration held in April 1917 to protest her country's impending entry into the war. Born in 1876 in Norfolk, Virginia, Cleghorn remained a member of the Women's International League for Peace and Freedom (the successor of the Woman's Peace party) until her death in 1959. She was also a member of the War Resisters League, the NAACP, and the American League to Abolish Capital Punishment. Reared Episcopalian, Cleghorn became a Quaker in adulthood and is buried in the Chestnut Hill Friends Burial Ground in Plymouth Meetings, Pennsylvania. Her "War Journal of a Pacifist, 1917" is extant in the archives of the Society of Friends Library at Swarthmore College.

Peace Hath Her Belgiums

Portraits and Protests. New York: Holt, Aug. 1917. 66.

"Uhlans": German cavalrymen, literally, but the term was used widely in the American press to refer pejoratively to German soldiers.

James Oppenheim

James Oppenheim was born in St. Paul, Minnesota, in 1882 and attended Columbia University between 1901 and 1903, though he did not receive a degree. During the same period he worked on the lower east side of Manhattan at the Hudson Guild Settlement House and subsequently taught school at the Hebrew Technical School for Girls in the same neighborhood. As much as his university education, Oppenheim's contact with working-class immigrants shaped his art; his poetry emerged from a radically progressive attitude honed by practical experience. Thus, when Oppenheim began writing and publishing free verse poetry first in *Songs for the New Age* (1914), then in *War and Laughter* (1916) and *The Book of the Self* (1917), his aims as a poet tended toward social criticism and philosophic exhortation—both qualities which in spite of his contemporary reputation as a "New Poet" have contributed to his obscurity today. When Oppenheim published *Seven Arts* from November 1916 to October 1917, he stood behind Randolph Bourne because he believed a journal of "arts and criticism" unwilling to do the latter work would not do justice to the former, either. Indeed, in August, September, and October 1917, Oppenheim wrote his editorials in free verse form, effectively merging the daily poem and the editorial, which were provisionally kept distinct in newspapers. Oppenheim published thirteen books of poetry, fiction, and popular psychology in his lifetime; he died in 1932.

Editorial

Seven Arts 2 (Aug. 1917): 489–92.

Scharmel Iris

Scharmel Iris was born in Florence, Italy, in 1889 and as a child immigrated with his family to Chicago. In his early career Iris received considerable recognition as a rising poet: his *Lyrics of a Lad* (1914) acknowledged, among the prior publishers of his work, the *Atlantic, Century, Little Review, Poetry,* and *Scribner's* in the United States and the *English Review* and *Blackwood's* in England. Woodrow Wilson dictated a preface for Iris's next collection, *Bread and Hyacinths* (1923). William Butler Yeats wrote a preface for Iris, as well, but it had to wait until 1953 to accompany Iris's third collection, *Bread out of Stone.* By this time, Iris's typically rhymed verse, especially ballad stanzas, had fallen far out of critical favor. Ironically, it was *Poetry,* the famous promoter of the "New Poetry," that virtually stood alone in championing Iris's work: one poem from *Bread out of Stone* had been previously published in the *Little Review,* thirty out of a total of fifty-three appeared in *Poetry,* and none were printed anywhere else. Other war poems in *Bread out of Stone* reveal that Iris was a partisan of the Allies and a celebrant of their soldiers' sacrificial death. "War-Time Cradle Song," while it may be read (and may be intended) as a condemnation of the autocratic governments of the Central Powers, is emphatic enough in its revolutionary anger to be directed toward any government for whom war service is compulsory.

War-Time Cradle Song

Poetry 10 (Sept. 1917): 302.
Bread out of Stone. Chicago: Regnery, 1953. 33.

Arthur Davison Ficke

Arthur Davison Ficke's popularity and influence as a poet was greatest during World War I, although his verse was largely traditional in form and romantic in tone. Born in 1883 in Davenport, Iowa, Ficke took his undergraduate degree at Harvard, returned to the University of Iowa for a law degree, and joined his father's law practice. All the while, however, he worked steadily on his literary art and art criticism. Between 1907 and 1917 he published seven collections of poetry, two plays, and two influential books on Japanese art. Ficke's art criticism and his appearance in the inaugural issue (and many subsequent issues) of *Poetry* single him out as one of the forward-thinking poets coming of age around World War I; but his first two poems in *Poetry* were sonnets, his best-regarded book was *Sonnets of a Portrait-Painter* (1914), and he and fellow poet Witter Bynner parodied the Imagists and other self-proclaimed "new poets" by posing as the "Spectrists." Under the names "Anne Knish" and "Emanuel Morgan," Ficke and Bynner published an anthology, *Spectra,* in 1916 and, before acknowledging their ruse in 1918, persuaded Alfred Kreymborg to feature them in a special issue of *Others.*

To the Beloved of One Dead

Scribner's 62 (Sept. 1917): 289.

Louis Untermeyer

For Untermeyer's biography see 290.

Battle Hymn of the Russian Republic

> *Masses* Sept. 1917: 27.
> Anthologized in Braithwaite (1917) 176.

"Let our white passion prevail / Till the terror is driven out": One crux of the poem is just what "the terror" refers to: with the Bolsheviks threatening the Russian republic from within and the German army occupying more territory by the day, the threats are multiple, yet Untermeyer's word choice offers a singular "terror."

"Turn all these fires to shake / Against their refuge of lies": Here lies a second crux. While the first half of the poem addresses "us" in republican Russia, the second speaks to "you" sympathetic readers elsewhere in the world. But who is the "they" and what is their "refuge of lies"? Imperial Germany? The Bolsheviks? Capitalist governments in the West more concerned with what Russia can do for them than what they can do for Russia?

Arturo Giovannitti

For Giovannitti's biography see 303–4.

When the Cock Crows

> *Solidarity* 27 Sept. 1917: 2.
> *Masses* Oct. 1917: 18–20.

"When the Cock Crows": The four gospels of the Christian New Testament record the story of Simon Peter, a disciple of Jesus, who during the night of his master's trial denies being his follower three times before the cock crows.

"the man who spoke against war and insulted the army": Frank Little, an IWW organizer, arrived in Butte, Montana, in mid-July to proselytize among miners then on strike against the Anaconda Copper Company. In his speeches to the striking workers, Little also spoke out against the draft and U.S. intervention.

"Molly Macguires": Molly Maguire was the generic name for any member of a secret Irish society founded in 1843 to resist British rule. In the United States, the term referred to militant unionists, particularly those in the coal fields.

"Albert Parson, George Engel, Adolph Fischer, August Spies": These four men were executed in 1887 for organizing the 1886 Haymarket labor demonstrations at which a bomb exploded, killing seven police officers.

"Leo Frank": In 1913 Leo Frank, a long-established Atlanta businessman and a Jew, was convicted for the rape of an employee. In 1915 Frank's death sentence was commuted, but a mob seized him from the state penitentiary in Marietta and lynched him in the town square.

"Joe Hill": See his biography on 279–80.

"I know what they promised to him, for I have heard thrice the bargains": This refers to Giovannitti's own experience as a radical organizer jailed and falsely accused of crimes. Most famous of these was Giovannitti's imprisonment and trial in Lawrence, Massachusetts, in 1913.

"Behold! I announce now to you a great tiding of joy": Appropriation of the angel's greeting to the shepherds announcing Jesus' birth in the Christian gospel of Luke.

Bernice Evans

The little we know about Bernice Evans may be gathered from her publication of "The Sayings of Patsy" in the *New York Call*. She was probably, though not certainly, an editor on the *Call's* staff because the "Sayings" appeared in thirteen different Sunday editions in the fall and winter of 1917–18, including six straight weeks beginning on 23 September. No book publications are attributed to Evans, and the occasional awkwardness of her verse and especially the endings of some poems suggest she was a classic journalistic poet: writing quickly to meet close deadlines and striving for timeliness rather than artistic polish. Within this context, the poems' trenchant, unflinching criticism of the U.S. mobilization is nothing short of remarkable because the *Call* was continually battling the postmaster over whether its content was subversive and therefore undeliverable by mail.

The Sayings of Patsy

New York Call 30 Sept. 1917: magazine sec., 13. Illus.

"You can't pick up / A magazine / these days . . .": The "Housekeeping magazines" such as *Ladies' Home Journal* and *Good Housekeeping* did indeed offer a variety of features and regular columns explaining how essential foodstuffs could be conserved without compromising health or displeasing the family palate.

"If these thrift-crazy folk / Would go after / The food speculators . . .": See the note for Berton Braley, "The Traitor, "The traitor who holds up a nation for gain" on 309.

Vachel Lindsay

For Lindsay's biography see 282–83.

The Soap-Box

Poetry 11 (Oct. 1917): 14–16.
Literary Digest 15 Dec. 1917: 36.

"Kerensky": Alexandr Feodorovich Kerensky, a leader in the March 1917 revolution that deposed Czar Nicholas, became premier of the Russian republic. Under his leadership republican Russia continued the war against Germany but, after initial successes, was beaten as badly as czarist Russia had been. Kerensky and the republic were in turn toppled by the Bolshevik Revolution of November 1917.

"Henry-George": Sandwiched here between the well-known Marx and Wilson, Henry George was a nineteenth-century American economist and journalist who advocated the single tax, a progressive reform. His book *Progress and Poverty,* published in 1879, was widely read and admired among late nineteenth-century reformers and radicals.

"And holy maiden soldiers who have cut away their locks": Partly out of desperation for soldiers willing to fight, partly as a publicity maneuver to shame Russian men into fighting, the Russian provisional government under Kerensky recruited a women's brigade that went into action in June 1917 with considerable military success but then, along with the rest of the Russian army, was defeated badly and disintegrated in the general retreat of July.

Katharine Lee Bates

For Bates's biography see 277.

The Retinue

Atlantic Monthly 120 (Oct. 1917): 508–9.
Four Lights 20 Oct. 1917: 1.
The Retinue and Other Poems. New York: Dutton, 1918. 1–3.
Anthologized in Eaton 137–38.

"But captain of a mighty train, millions upon millions": By the fall of 1917, conservative (and, in fact, fairly accurate) estimates of the war dead stood at seven million.

"Led by Kitchener of Khartoum, march the English legions": Lord Kitchener was "of Khartoum" by dint of his leadership of an Egyptian colonial army that had crushed a rebellion in Sudan in the 1890s (see the note for William Lloyd Garrison Jr., "[The Anglo-Saxon Christians, with Gatling gun and sword,]" "The mahdis and the sirdars along the great Soudan" on 278). Kitchener was appointed British secretary of war soon after hostilities began and became famous for overseeing the recruitment and training of England's huge volunteer army of 1914 and 1915. Just at the outset of a diplomatic mission to Russia in June 1916, he was drowned when the ship transporting him struck a mine and went down off the Orkney Islands of Scotland.

McLandburgh Wilson [Florence McLandburgh]

For McLandburgh's biography see 285.

Made Safe for Democracy

The Little Flag on Main Street. New York: Macmillan, Oct. 1917. 3–4.

"They've taken the men folks and used 'em for slaves . . .": The forced labor of Belgian men deported to Germany, the rape of Belgian women, and the dismemberment of Belgian children were atrocities trumpeted by Allied propaganda that, though unproven, were reported widely in the American press.

Company for Dinner

The Little Flag on Main Street. New York: Macmillan, Oct. 1917. 123.

Lola Ridge

Born in 1883 in Ireland, Lola Ridge was raised in Australia and New Zealand and im-migrated in 1907 to the United States, where she was always an exponent of radical causes. Relatively obscure as a poet when "Bread" appeared in the *New York Call*, Ridge was hailed (and disparaged) in 1918 when her lengthy piece "The Ghetto," focusing on Jewish Americans on the Lower East Side of Manhattan, appeared in the *New Republic*. It was the title poem in her first collection appearing later that year, and its critical success led to jobs as the overseas editor for the English avant-garde magazine *Broom* and as the guest editor for several issues of *Others*. Ridge's later collections were *Sun-Up* (1920); *Red Flag* (1927), inspired by the development of the Communist International; *Firehead* (1929), written in response to the Sacco and Vanzetti case; and *Dance of Fire* (1935). She died in 1941.

Bread

New York Call 19 Oct. 1917: 10.

("Women's demonstration against the high cost of living . . ."): During the war, bread riots and demonstrations were not uncommon in working-class neighborhoods. Demonstrations took place in January 1915 in Chicago, in December 1916 in New York City, and in February and March 1917 in New York City, Philadelphia, and Boston.

"They heard at their councils: / Bread!": The reference here is almost certainly to workers' councils, a socialist style of labor organization prevalent among recent Jewish immigrants, and in 1917 especially inspired by the Russian Revolution. In the summer of 1917 socialist and predominantly Jewish labor organizations such as the International Ladies' Garment Workers' Union and the Amalgamated Clothing Workers of America were primary supporters of the most radical of all pacifist groups to form during the war, the People's Council of America for Democracy and Peace—and perhaps it is this group, as well, that Ridge means to suggest by her reference to "councils."

Mary Alden Hopkins

Mary Alden Hopkins was active in the New York branch of the Woman's Peace party and was one of the rotating group of members who edited *Four Lights*. She also regu-larly published pieces in this four-page bimonthly bulletin, including "The Picket," published in the final issue of *Four Lights*, and the scabrous "Woman's Way in War" in the 2 June 1917 issue, which was deemed seditious by the post office and not deliv-ered (even though the Espionage Act empowering the post office to act as censor was not passed until June 15). Hopkins's satire was indeed sharp, even ruthless: "Accustom your children gradually to the sight of blood. . . . Women have often been accused of being essentially producers and conservers. Now is the time for them to lay forever that slander and prove that they are glad and eager to destroy joyfully all that the ages— and other women—have produced" (*Four Lights* 28 July 1917: 4). In "Who's Who among the Editors of the Four Lights," Hopkins wrote that her family lineage went back to the Plymouth colony, that her ancestors fought in the French and Indian War

and the Revolutionary War, but that "the ancestor with whom I feel the most sympa-
thy at present is the one who was hanged as a witch by the Salem judges" (*Four Lights*
28 July 1917: supp.)

The Picket

Four Lights 20 Oct. 1917: 2.

"The Picket": Refers to the National Woman's party picket line outside the
White House.
"Men tell us women / Not to ask for suffrage now": In 1917, the Wilson admin-
istration took the position that any action or discussion of the suffrage
amendment would interfere with the war mobilization.

Bernice Evans

For Evans's biography see 315.

The Sayings of Patsy

New York Call 21 Oct. 1917: magazine sec., 12. Illus.

"It certainly is / Cruel / To make him / Carry around / All that money, / Too":
The stick-figure illustration accompanying the poem shows a soldier push-
ing a wheelbarrow heaped full of silver dollars.

Carl Sandburg

For Sandburg's biography see 281–82.

The Four Brothers

Chicago Evening Post 29 Oct. 1917: 8.
Poetry 11 (Nov. 1917): 59–66.
New York Globe and Commercial Advertiser 14 Nov. 1917: 10.
Cornhuskers. New York: Holt, 1918. 143–47.
Christian Century 4 July 1918: 11. Excerpt, facsimile of Sandburg holograph.

"A million, ten million, singing, 'I am ready'": On 5 June 1917, national draft
registration day, 9.5 million U.S. men between the ages of twenty-one and
thirty were enrolled.
"Three times ten million men say: No": Sandburg's estimate of the number of
Allied military personnel would have included the several millions in the
Russian armies who by the fall of 1917 had said no not only to the czar—
which the poem celebrates—but also to fighting at all—which the poem
overlooks in its strong alliance of the "four brothers."
"The graves from the Irish Sea to the Caucasus peaks are ten times a million":
A slightly high estimate of those killed in the war at the time, but quite close
to many estimates for the final death toll.

James Weldon Johnson

Born in Jacksonville, Florida, James Weldon Johnson (1871–1938) was the first African American lawyer to be admitted to the Florida bar since Reconstruction. Johnson was the well-known author of the (actually fictional) *Autobiography of an Ex-Coloured Man* (1912), an advocate of black arts, a song and poetry anthologist, an elder statesmen of the Harlem Renaissance, and a lifelong political activist. Beginning in 1916 and continuing through 1930, Johnson was a field officer with the NAACP. Later he was a U.S. consul to Venezuela and Nicaragua and a teacher at Fisk University. When published in the *Crisis,* "To America" was surrounded by an elaborate drawing by Laura Wheeler: a grouping of black women stand, kneel, or sit—one in supplication with chains on her hands, another bent and exhausted, another protecting a winsome child—as a white woman on a pedestal stands oblivious, her eyes closed, leaning against a Grecian column and wearing Old Glory garb a la Howard Chandler Christy posters.

To America

> *Crisis* 15 (Nov. 1917): 13. Illus.
> *Fifty Years and Other Poems.* Boston: Cornhill, 1917. 5.

Woman's Suffrage Prisoners at Occoquan Work House

By the late summer of 1917, White House suffrage picketers were serving their sentences for "obstruction of traffic" at the Occoquan Work House, the women's prison in Arlington, Virginia. Conditions were brutal: suffrage prisoners were placed in solitary confinement, hunger strikers were force-fed, and the forty-one new arrivals of 14 November were beaten and hurled into their cells. When conditions were publicized by the press—particularly the outrage of 14 November—Woodrow Wilson ordered the immediate release of the prisoners and shortly thereafter announced his public support for what was to become the Nineteenth Amendment. "We Worried Woody-Wood" was one of many songs invented and sung by suffrage picketers while in prison. It was performed at a welcoming party on 4 November by ten prisoners who had just been released from sixty-day terms.

[We Worried Woody-Wood]

> *Suffragist* 10 Nov. 1917: 4.

"Woody-Wood": Term of mocking endearment for Woodrow Wilson.

"We asked him for the vote, / But he'd rather write a note": Wilson's several diplomatic "Notes" to Germany had been instrumental in averting war in 1915 and 1916 and were widely publicized.

"We asked them for a brush, / For our teeth. . . . We asked them for a night-ie . . .": Newspaper reporting about conditions in the prison worked as a public relations boon in part because many readers felt outrage at middle- and upper-class women being treated like working-class criminals. Race prejudice played a role as well; a large proportion of inmates at Occoquan were black. As the *Masses* editors remarked, "It appears the warden of the Occ[o]quan workhouse called some of the pickets' bluffs by demanding that they eat at the same board with negro prisoners. '*Gentlewomen,*' we read, 'compelled to eat with negroes!'" ("Calling").

"And they looked—hightie-tightie": The sense of this slang appears to describe the prison matrons as "high and mighty," taking a superior attitude, and "tight," as in stingy.

"Don't quote the President": One of the picketers' most successful strategies for devising slogans was to quote from Wilson's numerous pronouncements about the importance of democracy, which reportedly infuriated Wilson and effectively insulated the picketers from prosecution under the Espionage Act.

Zelda

It may not be possible to discover which editor at the *New York Call* or which favorite of the paper went by the pen name Zelda. The author might be Zelda Stewart Charters, who published "War Song for the Socialist Suffrage Campaign of 1917" in the 7 October issue, although "Zelda" appears to be used as a pseudonym here. In any case, the poem exhibits the puckish wit and free verse that the *Call* seems to have inspired, or demanded, from its authors.

To the Patriotic Lady across the Way

New York Call 20 Nov. 1917: 8.

"She wore a Liberty loan button": The button indicates that the woman has subscribed to one of the five war bond issues offered by the federal government to finance the war mobilization. The Liberty Loans offered investors a 3.5 percent fixed rate over thirty years. The rate was at least half a point below the current bond market, so middle- and working-class Americans who oversubscribed were in fact making a patriotic sacrifice. Income on the bonds was nontaxable, however, a policy which brought a financial windfall to banks and Americans rich enough to be subject to the federal income tax.

"And her knitting needles clicked / Through some soldier's sweater": The Red Cross and other service organizations encouraged donations of hand-knitted sweaters, mufflers, mittens, and, most famously, socks to be distributed to U.S. soldiers in France. The upper- and middle-class women who did the largest share of this voluntary patriotic service were dubbed "Sister Susies." Their efforts were reputedly used "for cleaning guns and swabbing decks" more often than for their intended purposes (Anthony).

Amelia Josephine Burr

Amelia Josephine Burr was born in New York City in 1878 and graduated from Hunter College. Although well enough known before the war as the author of gentle, humorous poetry in a popular style comparable to Edgar Guest's, she came into her own during the war, becoming one of the most prolific of all American war poets. Her collections *In Deep Places* (1914), *Life and Living* (1916), *Silver Trumpet* (1918), and *Hearts Awake* (1919) all contain or consist entirely of poems about the war. She also placed at least sixty-five individual poems in journals including *Bellman, Bookman, Current Opinion, Current History Magazine* (of the *New York Times*), *Daughters of the Ameri-*

can Revolution Magazine, Everybody's Magazine, Good Housekeeping, Literary Digest, The Nation, Outlook, and *Woman's Home Companion.* She was, in addition, a founding member of the Vigilantes, so her poems were both featured in the *Fifes and Drums* anthology and broadcast by the Vigilantes syndicate to practically countless numbers of small newspapers.

Father O'Shea

> *Outlook* 117 (21 Nov. 1917): 462.
> Anthologized in Braithwaite (1918) 135–36.

> "Father O'Shea was his regiment's pride. / Sturdy, fine sons of the emerald
>   sod": The regiment referred to is almost certainly the Fighting 69th of the
>   New York National Guard, later designated the 165th regiment of the U.S.
>   Army. The regiment consisted almost entirely of Irish American volunteers
>   from New York City and was among the first American units to be brought
>   into line on the Western Front.
> "'It's clean wheat for heaven the Berthas will reap'": Berthas were German
>   heavy artillery, named so by arms manufacturer Gustav Krupp in honor of
>   his wife. The Krupps steel and munitions plants in Essen were the largest in
>   Germany.
> "There were women with eyes that were shallow and bold / In the quarter in-
>   closed . . .": Whereas French military authorities established, licensed, and
>   regularly inspected brothels near military camps in the rear, the U.S. Army
>   warned its trainees of the dangers of venereal disease, prohibited soldiers in
>   France from visiting prostitutes, and discouraged fraternization with French
>   women.

Bernice Evans

For Evans's biography see 315.

The Sayings of Patsy

> *New York Call* 30 Dec. 1917: magazine sec., 12. Illus.

> "There's a / Horrible Grin, / Up on Oyster Bay": Oyster Bay was Theodore
>   Roosevelt's residence.

1918

McLandburgh Wilson [Florence McLandburgh]

For McLandburgh's biography see 285.

Poetic Justice

> Newspaper clipping. 1918. Peace Poems subject file, box 2, folder W. Swarth-
>   more College Peace Collection, Swarthmore, Pa.

"To make him kiss the flag / Atonement will not suit": Not infrequently, American dissenters (or those thought to be dissenting or, sometimes, those simply of German or Austrian ethnicity) were forced by patriotic mobs to kiss the flag, often after being otherwise humiliated and, on a few occasions, before being killed. Just in the state of Illinois, such incidents occurred in the towns of Alton, Athens, Collinsville, La Salle, and Pocahontas (Schaffer 21–23).

"On war stamps make him spend": See the note for Zelda, "To the Patriotic Lady across the Way," "She wore a Liberty loan button" on 320. The certificates for Liberty Loans had a gummed backing so they could be collected and pasted together into books provided for the purpose.

Anonymous

The *Detroit Labor News* was affiliated with the American Federation of Labor, which early on, even before the war declaration, had agreed to cooperate with the mobilization and whose chairman, Samuel Gompers, was the sole labor representative on the War Industries Board. Pledges of loyalty did not, however, keep this *Detroit Labor News* writer from taking a swipe at Herbert Hoover's food conservation measures—albeit anonymously.

O, You Hoover!

Detroit Labor News 1 Feb. 1918: 4.

"My home it is heatless": Reference to the wartime increase in the prices of fuels for heating.

"The barrooms are treatless": Many communities went dry as a war measure to save grain products. This wartime development helped the Prohibition movement build momentum for the final drive for a national amendment.

"My stockings are feetless": Apparently, the patriotic knitting campaigns had given soldiers more socks than they needed but left the folks at home with fewer than necessary.

Baker Brownell

Before the war, Baker Brownell (1897–1965) was educated as a philosopher at Harvard, Tübingen, and Cambridge Universities. After the war he had a distinguished twenty-year career as a Northwestern University philosophy professor. In the 1920s he was also an editorial writer with the *Chicago Daily News* and the *Chicago Tribune*. During the war Baker was a soldier—and a soldier-poet featured in *Poetry* magazine. As an enlisted man in the army, Baker was sent to help patrol the border during the Mexican disputes of 1916. After the declaration of war with Germany he gained commissions as a second lieutenant in the army and later as an ensign with the navy. His poems of March 1918 indicate acquaintance with army training camps but not with combat (which this early would in fact have been rare for a U.S. serviceman).

Freebourne's Rifle

Poetry 11 (Mar. 1918): 316–17.

"'It's an old gun,' the major said": Training in the U.S. Army was hampered by a shortage of rifles. Private Freebourne may be lucky in having a gun at all; some infantry soldiers drilled with stick-guns, others received their rifles only just before embarkation and never fired them in stateside training camps.

"To the Q. M.": To the Quartermaster.

Lucian B. Watkins

Born in 1879 in Chesterfield, Virginia, and educated at the Virginia Normal and Industrial Institute in Petersburg, a traditionally all-black institution, Lucian B. Watkins worked as a teacher for some time after his graduation. Throughout his adult life he was regularly featured in the *Richmond Planet,* a black newspaper, as both a poet and a correspondent. He evidently chose a career in the military no later than 1913, as in October 1917 he reported to the *Planet* after a four-year tour of duty in the Philippines. By 1917 he had risen to the rank of first sergeant in the Army Medical Department and was on his way to service in France. En route to Europe, Watkins wrote glowingly of the justice of the American cause and its benefits for African Americans: "This war is going to put the true gold stamp on real men and women the world over; good citizenship in black men and women will be appreciated; intelligence and thrift will become colorless; lynch lawlessness is going to become unpopular. . . . When I think about this war and its significance, I am glad to be a part, however small[,] of this great movement for the betterment of the world" (1). This optimism seems to have been dampened quite soon by events at home, including the Houston riot and the lynching of a black man in Tennessee, which Watkins refers to in "The Negro Soldiers of America." His health was shattered while in France, and he died in a stateside military hospital in 1921.

The Negro Soldiers of America: What We Are Fighting for

Richmond Planet 2 Mar. 1918: 1.

John Pierre Roche

John Pierre Roche (1889–1960) is a prime example of someone who felt summoned to versify about the war but otherwise did not consider himself a poet. The only books of poetry he ever published—self-published—were about his experiences as a soldier, *Rimes in Olive Drab* (1918) and *Rimes from France* (1928). Born in Aberdeen, South Dakota, Roche served in the U.S. Army from 1917 to 1919, received a commission as an officer, and was sent to France assigned to headquarters of the 87th Infantry Division. His military service amounted to a three-year hiatus from a successful career in advertising: having gotten a start in Chicago soon after his 1911 graduation from Columbia, Roche in 1926 founded his own firm at which he remained a partner until his death. In March 1918 Roche was featured, along with the better-known American soldier-poet Charles Divine, in a *Literary Digest* review of army training camp poetry. Note that U.S. soldiers did not see significant combat until late spring 1918. Twice as many U.S. soldiers died in training camps from influenza as were killed in France in combat. The

Literary Digest calls Roche "humorous, thoughtful, and poetic," and quotes "You Were So White, So Soft" as "an example of his first quality."

"You Were So White, So Soft"

Rimes in Olive Drab. [Houston, Tex.]: by the author, 1918. [26].
Literary Digest 23 Mar. 1918: 47.

Covington Ami [Covington Hall]

Although born into a patrician Southern family, Covington Hall grew up amid economic uncertainty: his father separated from his mother soon after Hall was born in 1871, and his mother's family, always of uncertain finances in Hall's youth, lost its sugar cane plantation in 1891. At about the same time, Hall's beloved half uncle and guardian through much of his childhood, Ami Woods, died; it was in tribute to this uncle that Hall regularly wrote under the pen names Ami, Covami, or, as in the poems reprinted here, Covington Ami. Thereafter Hall supported himself in various professions, making money by selling insurance, practicing law, and teaching college. Most notably, however, Hall was a labor organizer, reporter, and poet. In 1913 and 1914 he edited the *Lumberjack,* the newspaper of the Brotherhood of Timber Workers, a Louisiana and East Texas union affiliated with the IWW. Later he worked as a labor organizer among loggers in the Pacific Northwest. Hall became especially prominent in the IWW after the highest-ranking union officials were rounded up in September 1917, as he published his poetry regularly in *New Solidarity* (the eastern organ of the IWW, replacing the suppressed "old" *Solidarity*) as well as the western organs of the IWW, the *Industrial Worker* and the *Lumberjack Bulletin*—the latter being a four-page newssheet that ran in weeks alternating with the more substantial former publication, to save expense. Immediately after the war—and the effective demise of the IWW—Hall was active in the Non-Partisan League of the Dakotas, and during the Great Depression he worked as a professor at the Minnesota Work People's College.

The Captain Said

Lumberjack Bulletin 9 Mar. 1918: 3.

"A rumor roamed that in her hold / Were oodle tons of purest gold": Almost as soon as they took power in Russia, the Bolsheviks were widely believed to be financing the most radical labor unions and political groups in the United States in the hope of fomenting an American revolution. The rumors were no more true than the earlier ones that German gold was bankrolling these groups.

"And Mimic Men mussed up the air": During the short breaks between reels at movie theaters, liberty bonds were hawked and other patriotic messages were conveyed by volunteers dubbed "Four-Minute Men."

"They chased a clue, they smelt a rat, / And swore they saw a sabby cat": The IWW symbol for sabotage (much talked about in the union but seldom used) was the black cat. This image was popularized by Ralph H. Chaplin; for a sample see the illustration on 122.

Wallace Irwin

For Irwin's biography see 278.

Ode to Tonsilitis

> Press release. Apr. 18. Vigilantes Press Releases, ca. Apr. 1918. Hermann Hagedorn Collection, Manuscript Division, Library of Congress.

> "Since Senatorial Rules decree once more": In March 1917, Robert M. La Follette and ten other senators successfully filibustered legislation to arm U.S. merchant ships. Wilson denounced the recalcitrant senators as "a little group of wilful men, representing no opinion but their own" who had "rendered the great government of the United States helpless and contemptible" (qtd. in Sullivan 5:269). Later that month, the Senate passed cloture rules closing debate for any measure on which a two-thirds majority wished to vote.
> "That one wild donkey still may hold the floor": La Follette was the dominant figure of Wisconsin politics in his time—a progressive Republican who served in the U.S. Senate from 1906 to 1925. La Follette was one of only two senators who voted against the war resolution. Although denied the filibuster, he continued to attempt liberalization of the war legislation coming before Congress.
> "And Robert spurns the Flag beneath the Ford": Although Henry Ford had dedicated his auto assembly plants to war production from the very beginning of mobilization, he was still remembered as the backer of the Peace Ship debacle. The line also appears to invoke the interventionists' charge that opponents favored neutrality because of the economic benefits it conferred.

Wallace Stevens

Written in 1917, "Lettres d'un Soldat" was inspired by the letters of the French soldier and painter Eugène Emmanuel Lemercier, missing in action on the Western Front in April 1915. Available in book form in French since 1916 and in English in 1917, the letters were excerpted by Stevens to supply epigraphs for each poem, providing a dialog between Lermercier's first-hand account of the war and Stevens's commentary. But "Lettres" was gradually dissected and largely abandoned in the end: Out of as many as seventeen poems, Stevens sent thirteen to *Poetry* in September 1917 and, together with Harriet Monroe, later reduced the number appearing in the May 1918 issue to nine. Only three of these, plus one rescued from the original manuscript, were selected by Stevens for publication in his books, and then with the excerpts from Lermercier's letters omitted. For Stevens's biography see 286.

From Lettres d'un Soldat

> *Poetry* 12 (May 1918): 62–65.
> IX (as "The Death of a Soldier"), VII (as "Negation"), and V (as "The Surprises of the Superhuman"). *Harmonium.* Rev. ed. New York: Knopf, 1931. 166–68.
> VI and VIII (renumbered VII). *Opus Posthumous.* Ed. Samuel French Morse. New York: Knopf, 1957. 14–15.

Translations of French epigraphs provided by Scott Fish.

The following appears in *Poetry* as an epigraph for the poem as a whole: *"Combattre avec ses frères, à sa place, à son rang, avec des yeux dessillés, sans espoir de la gloire et de profit, et simplement parceque telle est la loi, voilà le commandement que donne le dieu au guerrier Arjuna, quand celui-ci doute s'il doit se détourner de l'absolu pour le cauchemar humain de la bataille . . . Simplement, qu'Arjuna bande son arc avec les autres Kshettryas!" (Préface d'André Chevrillon)* [To fight alongside one's brother, in his place, within his rank, with eyes open, without hope of glory or profit, and simply because that is the law, such is the commandment that the god gives to the warrior Arjuna when he doubts whether he must turn away from the absolute to the human nightmare of battle. . . . Arjuna simply bends with the other Kshettryas!].

V

"J'ai la ferme espérance . . .": I have steadfast hope; but I especially have confidence in eternal justice, whatever surprise it causes the human idea that we have of it.

"palais de justice": Law courts.

"Uebermenschlichkeit": "Supermanliness," or having the qualities of the Superman, as described by Friedrich Nietzsche.

VI

"Bien chère mère aimée . . .": Beloved dear mother, . . . as for your heart, I have confidence in your courage, and at this hour my certitude is a great comfort to me. I know that my mother has achieved this liberty of the soul which allows the contemplation of the universal spectacle.

"O chère maman": O dear mamma.

VII

"La seule sanction . . .": The only punishment for me is my conscience. We must place ourselves in the hands of an impersonal justice, independent of every human factor; and in the hands of a useful and harmonious destiny in spite of every horror of convention.

"Negation": The intermediate moment of the Hegelian dialectic, wherein presence (thesis) becomes conscious of that which it lacks (its negation) and strives, consequently, for more inclusive being (synthesis).

VIII

"Hier soir . . .": Last night, coming back to my barn, drunkenness, brawls, cries, songs, howls. That is life!

IX

"La mort du soldat . . .": The death of a soldier is near to natural things.

Berton Braley

For Braley's biography see 309.

Consequences

New York Times 6 May 1918: 10.

He "wanted to go," but his wife said "No!": The important backdrop for this repeated line and, indeed, the entire poem is the prominence and leadership of women in the peace movement who asserted themselves in politics, military policy, and diplomacy, areas supposedly outside the "woman's sphere."

Vachel Lindsay

For Lindsay's biography see 282–83.

The Jazz Bird

Press release. [May.] Vigilantes Press Releases, ca. May 1918. Hermann Hagedorn Collection, Manuscript Division, Library of Congress.
As "The Modest Jazz-Bird." *Poetry* 14 (Aug. 1919): 258.

"The eagle said: 'Son Jazz Bird, / I send you out to fight'": Lindsay's tribute to black soldiers, mediated through the figure of the "Jazz Bird," refers first to the willing service of the 370,000 African Americans who were drafted and the roughly 30,000 who volunteered or already were service members. But in May 1918 he could have known of the first black American troops on the Western Front: the 369th Regiment was in action on 14 May and was among the first American units to fight. The 369th, 370th, 371st, and 372d Regiments fought with the French, first helping to stem German offensives and then joining the Allied counteroffensive. They were at the front longer than almost all units comprised of white Americans; though their officers and soldiers were often passed over for promotions and decorations by the U.S. Army, the French gave unit citations to three of the four regiments as well as honors to many individual soldiers.
"And the Jazz Bird spread his sunflower wings": "Sunflower" was argot for black America; as Du Bois remarked in the *Crisis*, "Thousands of young black men have offered their lives for the Lilies of France and they return ready to offer them again for the Sun-flowers of Afro-America" ("Essay" 72).
"At midnight on a haunted road . . .": Perhaps alerted by the *Poetry* editors to the instability of the lynching imagery in this stanza and the next two, Lindsay dropped these final three stanzas in the version published in *Poetry* magazine in 1919, "The Modest Jazz-Bird." Lindsay also made revisions of the stanzas that were reprinted: e.g., "And the Jazz Bird spread his sunflower wings" in the original becomes "So the youngster spread his sunflower wings."

John Curtis Underwood

For Underwood's biography see 308.

At Bethlehem

Poetry 12 (June 1918): 119–20.

"Bethlehem": See the note for Grace Isabel Colbron, "The Ballad of Bethlehem Steel; or, The Need for 'Preparedness'" on 299.

The Red Coffins

Poetry 12 (June 1918): 120–21.

Alice Corbin [Henderson]

A native of St. Louis, Missouri, Alice Corbin Henderson (1881–1949) was a long-time collaborator with Harriet Monroe on *Poetry*. She was the associate editor at the magazine's founding in 1912 and held that position until early in 1916, when she contracted tuberculosis. Relocating in Santa Fe, Henderson continued to publish reviews, commentary, and poetry in the magazine until 1933. Like those evident in the magazine she helped to shape, Henderson's attitudes toward the war closely mirrored mainstream liberal opinion. It was she who initiated and orchestrated the war poetry contest in fall 1914 that revealed the breadth of antiwar attitudes among American poets and also, quite unmistakably, her own antipathy. But Henderson, like Monroe, came to support the U.S. intervention in 1917–18. Henderson, who published her editorials under the initials A. C. H. but her poems under the name Alice Corbin, supported the Vigilantes syndicate with an announcement in the July 1917 issue of *Poetry* and at least one poem distributed through the organization. This poem, "The Planting of the Green," reveals Henderson writing in a rhyming, colloquial light verse typical of Vigilantes poetry but quite different from the poetry she published in her twenty-seven wartime appearances in *Poetry* magazine or in her collections of poetry published in 1912, 1920, and 1933. In short, at least for the duration of the war, Henderson was willing to shift her poetic register from high art to demotic verse.

The Planting of the Green

Press release. June 3. Vigilantes Press Releases, ca. June 1918. Hermann Hagedorn Collection, Manuscript Division, Library of Congress.

"The Planting of the Green": The title appropriates that of a popular Irish song, "The Wearing of the Green."

"Oh, Woody dear": Henderson affectionately adopts the familiar nickname for Woodrow Wilson used by the suffrage activists in "'We Worried Woody-Wood.'"

"It's just a mobilizin' camp / For answerin' the call!": The militarization of Auntie Sam's kitchen and Uncle Sam's farm simply embroiders the rhetoric of the Food Administration. *War Economy in Food with Suggestions and Recipes for Substitutions in the Planning of Meals* (1917) proclaims that "The question of planning meals grows daily more important, because it is more evident that food is to win or lose the war" (9).

Helen Topping Miller

A native of Fenton, Michigan, Helen Topping Miller was born in 1884 and died in 1960. She came to a literary career late, having been largely unknown at the time her "Sock Song" was sent from Morristown, Tennessee, snatched from the one hundred or so weekly entrants to the *New York Sun*'s "sock song" contest, and awarded the top prize for the week ending June 5. (This feat, incidentally, she repeated with another poem, "One! Two!" which imagines the similarity between a knitters' rhythmic movements and the marching of soldiers in France.) Between 1930 and her death, Miller became a prodigious and popular novelist, publishing fifteen books including *White Peacock* (1932), *Splendor of Eagles* (1935), *Last Lover* (1944), and *Slow Dies the Thunder* (1955).

[Sock Song]

> *New York Sun* 9 June 1918: sec. 3: 8.
> *Sock Songs.* Boston: Cornhill, 1919. 98.

> "Sock Song": This sub-subgenre of war poetry was the brainchild of editors at the *New York Sun,* who on 12 May 1918 issued a call for poems on the theme of "patriotic knitting." Entries in the contest, limited to ten lines in length but otherwise not restricted as to form, were intended both to "stimulate" the production of homemade socks sent to members of the American Expeditionary Force and to accompany the socks: "tucked in with socks to go overseas." The contest certainly stimulated production of patriotic verse about woolen hosiery. Within the first month of competition, over one hundred entries arrived at the *Sun* office, on average, each week, sent from sites as far afield as South Dakota, Missouri, and Tennessee. Later in the summer entries arrived from California, Indiana, Michigan, Montana, Virginia, and "several Canadian provinces." Every Sunday edition from 19 May through 10 November brought a fresh round of songs selected by editors for their (relative) excellence. First prize brought, in addition to notoriety, five dollars worth of wool yarn; second prize meant three dollars worth and third prize one dollar worth; honorable mentions were awarded to ten other poems. All 351 poems appearing in the *Sun* were reprinted in the 1919 anthology, where the *Sun* editor supplying the introduction prophesied, "while we have no idea that the anthologist of 2018 A.D. will make many of his choices from among our Sock Songs, to find him listing more than one writer herein represented will not surprise our Spirits in the least!" (Dounce ix). See also the note for Zelda, "To the Patriotic Lady across the Way," "And her knitting needles clicked / Through some soldier's sweater" on 320.

Allen Tucker

Allen Tucker, born in Brooklyn in 1866 (d. 1939), undertook professional training as an architect but eventually followed his inclination to become a painter; his interest in European art, initially in impressionism and later in expressionism, led him to join the avant-garde Association of American Painters and Sculptors, which put on the Armory Show of 1913. Soon after the war began, Tucker volunteered for the American Ambulance Service, a private organization working for the Allies in France; when the United States intervened, he transferred to the American Red Cross. What Tucker saw and experienced in France demanded expression in a medium besides painting, apparently: for the war, he also became a poet, publishing his work in the *New York Times, Scribner's,* and, eventually, his one collection of poems, *There and Here.*

The 367th Infantry

New York Times 12 June 1918: 10.

Crisis 16 (Sept. 1918): 227.

There and Here. New York: Duffield, 1919. 16–17.

"The Buffaloes, / The Black Regiment": The 367th Regiment was part of the
92d Infantry Division, the U.S. Army's single all-black division. The regi-
ment (and later the entire division) went by the nickname "the Buffaloes"
after the honorific title Native Americans gave to black soldiers who fought
them in the nineteenth-century frontier wars. Although some upper ranks of
the regiment were filled out by transfers from the 24th Infantry—the regi-
ment entangled with the Houston riot—the 367th was made up largely by
newly trained recruits and draftees. The 92d Division as a whole was pre-
vented from meaningful action until 10 November, the day before the armi-
stice. As some units of the 368th Regiment had broken and run in the Ar-
gonne offensive of September 1918 (as did many newly trained white
soldiers), the division was held back—officially because its soldiers were
considered unreliable, unofficially because this denied them a second chance
to prove themselves. For information on other black regiments who fought
in France see the note to Vachel Lindsay, "The Jazz Bird," "The eagle said:
'Son Jazz Bird, / I send you out to fight'" on 327.

Ajan Syrian

A biographical note in *Poetry* identifies Ajan Syrian as an immigrant from Syria (pre-
sumably the source of the author's surname, given immigration officers' infinite powers
for giving names and limited imagination in inventing them) and a resident of New
York City at the time his poems appeared. Twice during the war years he published
his work in *Poetry:* first in June 1915 with three poems not about the war, second in
August 1918 with three poems examining the war in the Middle East—"Armenian
Marching Song" and "Syrian Mother's Lullaby" besides the selection reprinted here.

The Prayer Rug of Islam

Poetry 12 (Aug. 1918): 237–39.

"*Makhir Subatu!*": Although this is a proper Arabic name, who exactly is being
referred to is unclear. The sources I have consulted do not identify any public
figures with that name and the contextual evidence in the poem is thin. My
conjecture is that Makhir Subatu is one of the master carpetmakers who
have summoned the poem's persona home, only, he feels, to betray him by
the genocide in wartime Turkey.
"These are the bones of men who loved their Christ": See the note for Lincoln
Colcord, *Vision of War,* canto 15, "dead Christians in Turkey . . . So many
massacred in Turkey" on 296–97.

Byron Beardsley

The byline in *Songs of the Trenches* tells us that Bryon Beardsley was a sergeant in the insurance office of the American Expeditionary Force's Quartermaster's Corps. Otherwise, no biographical information is available. The introductory matter to the volume explains that its poems were selected from the thousand or so poems submitted to a competition for American Expeditionary Force soldier-poets conducted by the *New York Herald* in the spring of 1918. Prior to the publication of *Songs,* just the two prize-winning poems and nine others had appeared; the September collection included a total of ninety-three poems "written on the decks of transports, in French villages, in muddy camps, in the trenches, beside cannon or camion, in hospitals" (xi)— actually, mostly transports, villages, and camps. No unit of the U.S. Army had yet been posted to the front at the time of the contest, so Beardsley's poem that anticipates "getting into the game" is typical of the collection.

The National Game

> *Songs of the Trenches.* Ed. Herbert Adams Gibbons. New York: Harper, Sept. 1918. 53–56.

> "A 'Boche' came up and toed the plate and tripled over Arras": In 1914 elements of the German army passed near Arras on their march toward Paris that ended at the Marne. In subsequent fighting the town was nearly leveled by shelling and came to lie just half a mile away from the front on the British side.

> "In the famous battle of the Marne he was tagged by General Joffre": Joffre was the commanding general of the French army from 1913 to the end of 1916. He was hailed as the hero of the Marne in 1914 but blamed for the failure of the combined English-French Somme offensive in 1916.

> "Canada singled o'er Vimy Ridge (he willingly paid the price)": Vimy Ridge was a German position north of Arras captured by Canadian troops in April 1917 in preparation for a major offensive. This later attack gained no ground, led to heavy casualties, and touched off large-scale mutinies in the French army.

> "Then Edith Cavel[l] walked up to the plate and came through with a sacrifice": See Robert Underwood Johnson's biography and the note for his "Edith Cavell" on 298. Here chronology is sacrificed to fit Beardsley's baseball scenario; Vimy Ridge was taken in April 1917, Cavell executed in October 1915.

> "Italy slammed an offensive, which rang with a sounding thud": By late summer 1917, a series of offensives had appeared to put the Italians in position to seize Trieste, the Austrian port on the Adriatic Sea. Then in October a combined German-Austrian offensive sent the Italian army into a rout that nearly defeated Italy altogether (described in Ernest Hemingway's *A Farewell to Arms*). The demoralization of the Italian soldiers was so complete that it was widely blamed on socialist and pacifist antiwar propaganda, supposedly fomented by German secret agents. The ten-volume *Literary Digest History of the World War,* for example, reports, "Somehow the word was spread (probably by enemy troops disguised in Italian uniforms, for a number of these were caught later and shot) that the war was over, and that there was nothing to do but 'go home'" (Halsey 9:94).

"So Hindenburg, who's catching, has called for the Kaiser's 'spitter'": Paul von
Hindenburg was the commanding general at the August 1914 battle of Tan-
nenberg, East Prussia, where the Russian army had been catastrophically
defeated. On account of continued successes on the Eastern Front and the
Verdun failure on the Western Front in 1916, Hindenburg was promoted to
chief of staff of all German armies, a position he held until the end of the
war. In the 1920s he was president of the Weimar Republic.

Sidney G. Doolittle

Sidney G. Doolittle was a driver with the Convois Automobiles, the French ambulance
service that made use of a significant number of American volunteers (E. E. Cummings
was one). While no other information about Doolittle is available, it is likely that he
had been in France for longer than most of the contributors to *Songs from the Trench-
es*; also, as an ambulance driver, he had probably been exposed to shell fire and had
certainly seen the war's physical damage to human bodies. His considerable cynicism
toward the folks on the home front may, then, be hard earned.

Enthusiasts

Songs of the Trenches. Ed. Herbert Adams Gibbons. New York: Harper, Sept.
1918. 90–92.

"They send me chewing-gum and strange things called sweaters, / And are al-
ways knitting miles of mufflers": See the note for Zelda, "To the Patriotic
Lady across the Way," "And her knitting needles clicked / Through some
soldier's sweater" on 320.

"They complain about the restrictions in America—/ 'Why, I can hardly get
enough meat for Rover!'": See the note to the anonymous "O, You Hoover!"
on 322.

Mary Carolyn Davies

For Davies's biography see 301.

Fire of the Sun

The Drums in Our Street. New York: Macmillan, Sept. 1918. 69–70.

Edward Ten Broeck Perine

Edward Ten Broeck Perine (1870–1941) was an accountant by vocation, a poet and avid
student of the theater by avocation. From 1911 until his death, he was a partner in the
family accountancy firm, Perine and Company. He was also a published author, writ-
ing of both his profession (*The Story of the Trust Companies,* 1916) and his amateur
enthusiasms (*Here's to Broadway!* 1930). "My Aunt's Little Note" was one of the first-
prize winners in the *New York Sun*'s weekly "sock song" contests. Although Perine was
in the minority as a male entrant, he was certainly not alone; and, indeed, although
the literature on patriotic knitting scarcely spoke of it, many men also did their bit
knitting for the troops.

My Aunt's Little Note

> *New York Sun* 1 Sept. 1918: sec. 2: 6.
> *Sock Songs.* Boston: Cornhill, 1919. 119.

> For information on the genre see the note for Helen Topping Miller, "Sock Song" on 328–29. See also the note for Zelda, "To the Patriotic Lady across the Way," "And her knitting needles clicked / Through some soldier's sweater" on 320.

Edith Matilda Thomas

For Thomas's biography see 281.

> "Verses"—for an Unknown Soldier

> *New York Times* 8 Sept. 1918: sec. 3: 1.

> For information on the genre see the note for Helen Topping Miller, "Sock Song" on 328–29. See also the note for Zelda, "To the Patriotic Lady across the Way," "And her knitting needles clicked / Through some soldier's sweater" on 320.

Edith Wharton

For Wharton's biography see 300.

> "On Active Service"

> *Scribner's* 64 (Nov. 1918): 619.

> "'On Active Service'": Military jargon used in obituary notices for any active duty military personnel who have died, particularly when the cause of death is not directly related to combat.
>
> "(R.S., August 12th, 1918)": The elegy is dedicated to Ronald Simmons, a thirty-ish American art student in Paris whom Wharton had come to regard fondly. Upon the U.S. declaration of war, Simmons had volunteered for the U.S. Army, been commissioned as an intelligence officer, and sent to a posting near Marseilles. In early August 1918 he contracted pneumonia and died in a military hospital. Although in her war work Wharton had daily confronted the death and ruin of many others and had responded sympathetically but stoically, she was devastated by this loss.

Edgar A. Guest

Born in Birmingham, England, in 1881, Edgar A. Guest immigrated to Detroit with his parents in 1891 and began working at the *Detroit Free Press* in 1895. Guest's facility at versification won him a poetry column for the *Free Press* in 1899 and kept him writing a poem a day for that paper—and presently, through syndication, for many others—over the next several decades. With the birth of radio he read his poetry on the airwaves; his lyrics were also popular on greeting cards. Guest once estimated that he had written and published some eleven thousand poems, only a fraction of which were collected in his sixteen books of poetry. Nearly all, however, might be described as fluent, genial, and moralizing. Like other poets, Guest wrote obsessively of the war during the U.S. intervention; selections from his wartime productions are contained in *Just Folks* (1917), *Over Here* (1918), and *The Path to Home* (1919).

At the Peace Table

Newspaper clipping. [1918]. Peace Poems subject file, box 1, file E-G. Swarthmore College Peace Collection, Swarthmore, Pa.
The Path to Home. Chicago: Reilly and Lee, 1919. 40–41.

"And over his shoulder a boy shall look—a boy that they crucified": One report of war atrocities, later entirely discredited, told of a British soldier captured in the initial retreat of 1914 who was crucified by the Germans.
"And the man that died in the open boat, and the babes that suffered worse": Submarine warfare, which endangered and killed civilians, was also numbered among German barbarisms. Another supposed atrocity—like the crucified soldier, never substantiated—was that German soldiers hacked the hands off Belgian babies.
"Shall sit at the table when peace is made by the side of a martyred nurse": Edith Cavell. See Robert Underwood Johnson's biography and the note for his "Edith Cavell" on 298.

Mary Carolyn Davies

For Davies's biography see 301.

Fifth Avenue and Grand Street

Braithwaite (1918) 26–27.

"She saw my pin like hers": Both women are wearing service pins, indicating that they have husbands on active military duty.

Fenton Johnson

Born in 1888 into a middle-class household in Chicago, Fenton Johnson was raised with opportunities had by few African Americans of his time. He attended classes at the University of Chicago, Northwestern, and the Pulitzer School of Journalism at Columbia University. With financial support from others (probably family members), he was able to self-publish three books of poetry—*A Little Dreaming* (1913), *Visions of the Dusk* (1915), and *Songs of the Soil* (1916)—and from 1918 to 1920 he was the founder, publisher, and editor of the *Favorite Magazine*. The poems in Johnson's books were written in the two manners made popular by Paul Laurence Dunbar: high diction treating conventional, romantic scenarios and black dialect portraying scenes from black life. Despite some good reviews, Johnson could not duplicate Dunbar's popularity. Indeed, by 1920 Johnson and his family had suffered grave financial losses, and while James Weldon Johnson and other writers of the Harlem Renaissance knew of Fenton Johnson, the movement offered little material assistance or artistic encouragement. During the 1930s, he participated in a WPA program for writers and produced outstanding new poetry, but otherwise he appears to have written nothing between then and his death in 1958. The period of the Great War was, in many ways, the peak of his career: besides publishing his books showing the influence of Dunbar, Johnson discovered the literary uses of black spirituals and of free verse and was discovered, in turn, by *Poetry* magazine and by *Others*. Johnson's poetic development beyond Dunbar's influence, which continued to be in evidence in later poetry but failed to save his career from obscurity, is well represented in "The New Day."

The New Day

Braithwaite (1918) 30–31.
Also anthologized in Johnson 142–44.

Mary Burrill

A native of Washington, D.C., Mary Burrill (ca. 1884–1946) was a longtime teacher of literature, oratory, and drama at the city's Dunbar High School, where Burrill herself graduated and which served a predominantly black neighborhood. She was also an accomplished dramatist and director, long active in community theater productions, and an activist on behalf of women as well as black Americans. These shared commitments to theater and to activism are reflected in Burrill's two extant plays: *They That Sit in Darkness,* about the importance of birth-control education in black communities, and *Aftermath,* about a veteran honored for patriotic valor in France who comes home to learn that his father has been lynched. Like "To a Black Soldier Fallen in the War," the latter play appeared in the *Liberator* (in 1919).

To a Black Soldier Fallen in the War

Liberator 1.10 (Dec. 1918): 11.
Crisis 17 (Feb. 1919): 186.

REPERCUSSIONS

John E. Nordquist

John E. Nordquist's work did not appear in *Solidarity* or other IWW publications until the entire union leadership of 1917 was jailed. By 1919, however, he had established himself as one of the chief Wobbly poets, publishing his lyrics in both *New Solidarity* and "The Little Red Song Book." Since after 1917 the union added relatively few new members and since it would be difficult to ascend to a leadership position so quickly, Nordquist most likely was a card-carrying Wobbly of the rank and file from sometime before the U.S. intervention. The parodic form and cantankerous rhetoric of "The Unemployed Soldier" certainly show that Nordquist had well internalized the Wobbly style as developed by Joe Hill, Richard Brazier, Ralph H. Chaplin, and the other IWW bards.

The Unemployed Soldier

New Solidarity 9 Feb. 1919: 3.

"'John Brown's Body'": Most famously, the tune used for "The Battle Hymn of the Republic."

"Now there is no job for us": Nearly all wartime agencies were terminated and most soldiers demobilized within a year of the armistice. Largely as a consequence, the economy went into recession in 1919–20, and many former soldiers were indeed left without a job.

"Soldier boys we'll join the union": Only a handful of soldiers became new members of the IWW; many who had been members before the war and had been drafted did, however, become active in the union again, often appearing at union meetings in uniform. Wesley Everest, the victim of the Centralia riot, was the most famous of these returning Wobbly soldiers. For more on the Centralia riot, see the part 7 introduction.

Wallace Irwin

For Irwin's biography see 278.

Thoughts Inspired by a War-Time Billboard

Commemorative booklet for the Victory Dinner of the Division of Pictorial Publicity, Committee on Public Information, 14 Feb. 1919.

Walton Rawls. *Wake Up, America!: World War I and the American Poster.* New York: Abbeville, 1988. 168–69.

"As mobilized Fishers and Christys implore": Posters by Harrison C. Fisher and Howard Chandler Christy. I have not annotated the proper names of the nine other creators of war posters mentioned unless Irwin uses nicknames or omits first names.

"Wallie Morg": Wallace Morgan.

"Blashfield": E. H. Blashfield.

"Charles Livingston Bull in marine composition / Exhorts us to Hooverize (portrait of bass)": Because Hoover admonished Americans to eat less meat and more fish, Bull's poster featured a large, freshly caught bass in a basket.

"Benda": W. T. Benda.

"There's the Christy Girl wishing that she was a boy": For a poster by Christy similar to the one here described see the illustration on 167.

"There's Leyendecker coaling for Garfield in jeans": Joseph Christian Leyendecker is the artist cited. Appointed in August 1917, Harry Garfield was the head of the U.S. Fuel Administration.

"Montie Flagg": In addition to the poster described by Irwin, James Montgomery Flagg was the creator of the ubiquitous Uncle Sam poster "I Want You for U.S. Army."

"And if brave Uncle Sam—Dana Gibson, please bow": This is the one overt clue that Irwin performed the poem publicly on an occasion when most, if not all, of the artists named were present.

Covington Ami [Covington Hall]

For Hall's biography see 324.

I Am Revolution

New Solidarity 26 Apr. 1919: 2.

Claude McKay

Claude McKay (1889–1948) was born in Sunny Ville, Jamaica, and immigrated to the United States in 1912. Although he was widely associated with the Harlem Renaissance of the 1920s, his longest stay in Harlem spanned the war years. McKay's association with left-wing politics dated from this period; by 1919 he was an associate editor of and contributor to the *Liberator,* and his poem "If We Must Die" was published both in that magazine and in the *Messenger,* the one avowedly socialist periodical in the U.S. black community. While not a poem specifically about the war, its defiant attitude voices the betrayal felt by many blacks after their armed service went largely unrewarded and clearly appropriates the ideologies of noble self-sacrifice and manly fortitude that saturated nationalist war propaganda. "The Little Peoples," also published in the *Liberator,* reflects further the specific terms of McKay's disillusionment and radicalization. Even as national self-determination was loudly proclaimed in the restoration of Belgium and the postwar reorganization of Eastern Europe and the Balkans, that principle was flouted for countries outside of Europe, where England, France, and Belgium maintained their holdings and added on those formerly held by Germany and Turkey. Radical politics dominated McKay's working life for the two decades following the war; he traveled to the Soviet Union several times, attended the Fourth International there, and except for two years back in Harlem (ca. 1921–23) remained in Europe until 1934.

The Little Peoples

Liberator 2.7 (July 1919): 21.
Anthologized in Braithwaite (1919) 110.

"The white world's burden must forever bear!": Inversion of colonialist rhetoric and ideology of the "white man's burden."

If We Must Die

Liberator 2.7 (July 1919): 21.
Messenger Sept. 1919.
Anthologized in Johnson 168–69.

Allen Tucker

For Tucker's biography see 329.

"Les Fleurs du Mal"

There and Here. New York: Duffield, 1919. 26–27.

"Les Fleurs du Mal": Variant of Charles Baudelaire's *Les Fleurs de Mal* (The Flowers of Evil), a collection of poetry published in 1857 and considered by many a ground-breaking moment in poetic modernism.

J. Eugene Chrisman

Little information on J. Eugene Chrisman is available. While allowing that the poem's persona and the author might be very different, we can guess from evidence internal to the poem that Chrisman was a former soldier in France who had faced German guns. Commenting on the poem, the editors of the *Literary Digest* allowed that "Flanders' Field has obviously been overworked . . . since the immortal first poem on that theme reached us" (for John McRae's original see 143) but also found that Chrisman's version was the most "sincere" to have come to their attention, as its lines "reveal, perhaps, the true psychology of the 'roughneck' soldier who may claim to be overfed with the sentimentalizings of those who don't know."

Poppies

Captain Billy's Whiz Bang. [1921]
Literary Digest 14 May 1921: 36.

"Poppies": For previous treatments of poppies as a poetic theme, cf. Alan Seeger's "Champagne, 1914–15" (113), Amy Lowell's "Orange of Midsummer" (157), and John McRae's ubiquitous poem "In Flanders Fields" (143).

"Château-Thierry": American troops fought in or near this town northeast of Paris on three occasions. Newly positioned in its vicinity within the French line, American troops first helped blunt German attacks in early June 1918, though eventually they were forced back; in July they helped stop the final German drive toward Paris and joined in the immediately following counteroffensive. Château-Thierry and the nearby Belleau Wood were famous in the United States as sites of American military triumph.

Brent Dow Allinson

An enthusiastic supporter of Wilson's policies of neutrality, Brent Dow Allinson composed a praising sonnet ("thou, who learned to labor and to wait / Through storm and stress with patient faith") that in the fall of 1916 was used to support the president's reelection campaign and, in the spring of 1918, was used by the *New York Tribune* to prove Allinson's disloyalty. A Harvard freshman in September 1915, Allinson duly registered for the draft in June 1917, served as a civilian officer in the U.S. Fuel Administration in the winter of 1917–18, and was appointed to a position in the State Department in February. It was then that a *Tribune* editorial attacked the State Department's appointment of a "pacifist" to serve in the "storm center," and officials responded by recalling Allinson to Washington from New York, where he had been waiting for passage to Europe. On 1 April 1918 Allinson, still in Washington, was forwarded his draft notice, which required him to report before a Chicago selective service board on 31 March. Although defended by the selective service board in Washington, D.C., Allinson was arrested for desertion on 28 April, transported to Chicago, court-martialed, and sentenced to prison. Allinson's sentence, initially a life term, was later reduced to fifteen years and then five years, and he was in fact released after two years in Leavenworth. His cause was championed by *Pearson's Magazine* in September 1920, even as he was being released. "Mr. Bryan Enters Arlington" is filed, with no date or site of publication identified, in Allinson's folder in the Swarthmore College Peace Collection. As it records the burial of William Jennings Bryan in Arlington National Cemetery, it cannot have been written earlier than 1925.

Mr. Bryan Enters Arlington

> Periodical clipping. ca. 1925. Peace Poems subject file, box 1, folder A. Swarthmore College Peace Collection, Swarthmore, Pa.

> "Oh, damn the rain / That's never stopped since April! . . .": Cf. the opening of T. S. Eliot's *The Waste Land.*

> "Is a strange absolution. . . . Where's that blond?": "Blond" is apparently a (not necessarily good-humored) dig at the black adjutant, to which John Abraham replies, "And I don' need those compliments you're throwin'!"

> "Stand by, Black Boy, and tell me all you see": The lieutenant of the poem had his eyes left behind in France when he was exhumed, although it is unclear how at the beginning of the poem he is able to identify his African American adjutant prior to his speaking.

> "Boy!—it's Mistah Bryan comin'": William Jennings Bryan, populist-leaning presidential candidate of the Democratic party in 1896, 1900, and 1908, and Woodrow Wilson's secretary of state until 9 June 1915.

> "Although in honesty you once resigned": Bryan resigned in the wake of the *Lusitania* sinking, believing Wilson's approach to be prejudiced against Germany. In the summer of 1915 he toured the country in support of pacifism. But in 1917, upon the U.S. declaration of war, Bryan publicly offered his assistance to the president in whatever capacity deemed useful.

> "More maddened than the Gadarenian swine!": In the Christian gospel of Mark, Jesus delivers a man from demon-possession and then, responding to the entreaty of the demons, permits them to enter a nearby herd of pigs who immediately drown themselves in the Sea of Galilee. Gadara was a city southeast of the sea.

> "In Florida!": Bryan's home state, where he resided after his resignation as secretary of state.

> "For what you did for God in Tennessee!": In 1925 Bryan was the unsuccessful celebrity prosecutor of John Thomas Scopes, the Tennessee teacher who had taught evolutionary theory in defiance of state law. Bryan's humiliating defeat to Clarence Darrow in the infamous "Monkey Trial" was almost literally the death of him.

> "'or crucify / Upon a cross of gold or war mankind!'": Allinson here interpolates a statement of Bryan's pacifism into his famous denunciation of the gold standard from the 1896 campaign, "Thou shalt not crucify mankind upon a cross of gold."

Sarah N[orcliffe]. Cleghorn

For Cleghorn's biography see 312.

Ballad of Gene Debs

> *Ballad of Gene Debs.* North Montpelier, Vt.: Driftwood, July 1928. Handbound booklet. Peace Poems subject file, box 1, folder C. Swarthmore College Peace Collection, Swarthmore, Pa.
>
> *Poems of Peace and Freedom.* Fulton, N.Y.: New York State Branch of the Women's International League for Peace and Freedom, 1945.

> "Ballad of Gene Debs": Eugene V. Debs was the foremost Socialist in the United States during the heyday of the party. He ran as the party's candidate for president in 1900, 1904, 1908, 1912, and 1920, polling nearly one million votes in each of the last two elections. Debs died in 1926.
>
> "A tall, thin, elderly man / Was pouring a great speech": On 16 June 1918, Debs addressed the convention of the Ohio Socialist party at Canton, deliberately choosing to test the Espionage and Sedition Acts by emphasizing the party's antiwar stance in his speech. For an abridged transcript of Debs's speech see Radosh 66–78.
>
> "Where is Rose Pastor Stokes?": Rose Pastor Stokes was a Russian-Jewish immigrant from the lower east side of Manhattan who married the millionaire Socialist and philanthropist Graham Stokes in a Cinderella romance widely publicized and also recreated fictionally in Anzia Yezierska's *Salome of the Tenements* (1923). When war was declared in 1917, Stokes joined her husband in resigning from the Socialist party over its antiwar position. By June 1918, however, she had rejoined the party, become estranged from her husband, and been arrested for speaking against the war. She was sentenced to ten years in prison but in 1921 won her appeal and did not go to jail.
>
> "As well as Kate O'Hare": Kate Richards O'Hare had chaired the platform committee that formulated the Socialist party's antiwar statement. She too was convicted under wartime sedition laws and received a five-year sentence, fourteen months of which she served before being pardoned in 1920.
>
> "And three good comrades, yours and mine, / Are locked into that place": Alfred Wagenknecht, Charles E. Ruthenberg, and Charles Baker, activists in the Ohio Socialist party, were in prison in Canton for having spoken against the war. Ruthenberg subsequently became the general secretary of the American Communist party and was later arrested three times on syndicalism charges.
>
> "'Arrest him!' the order / Came out to Terre Haute": Four days passed before a federal indictment was secured against Debs by the state of Ohio; he had meanwhile returned home to Terre Haute, Indiana. Debs also returned there, free on bond, in the weeks between his indictment and trial beginning 9 September 1918 in Cleveland.
>
> "'Is it to be a scrap of paper / For the bloody sake of war?'": See the biography for Henry Van Dyke [Civis Americanus] on 288. The remark appears to be a clear instance of Cleghorn's poetic license.
>
> "Three days from that day / The court convened again": On 11 September Debs made his statement to the jury; on 12 September the judge gave instructions to the jury and the jury reached its verdict; on 14 September the judge pro-

nounced sentence. Cleghorn's chronology has added a day, either in error or perhaps adopting the antiquated practice of including the day *of* a particular event in counting days *from* it (e.g., in the Christian New Testament Jesus dies on Friday and is raised on Sunday, the "third" day).

"'Again and again', / He said, 'I've met in council / With the union railroad men'": Reference to Debs's experience as a union official and, ultimately, president of the American Railway Union, which he led in the great Pullman strike of 1894. Debs's activity in the strike both catapulted him into prominence in the American labor movement and persuaded him that collective bargaining could not work, that instead political victory for the Socialist party would be the only way for workers to win their rights.

"That evening, at Moundsville, / He went the bars behind": Here Cleghorn appears to compress the chronology considerably. Debs began serving his sentence at the state penitentiary in Moundsville, West Virginia, in April 1919, only after the U.S. Supreme Court had denied his appeal on constitutional grounds.

"Dave Karsner": Karsner was a reporter with the *New York Call* who traveled with Debs from Terre Haute to the penitentiary.

"They moved Gene Debs from Moundsville . . .": Initially sent to a state penitentiary because of overcrowding in the federal prison system, Debs was transferred to the federal penitentiary in Atlanta in June 1919. From there Debs ran his presidential campaign as "Convict 9653."

"But when he had been three years in jail / The government let him go": Denied a pardon by Woodrow Wilson, Debs and other radicals imprisoned under the Espionage and Sedition Acts were given pardons on Christmas Day 1921 by Warren Harding.

✿ WORKS CITED

Addams, Jane. *Newer Ideals of Peace.* New York: Macmillan, 1911.

———. *Peace and Bread in Time of War.* New York: Macmillan, 1922.

Addams, Jane, Emily Balch, and Alice Hamilton. *Women at The Hague: The International Congress of Women and Its Results.* New York: Macmillan, 1916.

Anthony, Katherine. "The 'Sister Susie' Peril." *Four Lights* 14 July 1917: 1.

Baker, Ray Stannard. *Woodrow Wilson: Life and Letters.* 7 vols. Vol. 6, *Facing War.* New York: Greenwood, 1968.

Bell, Daniel. "The Background and Development of Marxian Socialism in the United States." *Socialism and American Life.* Vol 1. Ed. Donald Drew Egbert and Stow Persons. Princeton, N.J.: Princeton University Press, 1952. 213–405.

Bergonzi, Bernard. *Heroes' Twilight: A Study of the Literature of the Great War.* London: Constable, 1965.

Blake, Katherine Devereux. [O say can you see, you who glory in war.] Broadside. 1929. Peace Poems subject file, box 1, folder B. Swarthmore College Peace Collection, Swarthmore, Pa.

Bourne, Randolph. "War and the Intellectuals." *Seven Arts* 2 (June 1917): 133–34.

Braithwaite, William Stanley, ed. *Anthology of Magazine Verse for 1915.* New York: Gomme and Marshall, 1915.

———. *Anthology of Magazine Verse for 1916.* New York: Gomme, 1916.

———. *Anthology of Magazine Verse for 1917.* New York: Small, Maynard, 1917.

———. *Anthology of Magazine Verse for 1919 and Year Book of American Poetry.* Boston: Small, Maynard, 1919.

———. *Victory!* Boston: Small, Maynard, 1918.

"Branding the I.W.W." *Literary Digest* 31 Aug. 1918: 14–16.

Brisbane, Arthur. "Today." *Chicago Examiner* 18 Feb. 1918.

Broadhurst, Jean, and Clara L. Rhodes, eds. *Verse for Patriots, to Encourage Good Citizenship.* Philadelphia: J. B. Lippincott, 1919.

Browne, Porter Emerson. "The Vigilantes: Who and Why and What They Are." *Outlook* 119 (8 May 1918): 67–69.

"Calling the Bluff." *Masses* Sept. 1917: 27.

Cane, Melville, John Farrar, and Louise Townsend Nicholl. *The Golden Year: The Poetry Society of America Anthology (1910–1960).* New York: Fine Editions Press, 1960.

Case, Carleton B., ed. *Wartime and Patriotic Selections for Recitation and Reading.* Chicago: n.p., [1918].

Clarke, George Herbert, ed. *A Treasury of War Poetry: British and American Poems of the World War, 1914–1917.* Boston: Houghton Mifflin, 1917.

————, ed. *A Treasury of War Poetry: British and American Poems of the World War, 1914–1919.* 2d series. Boston: Houghton Mifflin, 1919.

Colcord, Lincoln. *Vision of War.* New York: Macmillan, 1915.

"Colored Men Lynched by Years, 1885–1917." *Crisis* 15 (Feb. 1918): 184.

Cornebise, Alfred E., ed. *Doughboy Doggerel: Verse of the American Expeditionary Force, 1918–1919.* Athens: Ohio University Press, 1985.

Creel, George. *How We Advertised America.* 1920. New York: Arno, 1972.

Cross, Tim. *The Lost Voices of World War I: An International Anthology of Writers, Poets, and Playwrights.* London: Bloomsbury, 1988.

Cunliffe, J. W., ed. *Poems of the Great War.* New York: Macmillan, 1916.

Davidson, Lucile. Letter to Fannie M. Witherspoon. 15 Oct. 1917. Collected Records of the Woman's Peace Party, Scholarly Resources microfilm edition, reel 4, box 5, folder 13. Swarthmore College Peace Collection, Swarthmore, Pa.

Degen, Marie L. *The History of the Woman's Peace Party.* Johns Hopkins University Studies in Historical and Political Science 57.3. Baltimore: Johns Hopkins University Press, 1939.

Dounce, Harry Esty. "Introduction." *Sock Songs.* Boston: Cornhill, 1919. vii–ix.

Dubofsky, Melvin. *We Shall Be All: A History of the Industrial Workers of the World.* Chicago: Quadrangle Books, 1969.

Du Bois, W. E. B. "Close Ranks." *Crisis* 16 (July 1918): 111.

————. "Documents of the War." *Crisis* 18 (May 1919): 16–21.

————. "An Essay toward a History of the Black Man in the Great War." *Crisis* 18 (June 1919): 63–87.

————. "Houston and East St. Louis." *Crisis* 15 (Apr. 1918): 269.

————. "Returning Soldiers." *Crisis* 18 (May 1919): 13–14.

————. "Young." *Crisis* 11 (Mar. 1916): 240–42.

Eaton, W. D., ed. *The War in Verse and Prose.* Chicago: T. S. Denison, 1918.

Eliot, T. S. "Tradition and the Individual Talent." *Selected Prose of T. S. Eliot.* Ed. Frank Kermode. New York: Harcourt, Brace, Jovanovich, 1975. 37–44.

Elliott, H. B., ed. *Lest We Forget: A War Anthology.* London: Jarrold, 1915.

Ellmann, Richard, and Robert O'Clair, eds. *The Norton Anthology of Modern Poetry.* 2d ed. New York: Norton, 1988.

[Erskine, John, ed.] *Contemporary War Poems.* Spec. bulletin of *International Conciliation* Dec. 1914.

————. Introduction. *Contemporary War Poems.* [Ed. John Erskine.] Spec. bulletin of *International Conciliation* Dec. 1914: 3–6.

Ferro, Marc. *The Great War, 1914–1918.* Trans. Nicole Stone. London: Routledge and Kegan Paul, 1973.

Finnegan, John Patrick. *Against the Specter of a Dragon.* Westport, Conn.: Greenwood, 1974.

Fussell, Paul. *Doing Battle: The Making of a Skeptic.* Boston: Little, Brown, 1996.

————. *The Great War and Modern Memory.* New York: Oxford University Press, 1975.

————, ed. *The Norton Book of Modern War.* New York: Norton, 1991.

Gilbert, Sandra M., and Susan Gubar. *No Man's Land: The Place of the Woman Writer in the Twentieth Century.* 3 vols. Vol. 2, *Sexchanges.* New Haven: Yale University Press, 1989.

Gilman, Charlotte Perkins. "National Woman Suffrage Conventions." *Impress* 26 Jan. 1895: 15.

Greene, Grace W. "Poems of the War." Periodical clippings scrapbook. Peace Poems subject file, box 2, Anthology of War Poems folder. Swarthmore College Peace Collection, Swarthmore, Pa.

Grumbine, Harvey Carson. *Humanity or Hate: Which?* Boston: Cornhill, 1918.

Halsey, Francis Whiting, ed. *Literary History of the World War.* 10 vols. New York: Funk and Wagnalls, 1919–20.

Hart, James A. "American Poetry of the First World War (1914–1920): A Survey and Checklist." Ph.D. diss., Duke University, 1964.

Henderson, Alice Corbin. "Poetry and War." *Poetry* 5 (Nov. 1914): 82–84.

"Hold the Fort: Grand Entertainment." *International Socialist Review* 20 (Nov.–Dec. 1917): 279.

Holman, Carrie E., ed. *In the Day of Battle.* Toronto: William Briggs, 1916.

Imperial German Embassy. ["Notice!"]. *New York Times* 1 May 1915: 15.

Johnson, James Weldon, ed. *The Book of American Negro Poetry.* New York: Harcourt Brace, 1931.

Kennedy, David M. *Over Here: The First World War and American Society.* New York: Oxford University Press, 1980.

Kipling, Rudyard. "For All We Have and Are." *New York Times* 2 Sept. 1914: 1.

Kramer, Aaron. *The Prophetic Tradition in American Poetry, 1835–1900.* Rutherford, N.J.: Fairleigh Dickinson University Press, 1968.

Lauter, Paul, ed. *The Heath Anthology of American Literature.* 2 vols. Boston: Houghton Mifflin, 1991.

Leavenworth Penitentiary warden. Letter to Assistant Attorney General Mabel Walker Willebrandt. Sept. 30, 1922. Inmate Case File 13104. U.S. Penitentiary Leavenworth. Bureau of Prisons. Record Group 129. National Archives and Records Administration. Washington, D.C.

Leed, Eric. *No Man's Land: Combat and Identity in World War I.* Cambridge: Cambridge University Press, 1979.

Levin, Murray B. *Political Hysteria in America: The Democratic Capacity for Repression.* New York: Basic Books, 1971.

Lewis, C. Day. "Introduction." *The Collected Poems of Wilfred Owen.* Ed. C. Day Lewis. 1931. New York: New Directions, 1965. 11–29.

Lewis, David Levering. *W. E. B. Du Bois: Biography of a Race, 1868–1919.* New York: Holt, 1993.

Marchand, C. Roland. *The American Peace Movement and Social Reform, 1898–1918.* Princeton, N.J.: Princeton University Press, 1972.

Marsland, Elizabeth A. *The Nation's Cause: French, English, and German Poetry of the First World War.* New York: Routledge, 1991.

Masters, Edgar Lee. "Mars Has Descended." *Poetry* 10 (May 1917): 88–92.

Meetings of the Executive Committee. 8 and 29 Oct. [1917]. The Vigilantes Minutes, 1917. Hermann Hagedorn Collection, Manuscript Division, Library of Congress.

Metzer, Milton. *Bread—and Roses: The Struggle of American Labor.* New York: Knopf, 1967.

Monroe, Harriet. "The War and the Artist." *Poetry* 11 (Mar. 1918): 320–22.

———. "War Poems." *Poetry* 10 (Aug. 1917): 271–78.

———. "What War May Do." *Poetry* 10 (June 1917): 142–45.

———. "Will Art Happen?" *Poetry* 10 (July 1917): 203–5.

Monroe, Harriet, and Alice Corbin Henderson, eds. *The New Poetry: An Anthology.* New York: Macmillan, 1917.

Murray, Robert K. *Red Scare: A Study of National Hysteria, 1919–1920.* 1955. New York: McGraw-Hill, 1964.

Nelson, Cary. *Repression and Recovery: Modern American Poetry and the Politics of Cultural Memory, 1910–1945.* Madison: University of Wisconsin Press, 1989.

Newman, Pauline M. "Lest We Forget." *New York Call* 24 Mar. 1918: magazine sec., 7.

Oppenheim, James. "The Song of the Uprising." *Seven Arts* 2 (Sept. 1917): 552–63.

Peterson, H. C., and Gilbert Fite. *Opponents of War, 1917–1918.* Madison: University of Wisconsin Press, 1957.

Pound, Ezra. "A Few Don'ts by an Imagiste." *Imagist Poetry.* Ed. Peter Jones. Harmondsworth, England: Penguin, 1972. 130–34.

Powell, Lyman P., and Charles M. Curry, eds. *The World and Democracy.* Chicago: Rand McNally, 1919.

Powell, Lyman P., and Gertrude W. Powell, eds. *The Spirit of Democracy.* Chicago: Rand McNally, 1918.

Preston, William, Jr. *Aliens and Dissenters: Federal Suppression of Radicals, 1903–1933.* Cambridge: Harvard University Press, 1963.

"Protesting Women March in Mourning." *New York Times* 30 Aug. 1914: 11.

Radosh, Ronald, ed. *Debs.* Englewood Cliffs, N.J.: Prentice-Hall, 1971.

Reilly, Catherine W. *English Poetry of the First World War: A Bibliography.* New York: St. Martin's, 1978.

———, ed. *Scars upon My Heart: Women's Poetry and Verse of the First World War.* 1981. London: Virago, 1982.

Rittenhouse, Jessie B., ed. *The Second Book of Modern Verse: A Selection from the Work of Contemporaneous American Poets.* Boston: Houghton Mifflin, 1919.

Sadler, Kate. "Lest We Forget." *International Socialist Review* 15 (July 1914): 30–32.

Salerno, Salvatore. *Red November, Black November: Culture and Community in the Industrial Workers of the World.* Albany: State University of New York Press.

Sanford, A. P., and Robert Haven Schauffler, eds. *Armistice Day.* New York: Dodd, Mead, 1928.

Schaffer, Ronald. *America in the Great War: The Rise of the War Welfare State.* New York: Oxford University Press, 1991.

Seeger, Alan. *Poems.* New York: Scribner's, 1916.

———. *Poems* manufacturing record. Manufacturing Records: Editions Published 1902–1955, box 21. Charles Scribner's Sons Archive. Manuscripts Division, Department of Rare Books and Special Collections, Princeton University Libraries, Princeton, N.J.

Silkin, Jon, ed. *The Penguin Book of First World War Poetry.* London: Allen Lane, 1979.

Slonimsky, Nicolas. *Music since 1900.* 4th ed. New York: Scribner's, 1971.

Smith, Barbara Herrnstein. "Contingencies of Value." *Canons.* Ed. Robert von Hallberg. Chicago: University of Chicago Press, 1984. 5–39.

Smith, Daniel M. *The Great Departure: The United States and World War I, 1914–1920.* New York: Wiley, 1965.

Some Imagist Poets, 1916: An Annual Anthology. Boston: Houghton Mifflin, 1916.

Stevenson, Burton, ed. *American History in Verse for Boys and Girls.* Boston: Houghton Mifflin, 1932.

———. *Poems of American History.* Boston: Houghton Mifflin, 1922.

"Subscribers—Please Read." *New York Call* 27 Dec. 1917: 8.

Sullivan, Mark. *Our Times, 1900–1925.* 6 vols. Vol. 5, *Over Here, 1914–1918.* New York: Scribner's, 1933.

Tompkins, Jane. *Sensational Designs: The Cultural Work of American Fiction, 1790–1860.* New York: Oxford University Press, 1985.

Towne, Charles Hanson, ed. *For France.* Garden City, N.J.: Doubleday, Page, 1917.

———. *So Far So Good.* New York: Julian Messner, 1945.

Tuchman, Barbara. *The Guns of August.* New York: Macmillan, 1962.

Tyler, Robert L. *Rebels in the Woods.* Eugene: University of Oregon Press, 1967.

Untermeyer, Louis. *From Another World.* New York: Harcourt, Brace, 1939.

U.S. Committee on Public Information. *The Battle Line of Democracy: Prose and Poetry of the World War.* Washington, D.C.: GPO, 1917.

U.S. Food Administration. *The Day's Food in War and Peace.* Washington, D.C.: GPO, 1918.

———. *War Economy in Food with Suggestions and Recipes for Substitutions in the Planning of Meals.* Washington, D.C.: [GPO], [1917].

Van Wienen, Mark W. *Partisans and Poets: The Political Work of American Poetry in the Great War.* New York: Cambridge University Press, 1997.

The Vigilantes. *Fifes and Drums.* New York: George H. Doran, [1917].

W., R. Y. Letter. "To the Editor of the *New York Times.*" *New York Times* 30 Aug. 1918: 10.

Walker, Robert H. *The Poet and the Gilded Age: Social Themes in Late Nineteenth-Century American Verse.* Philadelphia: University of Pennsylvania Press, 1963.

Walsh, Jeffrey. *American War Literature, 1914 to Vietnam.* New York: St. Martin's, 1982.

War Poems from the Yale Review. New Haven: Yale University Press, 1918.

War Poems from the Yale Review. 2d ed. New Haven: Yale University Press, 1919.

"War Will Probably Benefit World's Literature, Declares Prof. Brander Matthews of Columbia." *New York Times Book Review* 13 Sep. 1914: 2.

Watkins, Lucian B. "Back to God's Country." *Richmond Planet* 20 Oct. 1917: 1–2.

West, James E. "The Boy Scouts of America." *Journal of Proceedings and Addresses, National Education Association of the United States* (1916): 805–810.

Wheeler, W. Reginald. *A Book of Verse of the Great War.* New Haven: Yale University Press, 1917.

White, True Worthy. "Patriotic Celebration Program." *Atlanta Constitution* 4 June 1917, magazine sec.: 1.

Wilson, Woodrow. *The Messages and Papers of Woodrow Wilson.* Ed. Albert Shaw. 2 vols. New York: Review of Reviews, 1924.

"The Women's Manifestation." *New York Times* 30 Aug. 1914: 14.

Wood, Charles W. "Am I a Patriot?" *Masses* June 1916: 8.

"WPP Preamble and Platform Adopted at Washington, January 10, 1915." Collected Records of the Woman's Peace Party, Scholarly Resources microfilm edition, reel 3, box 3, folder 4. Swarthmore College Peace Collection, Swarthmore, Pa.

Wright, Chester W. *Economic History of the United States.* New York: McGraw-Hill, 1941.

Wright, Quincy. *A Study of War.* Chicago: University of Chicago Press, 1965.

"Writing Poems on War." *New York Times* 11 Aug. 1914: 8.

Wynn, Neil A. *From Progressivism to Prosperity: World War I and American Society.* New York: Holmes and Meier, 1986.

☙ ACKNOWLEDGMENTS

Changes in literary-critical attitudes about popular poetry are not just a matter of impersonal academic trends but result from the work of individual scholars, mentors, colleagues, and friends to whom I am deeply indebted for support and encouragement. Without their vision of a more open and inclusive definition of the poetic, without the freedom they allowed me for what could have seemed a quixotic adventure in bibliographic exploration, this anthology could never have come into print.

I have had the privilege of working with Cary Nelson for some fifteen years: as brilliant instructor, dissertation advisor, mentor, and now general editor of the American Poetry Recovery Series. To him must go the first and greatest share of my appreciation. I also heartily thank the other members of my dissertation committee—Janet Lyon, Robert Dale Parker, and Jack Stillinger—who with Cary shepherded so well *Partisans and Poets,* the critical study that provided the foundation for this volume. Others who have offered generous and constructive feedback during my decade and more of work on American World War I poetry include Alan Wald of the University of Michigan; Susan Schweik of the University of California at Berkeley; and Ronald Schaffer of California State University at Northridge. W. D. Ehrhardt read the complete manuscript at a late stage. The editors, readers, and board of the University of Illinois Press are likewise due much credit. Particularly I thank former director Richard Wentworth, current director Willis Regier, and the two unidentified referees of the manuscript.

Several institutions and departments have subsidized and supported the completion of this manuscript, in ways both large and small. For access to library collections and staff, I have Roanoke College and Virginia Polytechnic Institute and State University to thank. For gainful employment and library access during a particularly crucial year of my academic career, I am indebted to the University of Southern Maine. Most of all, though, I thank Augustana College, South Dakota, for the support in funds and community that allowed this book to happen. In particular, I thank the college for the assistance provided by the Granskou Award for summer 1997.

At all my academic affiliations, I have been surrounded by stimulating and encouraging colleagues who deserve my gratitude. An incomplete list must include the following: at Roanoke College, Pamela S. Anderson, Gary Gibbs,

Michael Hakkenberg, Michael A. Heller, Katherine Hoffman, and Sangeeta Tyagi; at Virginia Tech, Tom Gardner, Lillian S. Robinson, Leonard Scigaj, and Nancy Simmons; at the University of Southern Maine, Richard Abrams, Lucinda Cole, Eileen Eagan, Diana Long, Dianne Sadoff, and Richard Swartz; and at Augustana College, Carolyn Smith Geyer, Sandra Looney, Marilyn Carlson-Aronson, Nancy Dickinson, Debbie Hanson, Cheryl Jackson, Tim Jones, Jeffrey Miller, and Anne Windholz. Bill Geyer, whose professorship in modern American poetry, whose office, and whose very chair and file cabinets I inherited at Augustana, was gracious and constructive in his reading of the entire manuscript.

Scott Fish, professor of French at Augustana, generously supplied translations of the epigraphs for the Wallace Stevens poems. Many thanks, Scott.

A succession of outstanding work-study students at Augustana have assisted in several phases of this book's publication. Kudos to Erin Fresvik, Stacey Hesse, Lisa Maycroft, Amy Olson, Kyle Small, Brianna Smith, and Kristin Butler. They have helped in tasks ranging from locating poems and biographical information to checking sources and proofreading. All were enthusiastic, able, and persistent in what must have seemed at times an endless and tedious series of tasks. Two separate classes at Augustana have read portions of the manuscript as part of their coursework and supplied helpful feedback: thanks to the students in my 1998 course "Love and War: Gender, Popular Culture, and Modern War Literature" and my spring 1999 seminar "Modern American Poetry and Politics."

Over the decades since the Great War American literary critics were busy with other things, but librarians, archivists, and a fair share of antique dealers preserved the original texts of the poems upon which this anthology depends. It is my privilege to acknowledge the collections that house the texts and some of the librarians who helped me access them. Of note are the following special collections and archivists: the Special Collections and Archives of the University of Illinois at Urbana-Champaign; the Rare Book Room at the University of Virginia; the Swarthmore College Peace Collection, and especially curator Wendy Chmielewski; the Archives of Labor and Urban Affairs at the Reuther Library at Wayne State University, particularly research archivists Raymond Boryczka and Warner Pflug; the Rare Book and Special Collections Library at the University of Michigan, notably researcher Ed Webber; the Library of Congress Manuscripts Division; and the Rare Books and Special Collections Library at Princeton University, particularly archivist Margaret M. Sherry. The following general collections and library staff, many showing extraordinary prowess in the realm of interlibrary loans, provided absolutely essential support: the libraries of the University of Illinois; the Clemons and Alderman libraries at the University of Virginia; the Newman Library at Virginia Tech; the McConnell Library of Radford University in Virginia; the Fintel Library of Roanoke College and librarians Julie Beamer, Tom Davidson, Rebecca Heller, and Pat Scott; the University of Southern Maine Library and Cassandra Fitzherbert and Mary Beth Gendron; and—most important of all— the Mikkelsen Library at Augustana College and Becky Folkerts, Jan Enright, and Ronelle Thompson.

A portion of the general introduction was presented at "War in Memory, Popular Culture, and Folklore," a conference hosted in February 2000 by the Center for the Study of the Korean War and the National Archives–Central Plains Region, and has subsequently appeared in the conference proceedings. I am also most appreciative of the assistance provided by Tim Rives, archives specialist at the National Archives, in directing me to the Leavenworth Federal Penitentiary files of Charles Ashleigh and Ralph H. Chaplin.

The preservation of photographic and artistic renderings of the Great War is another realm of my indebtedness. Thanks to the following special collections for the permission to reproduce visual texts they have maintained and made available. the Museum of the City of New York; the Washington State Historical Society; the Joseph M. Bruccoli Great War Collection, Special Collections Library, University of Virginia Library; the Library of Virginia; the University of Minnesota, Twin Cities; the George C. Marshall Research Library, Lexington, Virginia; and the San Francisco History Center, San Francisco Library.

I can scarcely begin to spell out the contributions made by my family to the creation of this book. To them I can only say, thank you, for all you've done: William and Margaret Van Wienen; Marcia and Mark Van't Hof; Eveleen, Walter, Philip, and Nancy Windholz; my children, Nathaniel, Miranda, and Benjamin, whose sacrifices have been made unwittingly, for the most part, and all the more generously for that; and my wife, Anne Windholz, whose sacrifices have been given knowingly and unstintingly and, therefore, all the more generously as well. To her I really do owe everything.

Finally, a word of acknowledgment for those to whom this book is dedicated. My grandparents Henry and Margaret DeYoung and Peter and Martha Van Wienen have provided my vital link to the American generation that came of age during the Great War. Although all four died prior to its publication, I hope that in some small way their legacy continues to live in this book. My political education was enhanced in no small way by conversations overheard in Grandpa and Grandma DeYoung's kitchen. Grandma was the first person I knew to be a Democrat, driving Grandpa nuts by her obstinacy as election day would approach and she threatened, once again, to "cancel" his equally inevitable Republican vote. Grandpa and Grandma Van Wienen, who lived to know something of my research on World War I poems, provided further links to the past. The child of a German-born mother who died when he was one year old, Grandpa recalled how he had been the only student in his high school class who wished to take German for his foreign language requirement. For Grandpa's choice, his teacher made him an example to his classmates who, more astutely (or more cowardly), elected to take Latin that year of 1917. Grandma, whose wider memory recalled popular patriotic songs and recognized the names and faces of American and European wartime leaders, also observed something else in retrospect: "Ooooh," she said with her characteristic long and high exclamatory trill, "We were so *cocky* in those days! I guess we've gotten knocked down a peg or two since then." I am gratified to think that in their youth these people of candor and humor were likely readers, and even perhaps schoolhouse reciters, of some of the poems contained in this collection.

🌾 INDEX OF POEMS AND POETS

🔥 INDEX OF TOPICS

INDEX OF TOPICS

MARK W. VAN WIENEN is the author of *Partisans and Poets: The Political Work of American Poetry in the Great War.* He is an associate professor of English at Northern Illinois University.

THE AMERICAN POETRY RECOVERY SERIES

The University of Illinois Press
is a founding member of the
Association of American University Presses.

Composed in 10.5/13 Minion
with Minion display
by Jim Proefrock
at the University of Illinois Press
Designed by Dennis Roberts
Manufactured by Thomson-Shore, Inc.

University of Illinois Press
1325 South Oak Street
Champaign, IL 61820-6903
www.press.uillinois.edu